AF352567

Metapragmatics of Attentiveness

Pragmatic Interfaces

Series Editors:
Enikő Németh T., University of Szeged
Dániel Z. Kádár, Hungarian Academy of Sciences
Károly Bibok, University of Szeged

In the last two decades it has become increasingly clear that language and language use cannot be studied separately and independently of each other. This new approach assumes an interaction between grammar (phonology, morphology, lexicon, syntax and semantics) and pragmatics. An analysis of the interfaces between each component of grammar and pragmatics (the 'interface view') can also be applied to hard-pragmatics and soft-pragmatics research. Hard-pragmatics studies the field of language use from philosophical, linguistic and logical points of view, while soft-pragmatics explores phenomena of language use from a social and socio-cultural perspective.

The definitions hard- and soft-pragmatics, adopted around the 1980s, have become somewhat dated since pragmatics has become a field of its own, and so these two trends have merged to some extent. Also, various pragmaticians made important attempts to blend these approaches. Nevertheless, a border between these areas continues to exist: hard-pragmaticians rarely venture into socio-pragmatic issues, and, vice versa, soft-pragmatic studies rarely make use of formal tools of hard-pragmatics.

Pragmatic Interfaces fills an important knowledge gap in the field of pragmatics as the first major publication project devoted to studying grammar–pragmatics interfaces and merging of soft-pragmatics with hard-pragmatics. Through this merging many pragmatic phenomena could be essentially revisited. *Pragmatic Interfaces* follows an interdisciplinary approach, allowing scholars from different areas of grammar and pragmatics to collaborate.

Published:
Data and Argumentation in Historical Pragmatics: Grammaticalization of a Catalan Motion Verb Construction
Katalin Nagy C.
Face and Face Practices in Chinese Talk-in-Interaction: A Study in Interactional Pragmatics
Wei-Lin Melody Chang
Implicit Subject and Direct Object Arguments in Hungarian Language Use: Grammar and Pragmatics Interacting
Enikő Németh T.
Impoliteness in Corpora: A Comparative Analysis of British English and Spoken Turkish
Hatice Celebi
Politeness Phenomena across Chinese Genres
Edited by Xinren Chen

Metapragmatics of Attentiveness:
A Study in Interpersonal and Cross-cultural Pragmatics

Saeko Fukushima

SHEFFIELD UK   BRISTOL CT

Published by Equinox Publishing Ltd.

UK: Office 415, The Workstation, 15 Paternoster Row, Sheffield, South Yorkshire S1 2BX

USA: ISD, 70 Enterprise Drive, Bristol, CT 06010

www.equinoxpub.com

First published 2020

© Saeko Fukushima 2020

British Library Cataloguing-in-Publication Data
A catalogue record for this book is available from the British Library.
ISBN-13   978 1 78179 724 2 (hardback)
ISBN-13   978 1 78179 725 9 (ePDF)

Library of Congress Cataloging-in-Publication Data
Names: Fukushima, Saeko, date author.
Title: Metapragmatics of attentiveness : a study in interpersonal and
   cross-cultural pragmatics / Saeko Fukushima.
Description: Bristol : Equinox Publishing Ltd, 2020. | Series: Pragmatic
   Interfaces | Includes bibliographical references and index. | Summary:
   "This book examines attentiveness, which is briefly defined as a demonstrator's pre-emptive
   responses to a recipient's verbal or non-verbal cues or situations surrounding a recipient and a
   demonstrator, which takes the form of offering. It elucidates what attentiveness is, and addresses
   the importance of attentiveness in im/politeness research. It also suggests the importance of
   taking an interdisciplinary perspective in im/politeness research, the importance of non-linguistically manifested politeness and the heart perspective. Evaluation by a recipient of attentiveness
   is considered since recent research suggests that im/politeness resides in evaluation. Thus, both
   demonstration and evaluation of attentiveness are investigated in the book. Attentiveness may be
   demonstrated or evaluated differently within different cultures. Generation can be considered as
   one of the sub-groups of culture. Therefore, cross-cultural and cross-generational comparisons on
   demonstration and evaluation of attentiveness are included. Although some differences in demon
   stration or evaluation of attentiveness are found cross-culturally, similarities outweigh differences.
   This suggests that attentiveness, which is thought to be a virtue in Japanese culture, is not unique
   to Japanese culture, and that attentiveness is an important interpersonal notion elsewhere, too. It is
   also shown that attentiveness is one of the constituents of politeness, which indicates that attentiveness is closely related to politeness"-- Provided by publisher.
Identifiers: LCCN 2019013037 (print) | LCCN 2019980082 (ebook) | ISBN
   9781781797242 (hardback) | ISBN 9781781797242 (pdf)
Subjects: LCSH: Interpersonal communication. | Interpersonal
   communication--Japan. | Interpersonal relations. | Interpersonal
   relations--Japan. | Politeness (Linguistics) | Politeness
   (Linguistics)--Japan.
Classification: LCC P94.7 .F875 2020 (print) | LCC P94.7 (ebook) | DDC
   177/.1--dc23
LC record available at https://lccn.loc.gov/2019013037
LC ebook record available at https://lccn.loc.gov/2019980082

Typeset by Steve Barganski

To the memory of my parents, Takeshiro and Toshiko

Contents

List of figures and tables

Foreword

Japanese language use – in particular, politeness – has played an important role in pragmatic research since the 1980s. The Japanese language has not only enriched pragmatic knowledge due to its amazing history and complex pragmatic features, but also Japanese scholars have successfully changed Western hegemony in many key areas. Perhaps most importantly, the highly influential area of linguistic politeness has greatly profited from Japanese research. Japanese metapragmatics – i.e. language about language use – has emerged in many studies in the field because Japanese is extremely rich in metapragmatic expressions, in particular when it comes to politeness, impoliteness, humour and also other (less-studied) sociopragmatic phenomena such as bullying, exclusion, aggression and so on. Indeed, the Western spectator may feel puzzled by words such as *kikubari* 気配り – roughly 'successfully complying with what the other is expected to want without making the other name it' – because many lingua-cultures have their equivalents of such impressively deep meaning. It is thus a surprising fact that to date no book-length study has been dedicated to the interface between Japanese metapragmatics and interpersonal language use. This is a knowledge gap that Saeko Fukushima's book fills with great mastery.

When Saeko asked me to write a foreword for her book, I agreed without having seen the manuscript at that time. Normally, I would have felt concerned in committing myself to praising a book that I have not read – and what else could a foreword do than say nice things about the book in which it occurs? The fact that Saeko Fukushima is a prolific and highly respected figure in our field by itself would have not convinced me to write this foreword: sometimes eminent scholars write boring books! Rather, the reason why I enthusiastically agreed to write this short text at that point in time is that in her career Saeko has studied things from a very novel point of view. Anyone who is familiar with her work knows that what is coming in a new Fukushima publication will surely be both novel and entertaining. If Japanese pragmatics has had any flaw, it might be its conventional and somewhat inward-looking character. The past decades have witnessed the emergence of some very influential areas in Japanese pragmatics, and yet research on the field has often been schematic in the sense that it has over-prioritised certain themes such as honorifics and backchannelling and neglected many others such as metapragmatics. The cautious conservatism of Japanese scholars may be due to the danger of sticking out in Japanese society. In addition, a body of Japanese studies may occasionally occur as somewhat inward-looking in character from the Western spectator's point of view. That is, in Japanese pragmatics, the study of the above-mentioned influential themes is often aimed at 'internal' use by experts of the language, and often the implicit moral of many studies is that Westerners may ultimately not understand how Japanese language use works. When Saeko approached me to write this foreword, I knew that whatever I will find, the book will be neither over-conventional nor inward-looking. And I was right!

The volume the reader holds is a collection of thematically interrelated essays on Japanese metapragmatics and politeness, including intriguingly complex and interesting expressions such as the above-mentioned *kukubari*. The topics studied are not only relevant to academics and advanced students working on Japanese, but practically to any reader who has an interest in pragmatics and the Japanese lingua-culture, due to the explanatory power of Fukushima's work. So, if the reader is prepared for an academic tour de force and the exploration of a fascinating lingua-culture provided by an outstanding expert of the field, reading the present volume is a must.

Dániel Z. Kádár
Dalian University of Foreign Languages, China
Hungarian Academy of Sciences

Acknowledgments

Many people deserve my sincere appreciation. Without their warm love and support, I could not have accomplished this work. Firstly, I would like to express my sincere gratitude to Mami Kasai, who always cares about others and demonstrates attentiveness. She taught me the importance of attentiveness and showed me how to demonstrate attentiveness in many ways. Without her warm guidance and great love, I would not have been able to complete this book. Another person I would like to thank is my late father, who always acted with the spirit of attentiveness. He told me to care about others. As an instance of this, I remember his exact words: 'If you want to drink tea, the others want to drink it, too. So, make some tea for them first.' Without his way of bringing up children, I would not have had an interest in attentiveness. I am grateful to have been brought up by him.

I am also very appreciative for the support given to me by many other people, among others, Maria Sifianou, Michael Haugh and Yukari Ohashi. Maria, who has always been supportive in many ways, deserves my special gratitude. I thank Michael, who showed an interest in my concept of attentiveness and an understanding of it, for our discussions on attentiveness. Yukari, whom I thank for our longstanding friendship, always gave me statistical advice whenever I needed it.

I would like to thank the International Pragmatics Association and Equinox Publishing for kindly granting permission for me to use some passages from the following articles. These articles were revised in this volume.

> The International Pragmatics Association for permission to reprint 'Evaluation of politeness: Do the Japanese evaluate attentiveness more positively than the British?', originally published in *Pragmatics* 19(4) (2009), 'A cross-generational and cross-cultural study on demonstration of attentiveness', originally published in *Pragmatics* 21(4) (2011), and 'Evaluation on (im)politeness: A comparative study among Japanese students, Japanese parents and American students on evaluation of attentiveness', originally published in *Pragmatics* 23(2) (2013).

> Equinox Publishing for permission to reprint 'Emic understandings of attentiveness and its related concepts among Japanese', originally published in *East Asian Pragmatics* 1(2) (2016).

Finally, my gratitude goes to the editors of the *Pragmatics Interfaces* series, especially Dániel Z. Kádár, for his support and warm friendship. Any errors that may remain are entirely mine.

CHAPTER 1

Introduction

1.1 Why this book?

We cannot live alone. We have contact with other people. We sometimes do something for others with the intention of helping them without, or before, being asked. Or, we are sometimes helped by such an act. I call that 'attentiveness', which is the theme of this volume. Attentiveness is briefly defined as the demonstrator's pre-emptive response to the recipient's verbal and non-verbal cues or situations surrounding the recipient and demonstrator, which takes the form of offering (see Section 1.2). The main aims of this book are to clarify what attentiveness is, to examine how it works and to address the importance of attentiveness in im/ politeness research. Firstly, the concept of attentiveness is investigated from various aspects which are related to im/politeness and other relevant issues. Secondly, attentiveness is examined in relation to other concepts from an interdisciplinary perspective. Thirdly, it explores how attentiveness works (including the demonstration and evaluation of attentiveness) in different cultural settings. Fourthly, emic understandings of attentiveness in Japanese relational networks are investigated. Finally, it considers how attentiveness is related to im/politeness.

Interpersonal pragmatics and cross-cultural pragmatics are the realms which this volume attempts to explore. Attentiveness itself is an interpersonal notion, and there is an increasing focus on interpersonal relations, or what has been broadly termed the relational shift (Kádár and Haugh 2013: 50).[1] Attentiveness may enhance interpersonal relationships when it is evaluated positively, and the reverse case is also possible. One of the features of interpersonal pragmatics is interdisciplinarity (see, e.g., Locher 2015). For example, Haugh, Kádár and Mills (2013: 2) argue that 'interpersonal pragmatics is conceived of as inherently interdisciplinary or multidisciplinary in nature, and thus its aims are to build interfaces or bridges between the fields of Pragmatics and Communication and other related fields, not create yet further disciplinary boundaries'. Moreover, attentiveness and some of its related concepts are also in the realm of multiple disciplines. Thus, an interdisciplinary perspective is adopted in the investigation of attentiveness in this volume (see Section 2.3).

According to Huang (2012: 78), cross-cultural pragmatics means 'the systematic study of language in use, especially pragmatic differences across different cultures and languages'. Cross-cultural comparisons of the demonstration and evaluation of attentiveness are made in this volume (see Chapter 3). Cross-generational comparisons of attentiveness among the Japanese people (see Chapters 3 and 4) are also included in this volume, as intra-cultural variation in cross-cultural politeness is relatively neglected (Kádár and Haugh 2013: 243).

The investigations of attentiveness in this book align with the recent trend in im/politeness research. For example, Ogiermann (2015) acknowledges the importance of attentiveness in im/politeness research, although she does not use the term 'attentiveness'. More specifically, Ogiermann (2015: 35) argues that '[a]ccommodating somebody's wishes by "reading their mind" and providing them with what they need without being explicitly asked for it is certainly cooperative and considerate'[2] (emphasis is added where it coincides with attentiveness). She further argues that 'politeness is not so much about how we express our needs and involve others in satisfying them, but *how we attend to others' needs*' (2015: 35, emphasis added). This clearly shows that attentiveness is closely related to politeness (see Section 4.3). Thus, this volume aims to further the understanding of im/politeness in a broad sense through the lens of attentiveness.

Another important issue in recent im/politeness research is evaluation. Evaluation of attentiveness is dealt with in Chapter 3. There are many factors which would influence the evaluation of attentiveness. People of different backgrounds would evaluate certain behaviours differently. Different backgrounds may be called different 'cultures', although what the term 'culture' means sometimes varies between researchers. The issue of 'culture' is taken up in Chapter 3.

Attentiveness, which can be manifested either linguistically, non-linguistically or both (see Section 2.2.1), attracts its due attention in im/politeness research from the perspective of non-verbal aspect. It can be said that non-verbal aspect has been rather neglected in the field (see, e.g., Bargiela-Chiappini and Harris 2006; Eelen 2001). Indeed, Sifianou and Garcés-Conejos Blitvich (2017: 583) rightly argue that we may be missing an important aspect of politeness by confining ourselves to the study of verbal behaviour. Sifianou and Garcés-Conejos Blitvich (2017: 583) further contend that 'we may unwittingly even discriminate against social groups where non-verbal, non-linguistic behaviour may be equally or even more valued' (see also Eelen 2001; O'Driscoll 2013; Sifianou and Tzanne 2010). Haugh's (2018: 154) following statement shows the rather dominant status of the linguistic aspect in (im)politeness research: '(im)politeness research has for the most part remained anchored to language use'. Furthermore, Haugh (2011: 264) points out that much of the work on politeness in East Asia has thus far focused on linguistic forms. It is, therefore, definitely necessary to research im/politeness also from a non-linguistic perspective. Japanese (an East Asian language) data is incorporated in this volume, and attentiveness includes both linguistic and non-linguistic aspects. Thus, the present volume aims to fill the gaps in the field.

1.2 Definition of attentiveness

Attentiveness was initially investigated as one type of response to off-record requests[3] (Fukushima 2000: 91–92).[4] As off-record requests are indirect, attentiveness is related to indirectness and off-record requests.[5] Example (1.1) shows an off-record request and a response to that.

(1.1)

1   A: Are you going to the university tomorrow?

2   B: Yes. What time shall I pick you up?

(adapted from Sifianou 1993: 76)

A and B in Example (1.1) are friends. Line 1 is considered as an off-record request. In response to that, it is natural to interpret the question (line 1) in this case as a request and to 'make the offer' immediately (line 2). The reason why B makes an offer is that the addressee has given a lift to the person asking the question on many occasions (Sifianou 1993: 76). The addressee showed her 'eagerness to be of help without having been directly asked' (Sifianou 1997a: 171). In other words, B (line 2) makes a pre-emptive offer. This kind of response is what I call attentiveness.

A similar example can be found in Grainger and Mills (2016), who attempt to discover a relationship between in/directness and im/politeness.[6] Grainger and Mills (2016: 2) argue that:

> In English particularly, hints (or off-record statements) are also considered as an important part of indirectness; for example, in a sentence such as 'Well, you're going to the cinema tonight, aren't you? And my partner's using the car tonight', the speaker relies on the interlocutor to infer that they are hinting that they would like a lift. This allows a hearer to choose to pick up on the inference and offer a lift, or to choose to ignore the inference completely.

To offer a lift in response to the off-record request above is also an example of attentiveness. As shown in the example above, inference plays an important role in understanding the intention of a potential recipient of attentiveness and consequently in demonstrating attentiveness.

Attentiveness is a pre-emptive response, which takes the form of offering. A demonstrator of attentiveness pays attention to others by the work of *ki* ('spirit'), reads the atmosphere in a situation and anticipates or infers the other party's feelings, state, needs and wants through a potential recipient's verbal and non-verbal cues. Taking these into account, a demonstrator of attentiveness considers what kinds of attentiveness would be suitable in the given situation (see Section 2.2.3) and then decides on a suitable kind of attentiveness. Attentiveness is manifested linguistically and/or non-linguistically through a pre-emptive response which offers help to the other party. It can be said that one of the major characteristics of attentiveness is the nature of pre-empting. That is, one demonstrates attentiveness without or before being asked by a potential recipient.

There are some similar concepts to attentiveness. One of them is 'mindfulness', which is used mostly in intercultural communication. According to Ting-Toomey (1999: 16), '[*m*]*indfulness* means being aware of our own and others' behavior in the situation, and paying focused attention to the *process* of communication taking place between us and dissimilar others' (emphasis in original; see also Langer 1989). Attentiveness is similar to mindfulness in the sense of paying attention to others. Žegarac and Spencer-Oatey (2013: 441) acknowledge the relationship between paying attention to the needs of others and attentiveness, and Žegarac, Spencer-Oatey and Ushioda (2014) elaborate this, by exploring 'mindfulness' in intercultural interactions in detail. However, attentiveness in this volume would differ from mindfulness in that the former pre-empts the other party's needs or desires and does something for her/him in both linguistic and non-linguistic forms, whereas the latter does not necessarily include such an aspect. It may be said that mindfulness is focused more on a communication process.

Other similar concepts to attentiveness are 'social support', namely, a vital component of well-being and a principal benefit of having close, positive personal relationships (Floyd and Ray 2017), and 'supportive communication', namely, 'verbal and non-verbal behavior produced with the intention of providing assistance to others perceived as needing that aid' (MacGeorge, Feng and Burleson 2011: 317). MacGeorge et al. (2011: 329) state the following, drawing on Bolger, Zuckerman and Kessler (2000): '[s]upportive interactions can be initiated by a support provider who notices an apparent need and offers support. In fact, it may be desirable that social networks respond to the needs of their members and offer help without being asked'. Pre-emptive features may not necessarily be essential in social support, whereas they are distinctive features in attentiveness. Supportive communication may be more similar to 'helping behaviour' (see Section 2.3) than to attentiveness in the sense that it offers help where aid is necessary. Although pre-emptive features are desirable in supportive communication, as noted above, they are not necessarily needed. In a similar vein, pre-emptive features are not obligatory in social support. By contrast, pre-emptive features are absolutely necessary in attentiveness.

1.3 Data and methodology

Some different types of data are used in this volume, as each type of data has strengths and weaknesses (see, e.g., Kasper 2008; Jucker, Schneider and Bublitz 2018). Data in this volume includes questionnaires, focus groups, metapragmatic interviews (see Appendix 1 for transcription conventions) and field notes. Drawing on Babbie (1998), Kasper (2008: 291–292) argues that questionnaires provide information about what respondents believe, think, feel or know, but not about what they do in their social life. The responses in questionnaires may be the results of what the participants believe to be the best. It is possible to obtain data from many participants at the same time by the use of questionnaires. Thus, questionnaires are used especially when quantitative analyses are made (see Sections 3.3, 3.4, 3.5 and 4.3). The types of questionnaires used in this volume include a multiple-choice questionnaire, a rating scale questionnaire and an open-ended questionnaire.

A focus group, 'a carefully planned series of discussions designed to obtain perceptions on a defined area of interest in a permissive, nonthreatening environment' (Krueger and Casey 2009: 2), is used in Section 2.3 in order to obtain emic understandings of the concepts of consideration, empathy, altruism and helping behaviour in relation to attentiveness. Metapragmatic interviews, which offer insights into the metalinguistic awareness of cultural insiders or members (Kádár and Haugh 2013: 193), are used in Sections 3.4 and 3.5. Field notes were also gathered. As attentiveness in our daily lives sometimes occurs suddenly, it is often the case that audio- or video-recorders are not to hand. Attentiveness occurs subtly, too. In such cases, field notes are useful in gathering data. Field notes often appear in Section 2.2.

1.4 Structure of the book

Chapter 2 attempts to clarify what attentiveness is. In Section 2.2, the concept of attentiveness, the conditions needed for attentiveness to arise and the processes of attentiveness are clarified. Different kinds of attentiveness, namely, genuine attentiveness, reflexive attentiveness and business-oriented attentiveness, are explained. The conditions needed for attentiveness to arise include (1) willingness, which is motivated by empathy, (2) ability and (3) availability, including material and non-material things to perform a certain act of attentiveness. As for the processes of attentiveness, several stages leading up to the demonstration of attentiveness are explained. After attentiveness is demonstrated, evaluation of attentiveness follows.

Section 2.3 attempts to elucidate attentiveness further by scrutinising the relationship between attentiveness and the four concepts of consideration, empathy, altruism and helping behaviour, taking an interdisciplinary perspective. These four concepts are important from the heart perspective of politeness and interpersonal relationships. Moreover, consideration, empathy and altruism appear to be related to politeness. The above-mentioned four concepts are sometimes investigated within different disciplines. Thus, an investigation across disciplines is undertaken.

The focus of Chapter 3 is on how attentiveness works in different cross-cultural settings. Some issues on culture, which are related to Chapter 3, are considered first, and then the demonstration and the evaluation of attentiveness are compared cross-culturally and cross-generationally. In Section 3.3, a cross-cultural comparison (between British and Japanese participants) is made on the evaluation of attentiveness. In Section 3.4, cross-cultural (between Japanese and American participants) and cross-generational comparisons (between Japanese participants of two generations) are made on the demonstration of attentiveness. In Section 3.5, cross-cultural and cross-generational comparisons are made on the evaluation of attentiveness, using the same participants as in Section 3.4.

Chapter 4 investigates attentiveness cross-generationally in Japanese relational networks. Section 4.2 investigates emic understandings of attentiveness and its related concepts, namely, anticipatory inference and empathy, by the Japanese participants of two generations. Section 4.3 investigates attentiveness cross-generationally through the conceptualisation of politeness in Japanese.

Chapter 5 presents an overview and implications of this volume and suggests some ideas on the future prospect of research on attentiveness.

CHAPTER 2

What is attentiveness?

2.1 Introduction

The aim of this chapter is to elucidate what attentiveness is. In Section 2.2, I will clarify the concept of attentiveness, the conditions needed for attentiveness to arise, namely, anticipatory inference and empathy, and the processes of attentiveness, which lead up to demonstration and evaluation of attentiveness. The concept of attentiveness is investigated from various perspectives, namely, im/politeness, morality and moral order, *ki* ('spirit'), linguistic and non-linguistic aspects, social skills, reputation and interpersonal relationships. Relationships between a demonstrator and a recipient of attentiveness and the intentionality of a potential recipient of attentiveness are also investigated. Different kinds of attentiveness, namely, genuine attentiveness, reflexive attentiveness and business-oriented attentiveness, are explained with some data.

Section 2.3 attempts to further the understanding of attentiveness by investigating the relationship between attentiveness and some other related concepts, namely, consideration (*hairyo*), empathy (*omoiyari*), altruism (*ritashugi* or *aitashin*) and helping behaviour (*enjyo koudou*). These concepts are important in interpersonal relationships, as they entail the element of thinking about others. It can be said that these concepts are related to a 'heart perspective' of politeness (see, e.g., Fukushima 2015: 269–270; Intachakra 2012; Ruhi and Işik-Güler 2007).

Attentiveness is a pre-emptive response, which takes the form of offering, and the potential demonstrator of attentiveness seeks the well-being of the other party in cases of genuine attentiveness (see Section 2.2.1). In other words, the demonstrator of attentiveness tries to be of some help to the other party. Moreover, the demonstration of attentiveness is motivated by empathy (see Section 2.2.2). In this respect, is attentiveness similar to altruism, which also means helping others and is motivated by empathy? How about helping behaviour, which – as the term obviously implies – helps others? If attentiveness differs from these concepts, how different is it? An investigation of the relationship between attentiveness and these concepts may lead to further clarification of attentiveness.

The investigation in Section 2.3 is conducted through the lens of emic understandings. The importance of emic understandings (see, e.g., Eelen 2001; Fukushima and Haugh 2014: 166; Kádár and Haugh 2013; Linguistic Politeness Research Group 2011) is well acknowledged in the field. Emic understandings are important also from the perspective of metapragmatics (see, e.g., Blum-Kulka 2005 [1992]; Caffi 2009; Hübler 2011; Hübler and Bublitz 2007; Overstreet 2010; Verschueren 2000), as metapragmatics can be broadly defined as 'the study of awareness by ordinary or lay observers of the ways in which they use language to interact and communicate with others' (Kádár and Haugh 2013: 181). According to Eelen (2001: 35), 'metapragmatic politeness' is 'instances of talk about politeness as a concept, about what people perceive politeness to be all about'.

2.2 Concept, conditions and processes of attentiveness

Section 2.2.1 investigates the concept of attentiveness, including the examinations of some relevant issues to attentiveness. They include (1) im/politeness, (2) morality and moral order, (3) *ki* ('spirit'), (4) linguistic/non-linguistic aspects, (5) social skills, reputation and interpersonal relationships, (6) relationships between the demonstrator and the recipient and (7) intentionality. Then, three different kinds of attentiveness, namely, genuine attentiveness, reflexive attentiveness and business-oriented attentiveness are explained. In relation to business-oriented attentiveness, *omotenashi* (a Japanese style hospitality) is also explained. In Section 2.2.2, some concepts which can function as the conditions needed for attentiveness to arise, namely, anticipatory inference and empathy, are examined. Section 2.2.3 presents the processes of attentiveness which lead to the demonstration and the evaluation of attentiveness.

2.2.1 Concept of attentiveness

Attentiveness and im/politeness

Attentiveness is related to im/politeness. For native Turkish speakers, for example, a key criterion for politeness judgments is attentiveness to other's needs, wishes and emotions (Işik-Güler and Ruhi 2010: 632). Attentiveness (genuine attentiveness) (see the discussion below) is derived from the concern for someone's well-being (see Fukushima 2000, 2004). In this sense, the demonstration of attentiveness is an orientation to politeness. This politeness concern is derived from the demonstrator's side. Politeness can arise also from the recipient's side, as it is the recipient who evaluates attentiveness. A positive evaluation of attentiveness by a recipient could occasion politeness. Therefore, it can be said that politeness is located both in the demonstrator and the recipient of attentiveness (Fukushima 2015: 275).

We can see the connection between attentiveness and politeness in Examples (2.1) and (2.2). Sayuri (S) and Kumiko (K) in Example (2.1) are classmates.

(2.1)

1	S:	*Kumiko-chan, konaida no jyugyo no purinto mot-te-ru?*
		Kumiko, do you have the handout from the last class?
2	K:	*e, dono jyugyo desu ka?*
		um, which class?
3	S:	*ano ne, getsuyo sangen, ano jyugyo.*
		um, the class third period on Monday
4	K:	*getsuyo sangen tte iu to, watashi wa,*
		Monday third period huh … I …
5		*are-desu ne, ano eigo desu ne.*
		um … that English [class] huh
6	S:	*konoaida yasun-jat-te sa*
		I missed the class recently.[1]
7	K:	*a*
		oh
8	S:	*purinto, morat-ta mitai na-n-da kedo …*
		and it seems you got a handout but …
9	K:	*a, ii-desu yo*
		oh, that's fine.
10		*kopi shimasu ka?*
		Will you make a copy?

(adapted from Haugh 2015: 258–259)[2]

Although Sayuri wants a handout from the last class from which she was absent, she does not ask Kumiko explicitly. She only implies her needs in line 8. Kumiko infers Sayuri's needs and demonstrates attentiveness in lines 9–10. '[A] polite stance is indicated through the way in which Kumiko demonstrates attentiveness (*kikubari*) towards the implied needs of Sayuri' (Haugh 2015: 259). According to Haugh (2015: 260), 'the pre-emptive offer made by Kumiko is recognisably "polite" because it shows concern for the well-being of the beneficiary'.[3] As Sayuri needs a handout and Kumiko lets Sayuri make a copy of it, Sayuri must have evaluated Kumiko's attentiveness positively, which occasions politeness. However, there are cases in which attentiveness can be perceived negatively, such as meddling (see, e.g., Chang and Fukushima 2017; Fukushima and Haugh 2014), even when attentiveness is demonstrated for the sake of the well-being of the recipient.

In other words, attentiveness can be evaluated either positively or negatively by the recipient, which may occasion politeness or impoliteness.

Example (2.2) shows that the politeness concern is achieved interactionally by both the demonstrator and the recipient of attentiveness. In Example (2.2), a mother (M) and a daughter (D) are walking down the street towards the local train station. The mother notices that she has forgotten to bring a handkerchief.

(2.2)

1   M: *Mama, hankachi mot-te-ki-ta*

2   *to omot-ta-n-da kedo …*

         I thought I had brought a hankie along but …

3   D: (Passes her handkerchief to her mother)

4   M: *A, domo.*

         Oh, thanks.

(adapted from Haugh 2007b: 95)

According to Haugh (2007b: 95), '[t]he daughter's interpreting of her mother's utterance and her offer of a handkerchief were both accepted by her mother, and thus politeness also appears to have been retrospectively co-constituted through the daughter's response'. Haugh (2015: 264) cites the same example and he (2015: 265) states that 'this pre-emptive offer demonstrates attentiveness (*kikubari*) towards the implied needs of her mother, which is recognisably "polite", because it shows concern for her well-being (Fukushima 2004, 2009, 2011, 2013)'. Haugh (2015: 265) further argues that 'an orientation to a concern for "politeness" is arguably interactionally achieved by the two participants'. This suggests that the mother's attempt to solicit attentiveness by making an off-record request[4] and the attentiveness demonstrated by her daughter constitute politeness through interaction between mother and daughter, and that the attentiveness demonstrated by the daughter is polite because it was for the well-being of the mother. Furthermore, the mother evaluates her daughter's attentiveness positively, which leads to politeness.

Attentiveness, morality and moral order

Attentiveness is related to morality[5] and moral order (see, e.g., Haidt and Graham 2007; Haidt and Kesebir 2010; Haugh 2015; Kádár and Haugh 2013; Kádár and Márquez-Reiter 2015; Kádár 2017; Kádár and Fukushima 2018; Kádár, Parvaresh and Ning 2019; Spencer-Oatey and Kádár 2016). Bergmann (1998: 280) argues that '[m]orality is such a common and intrinsic quality of everyday social interaction that it is usually invisible to us, like glasses that provide a sharp sight of the area beyond although they themselves remain unseen'. According to Kádár et al. (2019), morality is a social skill, and humans develop a moral competence through socialisation. It is anchored to (or, at least, projected to) moral norms and related social ideologies (Kádár et al. 2019). Attentiveness is also a social skill which people develop through socialisation in light of moral norms and social ideologies. 'In general, attentiveness to others' needs is ideologically a moral issue', according to Cook and Burdelski (2017: 476).

Haidt and Graham (2007: 104–106) have listed five foundations of morality: (1) harm/care, (2) fairness/reciprocity, (3) ingroup/loyalty, (4) authority/respect and (5) purity/sanctity (see also Haidt and Kesebir 2010: 822). Among these, attentiveness is related to harm/care, as this type of morality includes concern for the suffering of others. All normally developed individuals dislike seeing suffering in others and have the potential to feel the emotion of compassion in response (Haidt and Graham 2007: 104). A potential demonstrator of attentiveness (in the case of genuine attentiveness) cares about a potential recipient of attentiveness and is concerned about her/him. Thus, a potential demonstrator demonstrates attentiveness so that s/he does not want to see a potential recipient suffer from something. In this sense, attentiveness is related to morality.

It is noteworthy that Haidt and Graham (2007) regard the five moral foundations above as universally available but are variably developed and manifested among different cultural groups (see Spencer-Oatey and Kádár 2016: 83). This may be related to, at least in part, some cross-cultural differences of the demonstration and evaluation of attentiveness (see Chapter 3).

According to Lempert (2013: 380–381), Sifianou (1992) argued that off-record requests (see Example [1.1]) provided addressees with the opportunity to express their generosity and solicitude for the interlocutor by offering, instead of avoiding imposition, as Brown and Levinson's (1978, 1987) theory would predict. Lempert (2013: 381) states that 'Sifianou linked this politeness behaviour to virtues of hospitality and generosity, and, more deeply, to *morally* inflected conceptions of personhood in Greece' (emphasis added). As 'solicitude for the interlocutor by offering' is very similar to attentiveness, we can see a connection between attentiveness and morality here.

Garfinkel (1967: 35) argues that 'the moral order consists of the rule governed activities of everyday life. A society's members encounter and know the moral order as perceivedly normal courses of action – familiar scenes of everyday affairs, the world of daily life known in common with others and with others taken for granted.' In a similar vein, Kádár and Haugh (2013: 67) define the moral order as 'what members of a sociocultural group or relational network "take for granted"'. It can be said that evaluations of attentiveness are grounded in the moral order. People have expectancies towards the moral order, and expectancies may differ cross-culturally. Thus, evaluation of attentiveness in different sociocultural groups or relational networks may differ (see Chapters 3 and 4). The moral order embodies moral values and norms, but people may not necessarily notice this embodiment until the moral order gets violated (Kádár et al. 2019) (see, e.g., Okano and Brown 2018 which depicts a case of violation of moral order by a celebrity in Japan).

Attentiveness and ki *('spirit'):* Kizukai *and* kikubari

Riley (2007: 217) lists attentiveness as one of the communicative virtues. Concepts of communicative virtues (CCV) (see also *kommunikative Tugend* in Hermanns 1993) were proposed by Marui, Nishijima, Noro, Reinelt and Yamashita (1996) as a 'higher-order notion' than politeness. Marui et al. (1996: 385) argue that what corresponds to 'politeness' in English language and culture represents only some of the components of *Höflichkeit* in German (Held 2005[1992]) or *teinei* in Japanese, and vice versa. According to Marui et al. (1996: 385), CCV are concepts which are historically developed and continually transformed in ongoing social interactions, concepts to which social members refer in evaluating the social behaviour of others as well as of themselves. Marui et al. (1996) treat attentiveness (they use the term *kizukai*) as one of the Japanese concepts of communicative virtues, and they (1996: 395) translate *kizukai* as 'reading others' needs'.

Kizukai or *kikubari* can also be found elsewhere. Lebra (2004: 44) argues that 'courtesy works on other's "face" – that is, honor or pride – calling on an etiquette or subtleties aimed at avoiding offense or embarrassment'. Lebra (2004: 44) calls such courteous sensitivities *kizukai* (or *kikubari*), meaning 'alertness and caring attention to other's needs or feelings'. 'Reading others' needs' and 'caring attention to other's needs or feelings' constitute a part of attentiveness in my terms.

As some of the previous studies above show, attentiveness is closely related to *kikubari* (lit. 'allocation of *ki*') or *kizukai* (lit. 'to make *ki* work') in Japanese. *Ki* is variously translated as (1) 'spirit, mind, heart', (2) 'mind, intention, will', (3) 'feelings, mood', (4) 'nature, disposition', (5) 'interest', (6) 'care, precaution, attention', (7) 'air', (8) 'atmosphere', (9) 'qi in Chinese philosophy' and (10) 'fragrance, taste' (Watanabe, Skrzypczak and Snowden 2003: 659–660). In this volume, *ki* can be understood as spirit, mind, care or attention. Hamano (1987: 106) contends as follows on *ki*: (1) *ki* is regarded as a changeable material, and perceived as something able to be seen or felt, for example, *ki no mijikai* ('short-tempered'); (2) *ki* is seen as attention toward others, for example, *ki wo tsukau* ('worrying' or 'paying attention') and (3) *ki* is thought to be something like radio waves between people, for example, *ki raku na* ('easy-going'). The second sense of *ki* in Hamano (1987) above applies most closely to attentiveness, namely, attention towards others.

Kizukai (which means *arekore to kokoro wo tsukau koto* 'to use heart on various occasions' [Shinmura 2018: 718]) consists of *ki* ('spirit') and the noun form of *tsukau* (which means *kokoro wo hataraka seru* 'to make heart work' [Shinmura 2018: 1934]). *Kikubari* consists of *ki* ('spirit') and the noun form of *kubaru* ('to allocate'). In the definition of *kikubari*, there are two orientations: to be alert so that there will be no inconveniences or failures, and to be attentive towards the other party (Shinmura 2018: 697). The former is self-oriented, as one is careful about what one is doing so that there would be no failures. The latter is other-oriented, which is more closely related to attentiveness in this volume (see Fukushima 2015: 274).

Ki ('spirit') and *kokoro* ('heart')[6] are often used interchangeably, according to Lebra (1993: 64). Hamano (1987: 110) also argues that *ki* is interchangeable with *kokoro*. There is also the term *kokoro kubari* (lit. 'allocation or distribution of *kokoro*'). Actually, *kokoro kubari* is listed as a meaning of *kikubari* in Shinmura (2018: 697). It can therefore be said that *kikubari* entails 'heart', and that attentiveness can be construed in relation to the heart.

Although attentiveness is closely related to *kikubari* or *kizukai* in Japanese, I am not proposing that it is unique to Japanese culture or Japanese language. The concept of attentiveness can be found also in other cultures, for example, in Greek, as shown in Sifianou (1993, 1997a) and Sifianou and Tzanne (2010), even though there is no single term (such as 'attentiveness') to describe such actions in Greek (Fukushima 2015: 273). The results of the study by Ogiermann and Suszczyńska (2011), which investigated the conceptualisation of Polish and Hungarian im/politeness, also show that attentiveness is found in other cultures. In Hungarian data, *figzelmesség* ('attentiveness/considerateness') was found. Polish participants associated being polite with *helping others* and *attending to their needs* rather than with using particular linguistic formulae (see also Ogiermann 2012). These results are closely related to the concept of attentiveness. Moreover, the concept of attentiveness is found in Zimbabwean culture. According to Grainger (2014), people in Zimbabwe do not make requests. It is presumed that they infer the other party's needs and pre-empt offers, which can be regarded as attentiveness.[7] And most probably some lexical forms of attentiveness can be found in other languages, too. For instance, *Aufmerksamkeit* in German may be equivalent to attentiveness (Fukushima 2015: 273).

Linguistic and non-linguistic aspects: cues, manifestations, and evaluation of attentiveness

Cues which may trigger attentiveness can be linguistic as well as non-linguistic. Line 1 in Example (1.1) ('Are you going to the university tomorrow?') is a linguistic cue.[8] Non-linguistic cues include, for example, the state of the other party (see Examples [2.3] and [2.4]; the author's own recordings and associated transcriptions). These cues are sometimes used to solicit attentiveness (see the discussion below), as in Example (1.1).

JP4,[9] who is a librarian at a university, in Example (2.3) recalls the attentiveness which she has received from some other librarians. A cue in this example is the state of being busy, which is non-linguistic. In the English translation, some words are added in { } for clarification.

(2.3)

1   JP4:   *Maa (.) isogashiku te koremo yaranakya (.) koremo yaranakya tte iu*
まぁ忙しくてこれもやらなきゃこれもやらなきゃっていう
Well, when I am busy {with work}, I also need to do this and that,

2   *jibun no shigoto no naka de (0.6) ano aiteru kata ga (.)*
自分の仕事の中で、あの、あいてる方が、
in such a working situation, some other {librarian}, who is not fully occupied with her work,

3   *ano chotto tetsudaou ka (.) to iu koe wo kakete kureru toki desu.*
あのちょっと手伝おうかという声をかけてくれる時です。
talked to me, 'Shall I help you a bit?'

JP1, who is in her fifties, in Example (2.4) has a limp. A cue is the physical state of JP1, namely, non-linguistic. She recalls the attentiveness she has received.

(2.4)

1   JP1:   *Kou yorikakatte iru to (.) maa isu wo motte kite kuretari toka (.) hai (.)*
こう寄りかかっていると、まぁ椅子を持ってきてくれたりとか、はい、
When I lean over the wall like this, someone brings me a chair. Yes.

2   *ano wazawaza toumawari nan desu keredo (.) ano erebeeta no hou e itte kuretari toka (.)*
あのわざわざ遠回りなんですけれど、あの、エレベーターの方へ行ってくれたりとか、
Although it is a detour {for them}, someone {who is with me} goes to the elevator.

3   *souiu kokoro zukai wo shite itadakeru toki wa arimasu.*
そういう心遣いをして頂ける時はあります。
I receive that kind of attentiveness.

Not only the cues of potential recipients of attentiveness, but also attentiveness can be demonstrated linguistically (e.g., offering help linguistically, giving advice), non-linguistically (e.g., doing something for the other party. Handing a handkerchief in Example [2.2] is an example of attentiveness demonstrated non-linguistically), or both linguistically and non-linguistically. Example (2.5) (noted down by the author) includes attentiveness manifested linguistically (namely, offering help in line 2) and non-linguistically (namely, an action to move a refrigerator after the conversation). Example (2.5) takes place in the corridor at the university immediately after the great east Japan earthquake in March 2011. The author bumps into H (a British male). S (the author) is trying to tidy up the mess in her office. We can see chaotic situations in every office. Right after the conversation (Example [2.5]), H comes to S's office and moves the refrigerator back.

(2.5)

1	S:	My office is in chaos, too. The refrigerator has moved.
2	H:	Can I help you put it back? I am strong.
3	S:	That would be very helpful.

(adapted from Fukushima 2011: 551)

Manifestation of attentiveness involves offering both material things (such as lending a pen) and non-material things. Non-material things can be classified roughly into two: tangible (e.g., moving the refrigerator back as in Example [2.5], or opening the window when it is hot) and intangible (e.g., making suggestions or giving advice). Cutrona and Suhr's (1992) five categories of 'social support' might be helpful in understanding the different manifestations of attentiveness:[10] tangible support (the provision of money, services or other material resources), informational support (the provision of facts and information to aid decision-making), network support (spending time with others to promote affiliation and connectedness), emotional support (expressions of love, empathy and encouragement) and esteem support (expressions that bolster the recipient's confidence and self-concept). Example (2.6) (noted down by the author) is an example of attentiveness demonstrated non-linguistically, offering a material thing, which is tangible support in Cutrona and Suhr's (1992) terms. The background is that four people (a Taiwanese, a New Zealander and two Japanese) happened to sit at the same table at a conference dinner. A Taiwanese (M) usually uses her English name. As S (the author) wanted to know her Chinese name, S talked to her. Immediately after line 3, Y, who happened to sit next to S, handed S a ballpoint pen without saying anything.

(2.6)

1	S:	What is your Chinese name? Could you possibly mark your name in the conference book, so that I can remember it? Otherwise, I cannot recognise your paper written in your Chinese name.
2	M:	Here (indicating her name in the conference book).
3	S:	Oh, your presentation is already over.

(adapted from Fukushima 2013: 279)

I did not ask Y to lend me a ballpoint pen. Y pre-empted my need and demonstrated attentiveness. Actually, I had not even thought of borrowing a pen. In this case, attentiveness was non-linguistically demonstrated; and a trigger for attentiveness to arise was a verbal cue (mentioning of marking M's name in the conference book in line 1) and a situation, namely, a conference dinner. It is often the case that people may not have a pen to hand at a dinner table, and it would be sometimes difficult to catch/remember foreign names. Attentiveness demonstrated in this case was with a low degree of imposition, that is, it did not take the demonstrator much time, effort or financial burden to demonstrate attentiveness. I evaluated Y's attentiveness very positively, although I did not have the intention of receiving attentiveness (see further discussion below).

Evaluation also entails both linguistic and non-linguistic aspects. When a recipient of attentiveness evaluates attentiveness, evaluation itself is non-linguistic, rather it is cognitive. However, when the evaluation is articulated, it becomes linguistic. When the evaluation is presented only through behaviours (e.g., smiles or frowns), it is non-linguistic.

Attentiveness and social skills, reputation and interpersonal relationships

Attentiveness can be regarded as one of the social skills[11] or a sign of maturity (see Example [4.14]). Miyahara (2004: 284) argues that a person who is able to observe subtle, social norms associated with the following attributes is regarded as mature and competent (Fukushima 2015: 274). These attributes include four characteristics of Japanese communication (Tsujimura 1987): *ishindenshin* ('communication without language'), taciturnity or passivity, indirect communication and respect for reverberation, and sensitivity towards *kuuki* (lit. 'air' but here, rather, 'atmosphere'). Tsujimura (1987: 124) states that *kuuki* is a mental phenomenon which exerts a pervasive pressure on us and on our behavioural patterns. The last attribute, namely, *kuuki*, in particular is related to attentiveness, as one must read the atmosphere in order to demonstrate attentiveness. Those who can demonstrate attentiveness as expected are evaluated positively, being called *kigakiku* 'attentive' (Fukushima 2011: 550). Those who are regarded as *kigakiku* can gain reputation, as *kigakiku* is an ability, that is, one can make a quick judgment according to the situation (Shinmura 2018: 682) and can thus act accordingly (Fukushima 2015: 274). Example (2.7) (the author's own recordings and associated transcriptions) illustrates that attentive people are evaluated positively.

(2.7)

1   JS8:   *Yappa sukareru ningen tte ki ga tsuku koto ga dekiru hito dato omoun desu yo.*
やっぱ好かれる人間って気が付くことができる人だと思うんですよ。
Well, we like people who are attentive, I think.

2   *Watashi wa sore wo ki ga tsukeru youni narou tte doryoku wa shite irun desu kedo* (.)

私はそれを気が付けるようになろうって努力してはいるんですけど、

I make efforts to be attentive, but …

3   *sono hito ga baito toka wo shite ite* (.)

その人がバイトとかをしていて、

4   *watashi ga kizukanaka tta koto ni* (.) *senpai ga kizuite yattete* (.)

私が気付かなかったことに先輩が気付いてやってて、

A senior at a part-time job demonstrates attentiveness, when I was not attentive.

5   *aa* (.) *erai naa toka* (.)

あぁ偉いなぁとか、

Well, I feel she is great, or something like that.

6   *yappa* (.) *dekiru hito wa sugoi na to omoi masu shi* (.)

やっぱできる人はすごいなと思いますし、

Actually, I think those who are attentive are great.

7   *sugoi yaku ni tatte iru no wo mite* (0.8)

すごい役に立っているのを見て、

On seeing that those who are attentive are helpful {at a part-time job},

8   *dekitara motto yaku ni* (.) *jibun mo taterushi tte* (.) *omoi masu.*

できたらもっと役に、自分も立てるしって思います。

I think I could be more helpful if I were more attentive.

JS8 in Example (2.7) admires her senior, who is attentive (lines 4–5), and JS8 tries to be attentive (line 2). JS8 evaluates her senior positively (lines 5–6), and states that people like those who are attentive (line 1). This shows that someone who is attentive (*kigakiku*) is evaluated positively, and this is in line with Hamano's (1987: 106) contention, namely that our personality is evaluated according to the way we pay attention to others. Žegarac and Spencer-Oatey (2013: 441) argue that one could be considered self-oriented because of a lack of alertness to the needs of others and will most likely fail to cooperate with them effectively in negotiating meaning and conveying messages. The lack of alertness to the needs of others may be the opposite of being attentive. Thus, it can be said that being attentive is important for one's personality (see Fukushima 2015: 274) (or social skills) and reputation as a consequence.

Example (2.8) (the author's own recordings and associated transcriptions) shows that one who cannot demonstrate attentiveness is not positively evaluated. Example (2.8) indicates further that attentiveness would help enhance one's reputation and would also promote group cohesion and interpersonal relationships.

(2.8)

<table>
<tr><td>1</td><td>JS7:</td><td>Tatoeba baitosaki demo (.) ki wo kubare nai hito tte yappari (.) chyotto arette (.) omou shi</td></tr>
</table>

例えばバイト先でも、気を配れない人ってやっぱり、ちょっとあれって思うし、

For example, at a part time job, there are some people who are not attentive. I feel awkward {I do not make a positive evaluation towards them}.

2 　*sugoku ki wo tsukau kata ga ite (.) taihen souda na toka omottari (.)*

すごく気を遣う方がいて、大変そうだなとか思ったり、

{On the other hand}, there is a person, who is very attentive. I think it may be hard for her/him {to be attentive to that extent}.

3 　*motto ki wo tsukawa nakute ii noni (.) toka wa omou koto wa aru kedo (.)*

もっと気を遣わなくていいのにとかは思うことはあるけど、

I sometimes think that it would be all right if s/he would not be so attentive, however,

4 　*ki wo tsukai sugita hito ni taishite (.) yadana toka (.) omottari wa anmari shinai to*

5 　*omou node (.) kizukawa nai hito yori mo (.) tsukau hito no hou ga (.)*

6 　*syuudan de iru toki wa (.) yappari ii kana tte (.).*

気を遣いすぎた人に対して、やだなとか思ったりはあんまりしないと思うので、気遣わない人よりも、遣う人の方が集団でいるときはやっぱりいいかなって。

I do not make a negative evaluation towards people who are very attentive, I think. Thus, I feel more comfortable to be with someone who is attentive rather than those who are not attentive, when we are in a group.

7 　*Nanka (.) baito saki toka kurasu toka (.) ironna tokoro ni (.) nandarou (.)*

8 　*shiriai ga dekite iru to (.)*

なんかバイト先とかクラスとか、いろんなところに、何だろう、知り合いができていると、

Well, at a part-time job or in a class, in many places, well, how to put it, I get acquainted with people.

9 　*sono tokoro dokoro deno (.) funiki toka (.) kuuki toka ga attari suru no de (.)*

その所々での雰囲気とか空気とかがあったりするので、

As there are different atmospheres at different places,

10 　*soko de umaku iku tame ni wa (.)*

そこでうまくいくためには、

in order to get along with people {at different places},

11 　*uun nandarou (.) sono ba de ki wo tsukatta hou ga (.) jibun mo raku dashi (.)*

12 　*mawari tomo umaku iku kana (.) to omoi masu.*

うぅん何だろう、その場で気を遣ったほうが自分も楽だし、

周りともうまくいくかなと思います。

> well, how to put it, it would be better to demonstrate attentiveness at each place. In
> that way, I feel comfortable and get along with others, I think.

According to JS7, she would make a negative evaluation towards those who are not attentive (line 1), and she has never made a negative evaluation towards someone who was very attentive (lines 2–4). This shows that one's reputation is related to the demonstration of attentiveness. According to JS7, attentiveness may help promote group cohesion (lines 5–6) and interpersonal relationships at different places (lines 7–12). It is interesting to note that JS7 herself feels comfortable or at ease by demonstrating attentiveness (line 11) at different places, including at a part-time job or in a class. She may feel comfortable because she can get along with others by demonstrating attentiveness (line 12). This shows that attentiveness helps construct good interpersonal relationships and that having good interpersonal relationships may outweigh the cost (e.g., time, energy and so on) required to demonstrate attentiveness.

Relationships between the demonstrator and the recipient of attentiveness

Marui et al. (1996: 396) claim that '[i]n the case of *kizukai* such manifestations can take the form of offering things or services to show friendliness, especially in relationships which are neither too close nor too distant'. However, attentiveness is demonstrated in every degree of familiarity between a demonstrator and a recipient, namely, from very familiar (close friends) to not very familiar at all (strangers) (see Section 3.4). With regard to the relationships between a demonstrator and a recipient of attentiveness, an interesting cross-cultural difference was found in Fukushima and Haugh (2014), which compared Japanese and Taiwanese emic understandings of attentiveness and its related notions. The Taiwanese participants would demonstrate attentiveness only to insiders but not to outsiders such as strangers, although such a distinction was not found among the Japanese participants.

Attentiveness is demonstrated in all kinds of relationships, regardless of status differences, that is, among status equals (e.g. among friends or colleagues), from status inferiors to superiors (e.g. from a student to a professor) and from status superiors to inferiors (e.g. from a professor to a student) (see, e.g., Fukushima 2004), although there are differences in terms of frequency of occurrence. Social relationships between a potential demonstrator and a potential recipient, or *tachiba*, namely, the 'place one stands' (Haugh 2005: 47) of a potential demonstrator and a potential recipient may influence the decision of a potential demonstrator to demonstrate attentiveness. When there is a difference in status between a potential demonstrator and a potential recipient of attentiveness, for example, attentiveness may be demonstrated with different frequency. For example, a junior may be expected to demonstrate attentiveness to a superior. This is in line with Lebra's

(2004: 45) contention, that is, 'when vertical distance is involved, the inferior self must be all the more alert, ready to employ *kizukai* at any instance to make the superior other feel comfortable' (emphasis added). Example (2.9) shows the different frequencies of demonstrating attentiveness. The Japanese student in Example (2.9) sometimes meets the personnel at a company at which she is going to work after graduation.

(2.9)

1   JS4:   *Eetto: (.) toki to baai ni yori masu. Ano (.) toku ni (.) ano: (.)*
　　　　　　えっとー、時と場合によります。あの特に、あのー
　　　　　　Um, it depends on the time and situation. Um, especially, um,

2   　　　　*meue no hito toka: (.) chotto syakaiteki na tachiba ga chigau hito no toki toka wa*
　　　　　　目上の人とかー、ちょっと社会的な立場が違う人の時とかは
　　　　　　when {I'm} with superiors or those with a social place/role that is different {to mine},

3   　　　　*jibun ga sossen shite ki wo tsukatte nanika wo suru to iu no wo (.)*
　　　　　　自分が率先して気を遣って何かをするというのを

4   　　　　*kangaeterun desu kedo (.)*
　　　　　　考えるんですけど
　　　　　　I show initiative in paying attention to {their} feelings, and think about what I can do.

5   　　　　*dousedai kurai no baai wa (.) mushiro (.) tabun (.)*
　　　　　　同世代くらいの場合は、むしろ多分

6   　　　　*ki wo tsukatte moratte iru gawa kana (.) to iu fuu ni kangaete i masu.*
　　　　　　気を遣ってもらっている側かなというふうに考えています。
　　　　　　But in the case of those who are about the same generation {as me}, instead, probably, I wonder if {I'm the one who} receives attentiveness, I think that way.

(adapted from Fukushima and Haugh 2014: 174)

JS4 in Example (2.9) would demonstrate attentiveness far more to her superiors (lines 2–4) than to her equals (lines 5–6). This confirms Lebra's (2004: 45) contention above.

The intentionality of a potential recipient of attentiveness

The discussion so far has included the aspect that a potential demonstrator of attentiveness would infer the needs of a potential recipient and s/he would demonstrate attentiveness. However, there are also cases in which a potential recipient of attentiveness would solicit attentiveness. Grainger and Mills (2016: 67–68), who compare table manners between middle and working classes in terms of in/directness, state that '[t]he rules in these "nice" (a euphemism for middle-class) houses consist in not directly requesting food at the table, but only indirectly manoeuvring your neighbour so that, through you offering them food, they will in turn offer you something'. Grainger and Mills (2016: 68) state that Fukushima (2015) calls this type of politeness 'attentiveness'. This is, however, related only to the case of attentiveness in which a potential recipient solicits attentiveness. I argue that there are two types of attentiveness: (1) where a potential recipient of attentiveness solicits attentiveness; and (2) where s/he does not solicit attentiveness, or s/he may not even think of receiving attentiveness in some situations. For example, A (line 1 in Example [1.1]) solicits attentiveness. It is obvious that A wants a lift. This is easily observed, because B has given a lift to A on many occasions in Example (1.1). Example (2.10) (noted down by the author) is another example in which a potential recipient solicits attentiveness. H and S (the author) are colleagues, and they usually commute to university by car. H lives in a city next to that in which S lives. After the meeting, H comes to S's office.

(2.10)

1	H:	Are you going back to ○○ {the name of the city in which S lives}?
2	S:	Yes.
3	H:	Today I came by train. My wife is using my car.
4	S:	Shall I give you a lift?
5	H:	Thank you.

The question in line 1 can be considered as a pre-request. It is obvious that S goes back to where she lives. H states that he came to university by train, which is the fact, and then he states the reason (line 3). As S can infer H's intention immediately, that is, H wants a lift, S gives an offer of a lift in line 4 and takes him back home (demonstrated attentiveness). The re-occurrence (B has given a lift to A on many occasions) in Example (1.1) and the background or common knowledge (H usually commutes to university by car) between a potential demonstrator and a potential recipient of attentiveness in Example (2.10) may help a potential demonstrator of attentiveness infer that a potential recipient of attentiveness solicits attentiveness in these cases.

However, in Example (2.5), S (line 1) does not have any intention of soliciting attentiveness. S just tells H the fact in a rather shocking state after a big earthquake. S does not seem to be physically strong enough to move the refrigerator back, whereas H looks strong. This may be why H offers to move the refrigerator back and demonstrates attentiveness. Also, in Example (2.6), S does not have any intention of soliciting attentiveness; however, Y kindly demonstrates attentiveness (handing S a ballpoint pen). As S is the author, we know that S does not have any intention of soliciting attentiveness in these cases. Otherwise, it is not always easy to detect whether a potential recipient of attentiveness solicits attentiveness or not. Indeed, O'Driscoll (2013: 179) argues that 'we see the limitations of exploring interaction through participant intentions'. One of the reasons for this is that we are not the participants, and another is that the participant her/himself may not know, as our motives for action in interaction, or any gathering, are often opaque to us, according to O'Driscoll (2013: 179).

A similar concept to one type of attentiveness, namely, a potential recipient of attentiveness solicits attentiveness, is 'support seeking' (or 'supportive communication' as mentioned earlier), which can be defined as 'intentional communicative activity with the aim of eliciting supportive actions from others' (MacGeorge et al. 2011: 330). An interesting contention MacGeorge et al. make is that members of collectivist cultures are less likely than members of individualist cultures to seek social support as a means of coping (2011: 330). Drawing on Gao (1996), MacGeorge et al. (2011: 330) state that one explanation for these cultural differences is that members of collectivist cultures may be comparatively hesitant to disturb the harmony of their in-groups by focusing the attention of group members on their distressed emotional states. Furthermore, MacGeorge et al. (2011: 330) explain that Asian philosophical and religious traditions (especially Buddhism and Taoism) promote the virtue of acceptance and endurance in the fate of adversity (Marsella 1993), making active support seeking seem inappropriate or superfluous (Wong, Wong and Scott 2006). Although further scrutiny seems to be needed with regard to these cultural differences, they may lead to interesting future studies.

In relation to the above-mentioned two different types of attentiveness (namely, a potential recipient of attentiveness either soliciting or not soliciting attentiveness), it is worth noting the differentiation between 'soliciting' (Haugh 2015) and 'prompting' (Haugh 2017; see also Haugh 2016b). 'Soliciting involves a speaker interactionally positioning another participant to pre-emptively initiate an action sequence for which that other person is thus held primarily responsible' (Haugh 2015: 262). The warrant for initiating an action sequence can be implemented by speakers through a number of interrelated practices, such as 'my side telling' (or 'fishing'), 'reporting', 'topicalising troubles' or 'noticing a deficiency' (Haugh 2015: 262-264). According to Haugh (2017: 186), '[p]rompting involves one participant inviting another participant to initiate some kind of social action, thereby avoiding accountability or having launched that social action sequence'. Haugh (2017: 186) further notes that:

> The term 'prompting' is equivocal with regards to putative intentions. We may be prompted to offer assistance to someone who has fallen down, for instance, by virtue of them having fallen down, without them having to say or otherwise indicate they need help.

Whereas 'soliciting' presupposes intentionality, 'prompting' does not in the same way as soliciting.

Genuine attentiveness and reflexive attentiveness

There are different orientations of attentiveness: genuine attentiveness and reflexive attentiveness. In principle, the former is displaying concern for the well-being of the recipient (or helping the other party), and the latter is for the benefit of the demonstrator. The benefit can be material or non-material. For example, one may receive some kind of gift in return (material benefits), or s/he gains credit or enhances her/his reputation (non-material benefits) as someone who is 'attentive' (*kigakiku*) (Fukushima 2011: 550; see Example [2.7]), or as a ploy to receive attentiveness from others in the future (see Example [2.12]). It would be possible that one can receive these benefits, even when s/he demonstrates genuine attentiveness. The difference between genuine attentiveness and reflexive attentiveness lies in the different motives of the potential demonstrator. That is, the demonstrator of genuine attentiveness demonstrates attentiveness, merely thinking of the well-being of the other party, whereas the demonstrator of reflexive attentiveness demonstrates attentiveness, trying to get the benefits as noted above, namely, for the sake of the demonstrator her/himself. Of course, these benefits can be obtained, only when the recipient evaluates the attentiveness positively. Reflexive attentiveness, however, does not necessarily have negative connotations. Even when reflexive attentiveness is demonstrated for the benefit of the demonstrator, it may also help the recipient.

Reflexive attentiveness is related also to the concept of reciprocity. Reciprocity is 'a generalized moral norm ... which defines certain actions and obligations as repayments for benefits received' (Gouldner 1960: 171). According to Burger, Sanchez, Imberi and Grande (2009: 12), people return favours out of self-presentation, that is, a concern for what the other person will think of them, and out of internal standards of behaviour. According to the internalised social norm account, people feel good about themselves when they 'do the right thing' and return favours (Burger et al. 2009: 12). The concept of reciprocity is included in the 'equity principle', which was proposed by Spencer-Oatey (2005b). That is, 'the belief that cost and benefits should be "fair" and kept roughly in balance' (Spencer-Oatey 2005b: 100). For Culpeper and Tantucci (2018), reciprocity means a constraint on human interaction such that there is pressure on an addressee to match the im/politeness threshold created by the addressor, thereby maintaining a balance of social payments. A demonstrator of reflexive attentiveness may try to gain some kind of benefit/favour in return, which can be explained from the concept of reciprocity. Some examples of genuine attentiveness and reflexive attentiveness are presented next.

Example (2.11) (the author's own recordings and associated transcriptions) illustrates genuine attentiveness.

(2.11)

1 JS2: *A (.) yappari tomodachi kara (.) chotto byouki gachi na toki ni (.)*

2 *daijoubu (.) toka sono go (.) kega wa dou (.) toka.*

あ、やっぱり友達から、ちょっと病気がちな時に

「大丈夫」とか「その後怪我はどう」とか。

Well, when I was ill, {I received emails} from my friend, {saying}, 'Are you all right?' or 'How is your injury?', or something like that.

3 *Ato (.) jishin ga atta toki toka ni (.)*

あと地震があった時とかに

4 *shingenchi sono hen datta mitai dakedo(.) jikka daijoubu (.) toka*

「震源地その辺だったみたいだけど実家大丈夫」とか

{I also received an email} when there was an earthquake, {saying that} the epicentre was around there. 'Is your home all right?', or something like that.

5 *souitta kizukai no meeru ga kuru to (.) yappari (.)*

そういった気遣いのメールがくると、やっぱり

6 *ki ni kake rareteru tte iu: no ga tsutawaru dake de ureshii desu yo ne.*

気にかけられてるっていうのが伝わるだけで嬉しいですよね。

When I receive that kind of email which contains attentiveness, after all, I feel happy, as I can sense that they are concerned about me.

JS2 feels 'genuine attentiveness' from the emails which she received from her friends. The senders of these emails are simply concerned about the receiver, when she was ill (lines 1–2) or when there was an earthquake near her home (lines 3–4). JS2 feels happy because she senses that the senders are concerned about her (lines 5–6). This kind of attentiveness, in which a demonstrator of attentiveness is genuinely concerned about the other party and does not seek for any reward or anything, can be termed 'genuine attentiveness'.

However, there are also cases in which a potential demonstrator of attentiveness demonstrates attentiveness for the benefit of the demonstrator. Such attentiveness is termed reflexive attentiveness (see Example [2.12]).

(2.12)

1 JS9: *Sukoshi demo kikubari ga dekireba (.)*

少しでも気配りができれば

2 *aite mo (.) aite ni mo kouinsyou wo atae rareru shi (.) kekkou (3.5) nan desu ka ne (.)*

相手も、相手にも好印象を与えられるし、結構、何ですかね

If {one} can just demonstrate a little attentiveness, the other person will also, one can make a good impression with others, to a large extent, what {to say},

3   *kouinsyou mo atae rareru shi* (1.0) *moshi jibun ga tanomitai toki mo*
好印象も与えられるし、もし自分が頼みたい時も
{one} can make a good impression, and if one wants something sometime,

4   *souyatte mae ni yattoku to ano:* (.)
そうやって前にやっとくとあのー
if one does that way, in the end,

5   *aite mo kou* (.) *mata kikubari wo kaeshi* (.) *kikubairi wo shite kureru you ni* (1.0)

6   *naru koto ga ooka tta node* (.) *daiji dato omoi masu.*
相手もこう、また気配りを返し、気配りをしてくれるようになることが多かったので、大事だと思います。
others will also return the attentiveness {in this way}, there were many cases where I have received attentiveness, and so {attentiveness} is important, I think.

(adapted from Fukushima and Haugh 2014: 173)

JS9 in Example (2.12) claims that attentiveness is important for creating a good impression of oneself with others (lines 1–3), and also because the recipients of one's attentiveness may reciprocate this in the future (lines 3–6). Here we can see the reciprocity which was mentioned earlier. These are some features of reflexive attentiveness, as they are for the benefit of the demonstrator of attentiveness.

Examples (2.13) and (2.14) (the author's own recordings and associated transcriptions) show some other features of reflexive attentiveness.

(2.13)

1   JS1:   *Kou nakama hazure ni sareru mitaina.*[12]
こう仲間外れにされるみたいな。
One would be isolated from a group, or something like that.

2   *De* (.) *sore ni naranai you ni tte iu node* (.) *kikubari wo* (.) *kou shinai to tte*
で、それにならないようにっていうので、気配りをこうしないとって
So, in order not to be excluded from the group, one should demonstrate attentiveness.

3   *omotte iru hito mo iru no kana tte omoi mashi ta.*
思っている人もいるのかなって思いました。
There may be people, who think that way, I thought.

4   *Jibun ga* (.) *sono syuudan kara habukare nai you ni tte* (.) *kou* (.)
自分がその集団から省かれないようにって、こう
In order not to be excluded from the group,

5   *ningen kankei wo umaku (.) kou enkatsu ni kouchiku shiteku tte iu node (.)*
人間関係をうまくこう円滑に構築してくっていうので
in order to construct good human relationships smoothly,

6   *kikubari toka (.) kizukai toka tte iu no (.) shiteru*
気配りとか気遣いとかっていうのしてる
one demonstrates attentiveness.

7   *hito mo iru no kamo shirenai na (.) tte omoi mashi ta.*
人もいるのかもしれないなって思いました。
There may be that kind of people, I thought.

(2.14)

1 JS2:   *Watashi nanka wa (.) sono wakai ningen to shite (.) kekkou sou ja nai (.)*
私なんかはその若い人間として結構そうじゃない。
I, as a young person, it is not necessarily so {to demonstrate attentiveness naturally}.[13]

2   *sakki* ○○ *san ga itte ta you na (.)*
さっき○○さんが言ってたような、
As ○○ {a name of JS1} said earlier {referring to example [2.13]},

3   *wari to negatibu na (.)*
割とネガティブな
out of a rather negative {motive, I demonstrate attentiveness}.

4   *nakama hazure ni sare taku nai (.) kowai (.) tte iu omoi kara (.)*
仲間外れにされたくない、怖いっていう思いから
I do not want to be excluded from a group. Out of a sense of fear,

5   *shinakya (.) kuuki yomanakya, mitaina.*
しなきゃ、空気読まなきゃ、みたいな。
I need to do {demonstrate attentiveness} and read the atmosphere, or something like that.

Examples (2.13) and (2.14) illustrate that participants demonstrate attentiveness in order not to be excluded from a group of their friends (lines 1–2 and 4 in Example [2.13] and line 4 in Example [2.14]). JS2 in Example (2.14) has a fear of being excluded from her friends (line 4). JS2 calls such a motive negative (line 3). It is important for her to read the atmosphere and demonstrate attentiveness so that she is not excluded from her peer group. Attentiveness demonstrated out of the motive of not being excluded from a group is for the sake of the demonstrator of attentiveness in the end. JS1 in Example (2.13) states that one demonstrates attentiveness also in order to construct good human relationships smoothly (lines 5–6). This is another motive for demonstrating attentiveness, but this motive is not necessarily exclusive for reflexive attentiveness.

O'Driscoll (2013) cites a situational context in which attentiveness is included, although he does not use the term 'attentiveness'. He drops in at a newsagent and there follows a conversation between the shop worker and him (the customer). He says, 'Cold today, isn't it?' and the shop worker says, 'It's that door. People open it and then it gets stuck'. In response to that, he offers to close the door (which is attentiveness in my terms) on the way out. O'Driscoll (2013: 179) states that the offer to close the door was the chance to present himself as a considerate person. This can also be considered to be one motive for reflexive attentiveness, as one can gain a good reputation as a considerate person when the recipient evaluates the attentiveness positively.

As we have seen so far, there are different types of attentiveness (genuine attentiveness and reflexive attentiveness). However, it is sometimes difficult to distinguish between them (see Example [2.15] [the author's own recordings and associated transcriptions]).

(2.15)

1   JS2:   *Sono (.) kikubari (.) kizukai ga (.) sono hontou ni aite no tame wo omotte deteru noka*
その、気配り、気遣いが、その、本当に相手のためを思って出てるのか

2   *sore tomo (.) jibun no tsugou tte ittara nan desu kedo (.)*
それとも、自分の都合っていったら何ですけど

Is attentiveness really derived from thinking of the other party, or is it rather for one's convenience, what {to say},

3   *jibun no shigoto no tame toka (.) jibun no (1.0) mentsu no tame toka (.)*
自分の仕事のためとか、自分の面子のためとか

such as for one's work, or for one's own face,

4   *hito kara jibun ga dou omowa reru no ka toka (.)*
人から自分がどう思われるのかとか

or how one is thought of by others?

5   *sou iu docchi ga douki to shite deteiru no kana tte iu no wa (.)*
そういうどっちが動機として出ているのかなっていうのは

What is the motivation?

6   *kekkou (.) senbiki ga muzukashii tokoro desu yo ne.*
結構線引きが難しいところですよね。

It is rather difficult to draw the line, isn't it?

As Example (2.15) shows, it is difficult to judge whether one demonstrates attentiveness for the well-being of the other party (namely, genuine attentiveness; line 1), or for oneself – for one's job or face, or how one is thought of by others – (namely, reflexive attentiveness; lines 2–4). As mentioned earlier, even reflexive attentiveness may help the other party. Moreover, one may receive some kind of reward even when one demonstrates genuine attentiveness when it is positively evaluated by the recipient. The motive to demonstrate attentiveness stated in line 4 (how one is thought of by others) may coincide with the above-mentioned example of presenting himself as a considerate person by closing the door (O'Driscoll 2013: 179).

Business-oriented attentiveness

People, especially those who are in the service business, demonstrate attentiveness in order to fulfil their duties. I term such attentiveness 'business-oriented attentiveness'. A Japanese professor, one of the audience in Fukushima (2014), cited an example of attentiveness she had received on a Japanese aeroplane. Immediately after she sneezed, a Japanese cabin attendant brought her a mask, which she greatly appreciated. What the Japanese cabin attendant demonstrated can be considered as business-oriented attentiveness, as she fulfilled her duties as a cabin attendant, namely, attending to passengers. Although this attentiveness is considered to be business-oriented attentiveness, it contains the element of thinking of the well-being of others (namely, genuine attentiveness). As this example shows, business-oriented attentiveness is also for the well-being of the other party (e.g., the Japanese lady who received the mask could avoid catching a cold by wearing a mask) on certain occasions. In other words, business-oriented attentiveness is demonstrated in order to fulfil their duties, especially in service industries, but it may also help the other party. It depends on the people and the occasions whether demonstrating business-oriented attentiveness is as a result of thinking about the well-being of the other party or merely out of a sense of duty. It also depends on how the recipient of business-oriented attentiveness evaluates it (e.g., the Japanese lady above appreciated the attentiveness demonstrated by a cabin attendant). If the evaluation by a recipient of business-oriented attentiveness is negative, the recipient does not feel that business-oriented attentiveness was for her/his own well-being.

Business-oriented attentiveness may also contain an element of reflexive attentiveness, namely, for the benefit of the demonstrator. As in the case of bringing the mask above, the cabin attendant may have elevated her reputation. It cannot be detected whether the cabin attendant had the intention of elevating her reputation or not, but the appreciation of the passenger would have made this possible. Thus, it can be said that business-oriented attentiveness contains the elements of genuine attentiveness and reflexive attentiveness, depending on the demonstrators, the evaluations by the recipients and so on.

What distinguishes business-oriented attentiveness from genuine attentiveness and reflexive attentiveness distinctively may lie in 'an issue of business productivity' (Cook and Burdelski 2017: 476). 'Ideologically *kikubari* is not directly linked to business profits. It is perhaps only in the business context in which *kikubari* is discussed in terms of job productivity and profits' (Cook and Burdelski 2017: 478). Examples (2.16) and (2.17) illustrate this. They are audiovisual recordings of new-employee orientation sessions at a small-scale IT company in Tokyo. The participants are two male superiors (Iino, in his 30s, who holds a managerial position, and Hata, in his 20s, who has worked for two years as a programmer) and four new employees, who are recent college graduates (Cook and Burdelski 2017: 475). Kato is one of the recent college graduates. The superior, Iino, explains how attentiveness can be applied to the business context. Just prior to this excerpt, Hata told the new employees to always ask themselves what others are intending in order to pick up on their unspoken needs (Cook and Burdelski 2017: 476). This shows that attentiveness is an important component of new-employee orientation.

(2.16)[14] (Inoue: superior, Kato: new employee)

1 → Iino: *eeto koo iu koto o yatte hoshii to iwareta toki ni*

Well, when (you) are told (by a customer), '(I) want (you) to do this',

2 → *sore de owari na no ka na tte iu no o kangaete hoshii to iu koto na n desu yo*

it is that (we) want (you) to think, 'Is that all (I need to do)?'

3 *ano kiita koto aru to omou n desu kedo*

Uh (I) think (you)'ve heard this before, but

4 *iwareta koto dake yatte ireba ii ka doo ka tte iu hanashi kiita koto nai?*

Haven't (you) heard whether or not it is okay to do just what you are told to do?

5 Kato: *sonna arimasu ne* [*h h h h*

(I) have heard such a thing h h h h.

6 Iino: [*h h h h*

7 *tte koto o koko wa iitai n desu yo*

In this part (of the orientation session) (we) want to say this (act proactively).

8 Kato: *hai*

Yes.

9 → Iino: *ano: tabun shigoto o yaru ue de iwareta koto o yatte ireba ii baai mo mochiron arimasu.*

Well, perhaps there are certainly times when it is okay to just do what (you) are told to do in (your) work.

10		Kato:	*un*
			Uh huh
11	→	Iino:	*arimasu kedo sore o bakka zutto yatteru to soko de oshi- oshimai ni natte shimau.*
			There are such times, but if you keep only doing so, you will come to a dead end.
12		Kato:	*hai*
			Yes.
13	→	Iino:	*hai sono saki o kangaete kudasai to*
			Well, please think ahead of that (= Do more than what you are told).

(adapted from Cook and Burdelski 2017: 476–477)

In Example (2.16), Iino, a superior, tells a new employee, Kato, the importance of attentiveness, first asking Kato whether all he needs to do is to just respond to the request in line 2. In other words, Iino tries to convey the importance of inference and attentiveness. That is, 'he encourages them to interpret the request beyond what is verbally stated and to proactively attend to what the customer might also need (before he or she asks for it)' (Cook and Burdelski 2017: 477). Iino emphasises the importance of thinking ahead (line 13), and Iino conveys to the new employees the importance of discerning when to display *kikubari* in their work (Cook and Burdelski 2017: 478). In Example (2.17), Iino summarises how attentiveness helps one's job productivity.

(2.17)[15] [Iino and Hata: superiors]

1	→	Iino:	*umaku okyakusan no yooboo o kumitotte ageru koto ga dekiru yoo ni naru to dondon shigoto ni tsunagatte iku n desu ne*
			Once (you) become skilful in picking up what clients want, (you) will get a lot of work.
2		Hata:	*soo desu ne*
			That's right.

(adapted from Cook and Burdelski 2017: 478)

Iino tells the new employee, Hata, that 'picking up what clients want' will lead to a profit (line 1). 'Picking up what clients want' means inferring the needs of the clients. This shows the importance of inference (see the discussion below) in business-oriented attentiveness. Example (2.17) illustrates that business-oriented attentiveness is important, as it leads to profit.

Example (2.18) (the author's own recordings and associated transcriptions) also shows an example of business-oriented attentiveness. JS2 works part-time at a tax office where people needed to pay tax. Obviously, the tax office is crowded with people.

(2.18)

1   JS2:   *Arubaito: wo shita toki ni* (1.0) *ano shigoto wo sumuuzu ni susume te iku no ni*
アルバイトをしたときにあの仕事をスムーズに進めていくのに

2   *kikubari tte hitsuyou nanda yo tte iu no wo*
気配りって必要なんだよっていうのを

When I worked part time, in order to proceed the work smoothly, attentiveness was necessary.

3   *chyokusetsu i tte kure ta* (.) *syokuin no kata ga ite:* (.)
直接言ってくれた職員の方がいて

That's what I was told directly by a clerk {who works at the tax office}.

4   *kore sugoku watashi ga ano uketsuke no shigoto datta toki ni:*
これすごく私があの受付の仕事だった時に

I worked at an information desk.

5   *okyaku san ga takusan kuru kara: sore wo sabaku no ni wa* (.)
お客さんがたくさん来るから、それをさばくのには

So, many people came. In order to deal with them,

6   *mou heya ni haitte kuru jiten de* (1.0) *nani wo shi ni kita hito nano ka tte iu no wo:*
もう部屋に入ってくる時点で何をしに来た人なのかっていうのを

7   *sono hito no te ni motte ru syorui toka* (.) *sono funiki kara* (.) *sasshite* (1.0)
その人の手に持ってる書類とかその雰囲気から察して

we inferred why they came to {the tax office}, as soon as people came into a room from the papers they had in hand, or from their atmosphere.

8   *ano saki ni jyunbi shite okeba: dondon kensuu wo konaseru kara*
あの先に準備しておけば、どんどん件数をこなせるから

We prepared {what was required} in advance. In that way, we can deal with many people.

9   *kichin to kansatsu: shite* (.) *nani wo motome rarete iru no ka tte iu no mo* (.)
きちんと観察して何を求められているのかっていうのも

10   *kou ki wo kubaru koto da shi* (.) *me wo kubaru koto tte iu no wo* (.) *kore iwarete:* (.)
こう気を配ることだし、目を配ることっていうのをこれ言われて

We observed {them} correctly, and we need to be attentive to what is required. That is what I was told {by a clerk at the tax office}.

11   *ishiki shiyou tte iu fuu ni* (1.0) *yatte mimashi ta.*
意識しようっていうふうにやってみました。

I tried to do so consciously.

12   *soredemo: sono* (.) *sono hito wa mou nannen mo souiu shigoto sarete ru kara* (.)
それでも、その、その人はもう何年もそういう仕事されてるから

13   *watashi ga zenzen kizukanaka tta koto (.) wo saki ni (.) kizuite*
          私が全然気づかなかったことを先に気づいて

          As that clerk has worked {in the tax office} for many years, s/he noticed what I hadn't
          at all.

14   *tatoeba kou (.) erebeetaa ni: (.) norou to shite iru hito ga ita ra:*
          例えばこうエレベーターに乗ろうとしている人がいたら

          For example, when s/he saw someone was about to get on an elevator,

15   *mou saki ni ugoite te botan oshite agetari toka (.)*
          もう先に動いててボタン押してあげたりとか

          s/he moved {went to the elevator} before {that person}, and s/he pushed a button of
          the elevator, or something like that.

16   *kurumaisu no hito ga: kita toki no taiou no shikata tte iu no wa*
          車いすの人が来たときの対応の仕方っていうのは

17   *kouiu yarikata ga arunda yo tte iu no wo (.) watashi ni misete kuretari toka shite (1.0)*
          こういうやり方があるんだよっていうのを私に見せてくれたりとか
          して

          S/he showed me how to deal with people who came with wheelchairs.

18   *shigoto wo sumuuzu ni (.) yaru no mo soudashi*
          仕事をスムーズにやるのもそうだし

          In order to proceed the work smoothly,

19   *sono issyun no deai demo:*
          その一瞬の出会いでも

          and even if an encounter was only for a moment.

20   *kou aite ni (.) sukoshi demo ii kanjyou wo (.) nokoshite moraou tte iu (1.0) no mo (.)*
          こう相手に少しでもいい感情を残してもらおうっていうのも

21   *kikubari ga kou (.) tasukeru youso nano ka na tte iu fuu ni wa omoi mashi ta.*
          気配りがこう助ける要素なのかなっていうふうには思いました。

          When we want to leave the other party with good feelings, attentiveness would be
          a help, I thought.

In Example (2.18), it is shown that attentiveness is important in business, namely,
to proceed the work smoothly (lines 1 and 18) and to deal with many people (lines
5 and 8). As shown in Example (2.17), Example (2.18) also shows the importance
of inference in the business context (lines 6–7). Observing the situation correctly
(line 9) is necessary to infer what is required (see also Section 2.2.3). In lines
20–21, JS2 states that attentiveness also helps in making the other party feel good,
which suggests that attentiveness contributes to constructing good human relationships in the business context, too.

In Example (2.19) (the author's own recordings and associated transcriptions), the importance of attentiveness in business is further shown.

(2.19)

1　JS1:　*Sono* ○○ *san ga sakki* (.) *baito de* (1.0) *subayaku okyaku sama wo sabaku tame ni*
その○○さんがさっき、バイトで素早くお客様をさばくために

2　　　　*kikubari ga* (.) *hitsuyou datte hanashi te ita n desu keredo* (.)
気配りが必要だって話していたんですけれど

○○ {the name of JS2} told us earlier, in order to deal with many people swiftly at a part-time job, attentiveness was necessary.

3　　　　*sono kikubari tte iu no wa* (.) *omoiyari kara* (.)
その気配りっていうのは、思い遣りから

4　　　　*o kyaku sama hitori hitori ni taishite* (.) *kono hito ga sugu o heya ni haireru you ni* (.)
お客様一人一人に対して、この人がすぐお部屋に入れるように

5　　　　*kono hito no tame ni* (.) *to iu o kyaku sama ni taisuru omoiyari kara suru n desu ka*
この人のためにというお客様に対する思い遣りからするんですか。

{Does one demonstrate attentiveness} from empathy, that is, thinking of each customer? {For example}, customers can get into a room soon.

6　　　　*soretomo* (.) *sono* (.) *shigoto* (.) *ga daiichi dakara* (.)
それとも、その仕事が第一だから

Or, as the work is the primary concern,

7　　　　*shigoto wo sugu* (.) *hake sasenakya ikenai kara tte iu*
仕事をすぐはけさせなきゃいけないからっていう

is it because one must deal with work efficiently?

8　　　　*docchi kara* (.) *sono kikubari wa umareru mono nan desu ka*
どっちからその気配りは生まれるもの何ですか。

From which {thinking of customers or doing work efficiently} is attentiveness derived?

9　JS2:　*Omoiyatteru koto wo* (.) *miseru* (.) *sono shisei wo miseru koto de* (.) *kou* (.)
思いやってることを見せる、その姿勢を見せることで、こう

By showing that one thinks of the other party, showing that attitude,

10　　　　*soko ni kou* (.) *nandaro* (.) *arasoi toka* (.) *jikan ga kakaru youna koto wo* (.)
そこにこう何だろ、争いとか時間がかかるようなことを

{one would like to avoid} disputes, or how to put it, or something which requires time.

11　　　　*kyokuryoku haijo shitai tte iu ito ga* (.) *soko ni aru na tte omotte.*
極力排除したいっていう意図がそこにあるなって思って。

There is an intention to avoid {those things} as much as possible, I think.

12   *hontou ni kokoro kara omotte itteru no ka douka tte naru to (.) hanhan tte kanji (.)*
本当に心から思って言ってるのかどうかってなると半々って感じ。

Whether one says {demonstrates attentiveness} from the bottom of the heart or not, I think it is fifty-fifty.

13   *nanka (.) hitotsu omoidashi ta no wa (.) chotto heya ni hairu toki ni dansa ga atte (.)*
何かひとつ思い出したのは、ちょっと部屋に入るときに段差があって

I remember one thing. There was a little gap when we entered a room.

14   *de (.) sono shokuin no kata ga ashimoto ki wo tsukete kudasai tte iu no wo (1.0)*
で、その職員の方が「足元気を付けてください」っていうのを

15   *iu hito to (.) iwanai hito ga ite (.) de (.) sore wa douiu chigai nandarou to omottara (.)*
言う人と言わない人がいて、で、それはどういう違いなんだろうと思ったら

That clerk {at the tax office} said 'Mind the gap' to some people, but s/he did not say that to some other people. I wondered what the difference was.

16   *kekkou karikari shiteru (.) kou (.) nanka iraira shinagara (.)*
結構カリカリしてる、こうなんかイライラしながら

To those who seemed to be irritated,

17   *soko ni you wo youji wo sumase ni kita tte iu hito ni taishite (.)*
そこに用を、用事を済ませに来たっていう人に対して

and came there to get things done,

18   *mou jizen ni koko (.) dansa arun de ki wo tsukete kudasai tte ittete (.)*
もう事前に「ここ、段差あるんで気を付けてください」って言ってて

{the clerk} said in advance, 'There is a gap here. So, mind the gap.'

19   *watashitachi nimo (.) kokoroyoku aisatsu shite kureru hito ni wa*
私達にも快く挨拶してくれる人には

To those who greeted us willingly,

20   *ashimoto ki wo tsukete kudasai tte itte naku te (.) de (.) kou okorarenai you ni (.) toka*
「足元気を付けてください」って言ってなくて、で、こう怒られないようにとか。

s/he did not say 'Mind the gap'. {S/he may have distinguished them}, not to be criticised, or something like that.

21   JS1:   *A (.) ato kara kureemu [tsuke rare nai you ni*
あ、あとからクレームつけられないように

Ah, s/he {did that so that s/he} may not be complained about later.

22	JS2:	[*Tsuke rare nai you ni*]
		つけられないように
		So that s/he may not be complained about

23 JP1: *hhh Arakajime yobousen wo hatte oku* [*mitai na.*
あらかじめ予防線を張っておくみたいな。
S/he took precautions beforehand, or something like that.

24 JP2:   [*Bunrui shite*] *iru no ka na tte* (.)

25   *omoi mashi ta.*
分類しているのかなって思いました。
S/he distinguished {them}, I thought.

26   *Hontou ni ashikoshi no warusou na kata ni mo itte iru no wa attan desu kedo* (.)
本当に足腰の悪そうな方にも言っているのはあったんですけど
S/he said {'Mind the gap'} to those who seemed not to be steady on their feet.

27   *kou* (.) *bimyou ni senbiki ga nasare te iru kanji ga shite* (.)
こう微妙に線引きがなされている感じがして
However, I felt that s/he drew a subtle line.

28   *sore wa kou* (.) *yappari shigoto ga todokoora nai you ni tte iu ito ga aru no ka na tte*

29   *hh iu fuu ni wa omoi mashi ta.*
それはこうやっぱり仕事が滞らないようにっていう意図があるのか
なっていうふうには思いました。
So, there was an intention, namely that the work would not go behind the schedule,
I thought.

In relation to Example (2.18), JS1 raised an interesting question in Example
(2.19), that is, whether attentiveness is demonstrated out of empathy, thinking
of the other party (genuine attentiveness; lines 3–5) or in order to proceed the
work swiftly (business-oriented attentiveness; lines 6–7) in the business context.
Avoiding disputes or problems is for the business's profit, as business productivity
will be lower if one needs to deal with many problems, which requires time (lines
10–11). JS2 states that showing the attitude of empathy (line 9) would help avoid
such problems. Thus, JS2 states 'fifty-fifty' (line 12) in answering the question by
JS1 above (lines 3–8). This is interesting, as showing the attitude of empathy may
not always coincide with thinking of that person from the bottom of the heart. It
is used rather as a strategy to avoid potential problems. JS2 cites an example of
'Mind the gap'. One says the same phrase to those who seem to be irritated (lines
16–18) and to those who are physically weak (line 26). In the former case, it can
be said that it is for the business (business-oriented attentiveness), that is, one
can proceed with the work smoothly (avoiding potential problems). However, in

the latter case, it is for the well-being of the other party (genuine attentiveness) even though it is in the business context. Example (2.19) also shows that business-oriented attentiveness contains an element of reflexive attentiveness. That is, the clerk at the tax office demonstrates attentiveness by stating 'Mind the gap' so that s/he would not be criticised later (lines 20–22). Although s/he would not receive any reward (such as enhancing her/his reputation), not being criticised is for the sake of the demonstrator her/himself. Thus, this can be considered as reflexive attentiveness as well.

So far, we have seen three types of attentiveness: genuine attentiveness, reflexive attentiveness and business-oriented attentiveness. Although they have some distinctive features, they are also interrelated. That is why it is sometimes difficult to distinguish them from each other. The common denominator among them is that one pre-empts the other party's needs. Next, *omotenashi* ('Japanese style hospitality'), which is related to business-oriented attentiveness, is investigated.

Omotenashi

Omotenashi, Japanese-style hospitality,[16] attracted due attention in the course of the 2020 Tokyo Olympics bid, proclaiming the high quality of service in Japan to the world (see, e.g., http://www.franceplusplus.com/2013/09/christel-takigawa-olympique/). *Omotenashi* consists of *o* (an honorific prefix) and *motenashi*, a noun form of *motenasu*. According to Shinmura (2018: 2913), *motenasu* has a variety of meanings: (1) 'to mediate' (*torinasu*), 'to cope with' (*shochi suru*), (2) 'to treat' (*tori atsukau, taigu suru*), (3) 'to be attentive so that the other party pleases' (*aite ga yorokobu you ni ki wo kubaru*), 'to entertain' (*kantai suru*), 'to treat' (*gochisou suru*), (4) 'to take care' (*mendou wo miru, sewa wo suru*), (5) 'to behave' (*jibun no mi wo shosuru, furumau*), (6) 'to praise' (*motehayasu*) and (7) 'to pretend' (*soburi wo suru, misekakeru*). *Omotenashi* when used in business (especially in service industries) or in ordinary parlance (*omotenashi* is demonstrated at an individual level, too) includes the meaning of the third and the fourth definitions above. This almost coincides with Yamajo's (2008: 3) understanding of *omotenashi*, namely, to invite guests, provide them with meals and gifts, and communicate with them closely. Yamajo (2008) contends that *omotenashi* in Japan is based on the tea ceremony. As background to the pursuit of restoring *omotenashi*, which is based on relationships of mutual trust, Yamajo (2008: i) states as follows: Japan has tried to catch up with advanced countries since the Meiji era. At the end of the twentieth century, we have succeeded in catching up with advanced countries, and Japan has become a mature society. In inverse proportion to material wealth, 'mind', such as empathy towards others and attentiveness, may have withered.

Kinjyo's (2014) understanding of *omotenashi* is closely related to attentiveness itself, that is, to be concerned for the other party, to empathise with the other party, to infer the other party's expectations and to do something wholeheartedly and casually or in a subtle manner in order to please the other party. In other words, *omotenashi* is the superlative form of *kikubari* ('attentiveness') (http://www.omotenaship.co.jp/omotenashi-organization/what-omotenashi/). Drawing on Nagao and Umemuro (2012) and Miyashita (2011), Terasaka and Inaba (2014: 90) state that *omotenashi* includes the following elements: one pleases the other party; one stands in the other party's position; one demonstrates *kikubari* ('attentiveness') matching the other party's purpose, situation and needs; and *reigi saho* ('manners'), based on Japanese traditional culture. Also, in the definition of *omotenashi* above we can see some aspects of attentiveness, that is, to think of the other party, to infer the other party's needs, wants and feelings, and to empathise with the other party (to stand in someone else's shoes [Lebra 1993: 72]). However, it is not necessarily the case that attentiveness (in my terms) includes manners[17] as in the definition of *omotenashi* above.

Kagaya, a Japanese-style inn (*ryokan*) in Ishikawa, Japan, has been selected by professionals as a top *ryokan* for over 30 years (ryokonet.co.jp). *Omotenashi* defined by *Kagaya* consists of accommodating the needs of guests without or before being requested or even expected to do so. In other words, service is provided before a guest requests or even expects it (http://www.pmaj.or.jp/online/1307/hitokoto.html). Here we can see a close connection between *omotenashi* and attentiveness. *Kagaya*'s business-oriented attentiveness is firmly grounded in the altruistic dimension and in the pre-emptive manner of attentiveness, although it looks to make a profit as well.

According to Terasaka and Inaba (2014: 92), a certain distance exists between customers and service providers, and formality and politeness have been used in association with service in Japan and also in association with *omotenashi*. This may be related to a sense of distance, which is related to a factor of *okuyukashisa* ('reserved elegance') or *sarigenasa* ('unpretentiousness' or 'subtleness'; Terasaka and Inaba 2014: 92)[18]. By contrast, service in the United States is expressed as friendly or intimate, which expresses frankness (Terasaka and Inaba 2014: 92). As *omotenashi* is based on *reigi* or manners, it shows respect to the other party. Thus, some kind of feelings of distance (not friendliness) arises in *omotenashi* (Terasaka and Inaba 2014: 92).

As is the case with attentiveness, *omotenashi* also has the possibility of being negatively evaluated despite its high quality of service. Some cross-cultural mismatches of expectation regarding service may arise. For example, while pre-empting the needs of guests in a rather formal way is regarded as ideal service in Japan (as in *omotenashi*), it may be seen as inflexible for non-Japanese customers, who prefer service provided in response to specific requests (see, e.g., Long, Fukushima, Kádár and Márquez-Reiter in preparation).

Some different cross-cultural preferences in service can be found also in Lee (2015), who investigated cultural differences between American and Japanese customers on their preferences regarding restaurant servers' attentiveness. The results in Lee (2015) show that server attentiveness had a positive effect on customer orientation,[19] customer satisfaction[20] and the amount of any tip for Americans, but not for Japanese customers. This may be related to the different expectations in service. While Americans prefer personalised and friendly service from servers, the Japanese value formal and unobtrusive service[21] (Lee 2015: 134). The results in Lee (2015) have some common tendencies with those in Long et al. (in preparation). Japanese customers expect a rather formal service without being directly asked, while American customers expect a personalised service being directly asked. Lee (2015) considers that the power distance norm can be used to explain dissimilar preferences in attentive service. Americans, who are characterised by their low power distance, discourage formalities in interactions between customers and servers and consider servers and customers equal (Lee 2015: 135). By contrast, high power distance in Japanese culture stresses status and formality. Customers see themselves in a superior position compared to servers (Lee 2015: 135). Lee (2015) also considers that Hall's (1976) high- and low-context communication (America's low-context communication and Japanese high-context communication) is able to address intercultural differences regarding preferences for attentive service.

2.2.2 Conditions needed for attentiveness to arise

In this sub-section, some conditions needed for attentiveness to arise are considered. The first condition is anticipatory inference. It is necessary for a potential demonstrator to read the other party's feelings, state, needs and wants. This anticipatory inference (see the discussion below) is made through observing the situations and the other party's state, considering the verbal and/or non-verbal cues of the other party, or through reading the atmosphere of a situation (Fukushima 2015: 276). Even when a potential demonstrator of attentiveness could infer the other party's needs, wants and feelings, s/he would not be able to demonstrate attentiveness. Other conditions for attentiveness to arise are a potential demonstrator's ability, availability and her/his willingness to demonstrate attentiveness (see Figure 2.1).

One cannot demonstrate attentiveness, if one does not have the ability needed in a situation. For example, if one cannot drive a car, one cannot demonstrate attentiveness by giving a lift. If one does not have something that a potential recipient needs, for example, a car, one cannot demonstrate attentiveness by offering a lift. While this is an example of availability from a material aspect, availability can also be non-material, such as time, knowledge, information and so on. Furthermore, attentiveness would not be demonstrated without a potential demonstra-

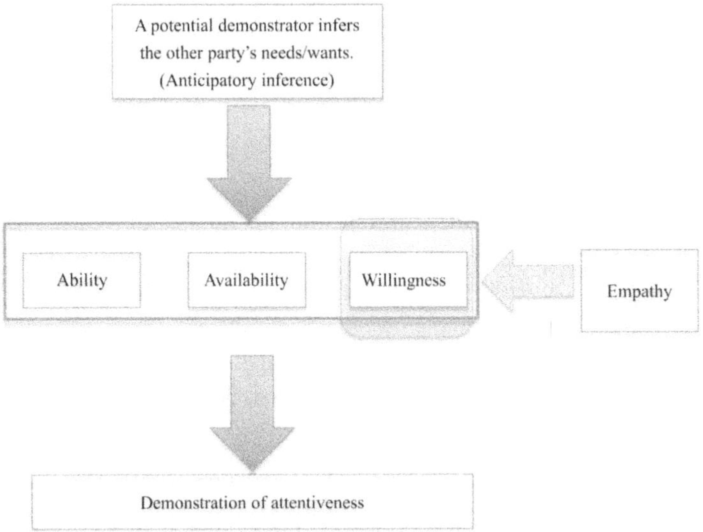

Figure 2.1: Conditions for the demonstration of attentiveness.

tor's willingness. For instance, observing a situation, somebody could infer the other party's wants and might have the ability and availability to demonstrate attentiveness, but s/he might not be willing to act accordingly for various reasons, such as disliking the other party. Therefore, willingness is absolutely necessary for attentiveness to arise (especially in genuine attentiveness).[22] Willingness may be motivated by empathy (see the discussion below) for a potential recipient. That is, if a potential demonstrator has empathy towards a potential recipient, it is likely that s/he would demonstrate attentiveness[23] (Fukushima 2015: 276–277), as the potential demonstrator has willingness to do so. In what follows, some explanations on anticipatory inference and empathy are given.

Anticipatory inference

Anticipatory inference is considered to be almost equivalent to *sasshi* in Japanese. Yamada (1997: 37) defines *sasshi* as the process of anticipatory guesswork required to fill out each other's communication, and it is a strategy where players try to understand as much as possible from the little that is said. Nishida (1977) defines *sasshi* as meaning conjecture, surmise or guessing what someone means (Gudykunst and Nishida 1993: 151). According to Gudykunst and Nishida (1993: 151), '[i]n its verb form (*sassuru*), its meaning is expanded to include imagine, suppose, or empathize with, and make allowances for others'.

Anticipatory inference is related to empathy. For example, a person with *omoi-yari* thinks s/he can know what some person wants, and that person does not have to say anything, according to Wierzbicka (1997: 276). This is possible through anticipatory inference. Moreover, anticipatory inference is definitely needed in implicit and indirect communication and for attentiveness to arise, as a potential demonstrator anticipates or infers the other party's needs, wants and sometimes also feelings, as mentioned earlier.

In relation to indirectness in Japanese, Wierzbicka (2003: 94) cites the following example:

> [A] man, usually a superior, will come into the room and say: *Kyoo wa iya ni atsui nee.* (It's awfully hot today, isn't it?) And one of his men will say *hai* ('yes'), and hurry to open the window or turn on the air conditioner. He may even apologise saying: *Doomo ki ga tsuki masen de …* (I'm sorry I didn't notice) … many Japanese seem to find pleasure in being with someone who understands them very well and so will sense their wishes and act to realise them without being asked.
>
> (Mizutani and Mizutani 1987: 36)

Wierzbicka (2003: 94) attempts to represent the attitude above as follows:

I want something

I don't want to say this

I will say something else because of this

I think this person will know what I want

'[T]his person will *know* what I want' is related to inference, namely that s/he will infer the other party's needs. In the example above by Mizutani and Mizutani, the elements of anticipatory inference and attentiveness exist. A subordinate apologises to his boss, as he could not infer the desire of his boss, and consequently he could not demonstrate attentiveness (act to realise his wish without being asked). This shows that anticipatory inference is one of the conditions for demonstrating attentiveness. Furthermore, the statement by Mizutani and Mizutani (1987: 36) shows that Japanese people like individuals who can infer the other party's wishes and demonstrate attentiveness, which may resonate with the contention by JS8 (line 1) in Example (2.7).

Clancy (1986) argues that anticipatory inference and indirect communication are important in Japanese communication. Clancy (1986: 216) contends that 'the Japanese style of communication can work only in a rather homogeneous society in which people actually can *anticipate* each other's needs, wants and reactions' (emphasis added). Furthermore, '[i]t is widely recognized that the communicative style of the Japanese is intuitive and indirect, especially compared with that of Americans … The basis of this style is a set of cultural values that emphasize *omoiyari* "empathy" over explicit verbal communication' (Clancy 1986: 213–214).

Ishii (1984; 1987: 125–126) characterises Japanese communication as *enryo-sasshi* ('restraint-inference') communication. Although restraint and inference are tacit traditional interpersonal norms (Ishii 1987: 127), Ishii points out that the traditional interpersonal sensitivity is lost because of recent mass media influences and the westernisation of lifestyle (1987: 128). However, Miyake (2011: 16, 188) argues that young Japanese people nowadays prefer the communication style of *sasshi* ('inference'). That is, they only imply their feelings of discomfort or dissatisfaction and they let the other party infer their intentions. Thus, it can be said that anticipatory inference is still important in Japanese communication (Fukushima 2016: 189).

Empathy

According to Bousfield (2016), empathy is important in im/politeness research, as it is what we rely upon in interaction both to be polite and to be impolite. Our understanding of empathy appears to be one defining common denominator for human responses to external stimuli involving humans (Bousfield 2016). In a similar vein, Yuuki (1991: 170) argues that empathy is a keyword which shows the fundamental existence of human beings. Empathy inevitably provides the foundation for, and leads us to, notions of 'morality' (Bousfield 2016). Morality (see, e.g., Haidt and Graham 2007; Haidt and Kesebir 2010; Kádár and Márquez-Reiter 2015; Kádár 2017; Pizziconi 2012; Spencer-Oatey and Kádár 2016) (see Section 2.2.1) plays a key role in evaluating actions, and it is now widely accepted that im/politeness entails an evaluative judgment (Spencer-Oatey and Kádár 2016: 74). Thus, empathy deserves investigation in im/politeness research.

Peterson and Seligman (2004: 330–331) treat empathy and sympathy together and argue that '[e]mpathy and sympathy are other-oriented emotions that commonly are defined as either (a) the ability to experience the affective state of another person or (b) a soft, tender emotion of pity and concern that is associated with imagining the plight of another person'. Pudlinski (2005: 267) argues as follows:

> [T]he practice of empathy involves demonstrating an understanding of another person's situation and/or feelings and communicating that understanding back to the person so that they feel understood ... In contrast, sympathy has been clinically defined as 'emotional identification with the patient's plight'.

According to Kupetz (2014: 4), empathy refers to the display of understanding of the other person's emotional situation. Likewise, Gladkova (2010: 273) argues that '[t]he essence of *empathy* is knowing and understanding the emotional state of another person' (emphasis in original). Wynn and Wynn (2006: 1386) point out that empathy is of importance in many walks of life and within different academic fields, including psychology, psychiatry, medicine and nursing science. 'As a general psychological phenomenon, empathy may be defined as the ability to imagine oneself in another's place and understand the other's feelings, desires, and reactions' (Wynn and Wynn 2006: 1386). Drawing on Duan and Hill (1996), Wynn and Wynn state that '[e]mpathy may be understood as a personality trait or as a situation-specific cognitive-affective state, where the empathic experience varies by situation' (2006: 1386).

Empathy, or *omoiyari*[24] in Japanese, can be roughly glossed as an attitudinal stance encompassing concern for the feelings of others (Fukushima and Haugh 2014: 168). Tao's (2010: 106) view is rather broad, and she argues that it is an other-oriented communicative behaviour, trying to maintain harmony in interpersonal relations. Lebra (1976: 38) defines *omoiyari* as 'the ability and willingness to feel what others are feeling, to vicariously experience the pleasure or pain that they are undergoing, and to help them satisfy their wishes', which is similar to the interpretations of empathy, as noted above. Lebra (1993: 72) argues that the most direct expression of empathy is to become another's *mi* (*aite no mi ni naru* 'to stand in someone else's shoes'). Hara (2006: 27) translates *omoiyari* as 'altruistic sensitivity' and states that *omoiyari* literally means sending one's altruistic feelings to others. Hara and Kim (2004: 2) argue as follows:

> [I]ndividuals at times talk to others indirectly because of altruistic and sympathetic feelings. In such a case, the individuals are tied by affectionate relations. This feeling of altruistic empathy is expressed by '*omoiyari*' (altruistic sensitivity) in Japanese. (emphasis added)

Travis (1998: 55) states that *omoiyari* essentially represents a kind of intuitive understanding of the unexpressed feelings, desires and thoughts of others, and doing something for them on the basis of this understanding. Wierzbicka (1997: 275) characterises *omoiyari* as an ability to read other people's minds and a willingness to respond to other people's unspoken feelings, wants and needs. It can be said that attentiveness and empathy mean almost the same, according to some researchers (e.g., Travis 1998). However, empathy itself does not include a demonstration of attentiveness in my view. Empathy motivates one of the conditions (namely, willingness) for demonstrating attentiveness, that is, attentiveness is not demonstrated without empathy, except in the case of reflexive attentiveness or business-oriented attentiveness (see Section 2.2.1). Uchida and Kitayama (2001: 276) advocate that *omoiyari* motivates prosocial behaviour.[25] Likewise, Muneuchi (2017: 56) states that *omoiyari* is altruistic, and that it is a psychological source which motivates various kinds of prosocial behaviour. Indeed, '[t]here is considerable evidence that feeling increased empathy for a person in need increases the *readiness to help* that person', according to Batson, Chang, Orr and Rowland (2002: 1657; emphasis added). 'The readiness to help' may be almost equivalent to willingness to demonstrate attentiveness. Although empathy and attentiveness differ, as noted above, they are closely related to each other. Attentiveness may be considered as one way of manifesting empathy (Fukushima 2016: 188).

In my view, *omoiyari*, or empathy, is to think of others from the bottom of one's heart; and one who has empathy is sincerely concerned with the other party. In other words, empathy is other-oriented, and it is closely related to interpersonal relationships. Empathy is an affective aspect of human beings. As the core of affective aspects may be the heart, it can be said that empathy is closely related to the heart (Fukushima 2015: 268–269). According to Yuuki (1991: 162), the original meaning of *omoiyari* is to make *kokoro* (the heart) work towards something or someone from afar. This may be partly related to type 1 of the non-demonstrable manifestation of attentiveness (see Section 2.2.3).

Empathy is said to be especially important in Japanese culture (e.g., Clancy 1990; Uchida 2011). According to Wierzbicka (1997: 275), it is generally regarded as one of the most important ideals in Japanese society. Lebra (1976: 38) states that '[f]or the Japanese, empathy (*omoiyari*) ranks high among the virtues considered indispensable for one to be really human, morally mature, and deserving of respect. I am even tempted to call Japanese culture an "*omoiyari* culture".

The importance of empathy in Japanese culture can be seen also from the following. Clancy (1986: 232–235) points out that cultivation of *omoiyari*, or empathy training, is conducted from early childhood in Japan (see also Burdelski 2010, 2013; Burdelski and Mitsuhashi 2010). For Japanese teenagers, empathy is an idealised self-presentation (Shimizu 1993 in Shimizu 2000: 229). Moreover, empathy ranked first in Japan among what parents desire for their children (Somucho 1995). And even at work in Japan, empathy is considered to be important. Example (2.20), a statement by an instructor in the business etiquette training provided for new employees in a Japanese company, lends support to this.

(2.20)

1   *Dakara, yasashiku ano <u>omoiyari</u> o motte aite ni tsumari ee jibun ga wakatteiru*

2   *kedo aite wa wakaranai deshoo to omou koto kara sutaato shite.*

(underscore added).

So speak kindly with consideration, and start with the idea that even if you understand what you mean, the addressee may not.

(adapted from Dunn 2013: 236)

The above is part of a statement by an instructor who said that 'speaking clearly and simply is also speaking kindly because it shows consideration towards the listener' (Dunn 2013: 236). Dunn translates *omoiyari* (line 1) as 'consideration' here.[26] The instructor in Example (2.20) states that it is important to have empathy towards the other party (line 1). 'Speaking kindly was not only a matter of memorizing appropriate "cushion phrases", but of actively anticipating customers' wants' (Dunn 2013: 237). 'Actively anticipating customer's wants' is closely related to business-oriented attentiveness (see Section 2.2.1). Thus, it may be said that empathy is important also in business-oriented attentiveness.

Empathy is considered to be important not only in Japanese culture, but also in some other cultures (e.g., Ran 2016). This may resonate with Lebra's following contention, at least in part.

> Self is more prone to 'become the other' when the latter is perceived as someone who is suffering, a victim, for example, of some stressful or painful condition. This type of surrogacy is the most psychological inner-oriented, empathy-driven (*omoiyari*), and perhaps most universal.
>
> (Lebra 2004: 205)

2.2.3 Processes of attentiveness

In this sub-section, the processes of attentiveness, which lead to the demonstration and the evaluation of attentiveness, are explained (see Figure 2.2). First, a potential demonstrator observes a situation, considering a potential recipient's verbal/non-verbal cues, if there are any, and reading the atmosphere of a situation (Stage 1). Then, a potential demonstrator anticipates or infers the other party's needs, wants and sometimes also feelings (Stage 2) (Fukushima 2015: 277).

In Stage 3, a potential demonstrator may consider a possible act of attentiveness before s/he demonstrates it. In other words, a potential demonstrator checks the attentiveness which s/he will demonstrate against the moral order, namely, 'a set of expectancies through which social actions and meanings are recognisable as such, and consequently are inevitably open to moral evaluation' (Kádár and Haugh 2013: 6), and s/he is likely to think of values (cultural and personal) and behavioural conventions which are culturally bound. Personal values or preferences are most likely determined by family and/or school education, religion, ideology, previous experiences and so on. Values or behavioural conventions may influence the kind of attentiveness s/he may demonstrate. A potential demonstrator may consider whether s/he is the right person to demonstrate attentiveness. S/he may also think that other people may or should demonstrate attentiveness. Other people may include those who are present in the situation in most cases, if the attentiveness needs to be demonstrated immediately. If the attentiveness could be demonstrated later, other people may also include those who are not present in the situation. When s/he thinks someone else is more suited to demon-

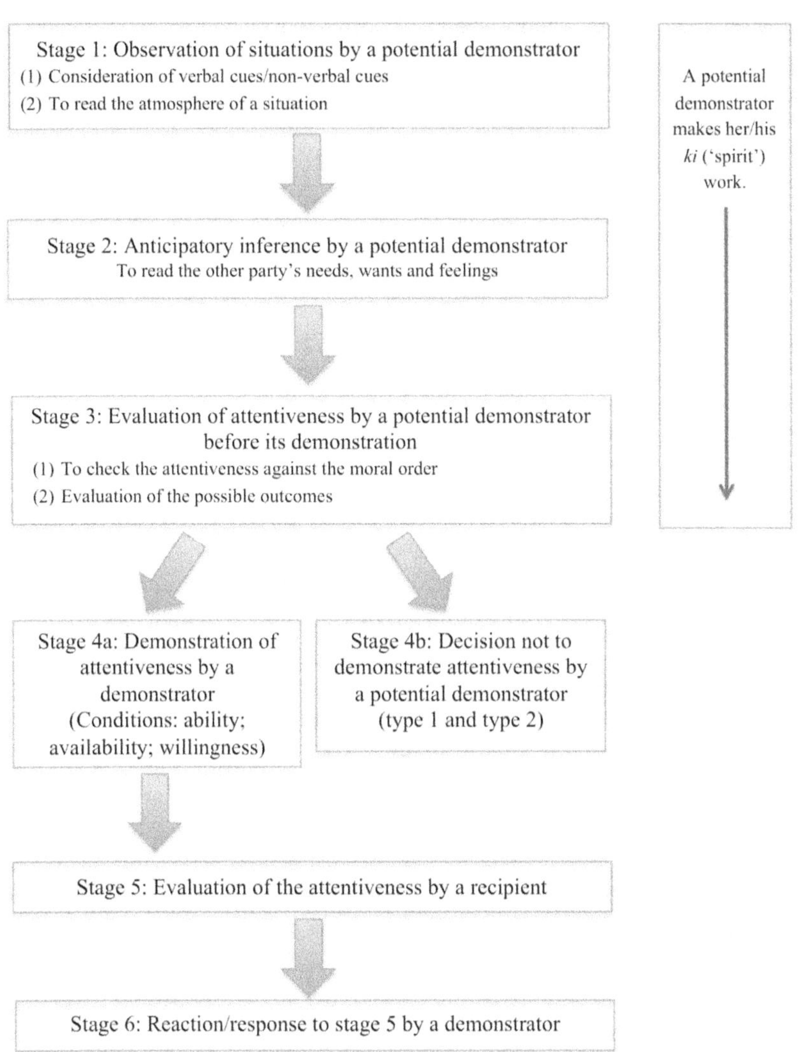

Figure 2.2: The processes of the demonstration and evaluation of attentiveness.

strating attentiveness, s/he may withhold demonstrating attentiveness. S/he does not want to be evaluated as a meddler.

A potential demonstrator may also consider the cost in terms of time, money, energy, psychological burden and so on, before demonstrating attentiveness. As shown in Section 2.2.2, if a potential demonstrator does not have the conditions of attentiveness (namely, ability, availability and willingness), attentiveness will not arise. Time, money, energy and so on, which will be required to demonstrate attentiveness, may be related to availability. A potential demonstrator her/himself may evaluate the possible outcomes. S/he may consider whether the intended attentiveness would help a potential recipient (especially in the case of genuine attentiveness), or on the contrary, it would be intrusive or meddlesome, as attentiveness can be sometimes perceived negatively. S/he may sometimes think of the consequences, such as receiving positive evaluation, too. In other words, s/he may think of the benefits s/he may get in the case of reflexive attentiveness (see Fukushima 2015: 277–278). However, there may also be cases in which a potential demonstrator may not think of the above, when the degree of willingness is very high. Or, a potential demonstrator may not be always conscious about the above.

Until a potential demonstrator reaches Stage 4 in Figure 2.2, s/he makes her/his *ki* ('spirit') work (Fukushima 2015: 278). As previously mentioned, *ki* here means 'attention towards others' (Hamano 1987: 106). In Stages 1–3, a potential demonstrator always pays attention to others, including the situation. Stages 1–3 can recur (Fukushima 2015: 278). A potential demonstrator may think of an appropriate form of attentiveness which s/he would demonstrate, going through these stages.

Two different decisions are possible after Stage 3. One of them is to demonstrate attentiveness (Stage 4a), and another is not to demonstrate attentiveness (Stage 4b). These decisions are the results of Stages 1–3, and they may be partly influenced by cultural conventions, personal values and so on. There are cases in which attentiveness is not demonstrated, even after a potential demonstrator could infer the other party's needs or wants (Stage 4b) (see Fukushima 2015: 278).

The decision not to demonstrate attentiveness in Stage 4b includes two different types: type 1 and type 2 of non-demonstrable manifestation of attentiveness. Type 1 is that a potential demonstrator decides not to demonstrate attentiveness, considering the situation or the state of the other party (Fukushima 2015: 278). This type of attentiveness is also important, although it is difficult to observe. A potential demonstrator in type 1 has empathy towards a potential recipient, but s/he withholds demonstration of attentiveness, thinking of the negative effects of attentiveness, such as meddling or hurting the other party's feelings. Some other reasons why a potential demonstrator withholds demonstrating attentiveness may include the following. Attentiveness may intrude on private territory, or fault/criticise the recipient (incapability). Or, one believes that a recipient may feel attentiveness as a burden or an imposing action.[27] In addition to these reasons, Harada (1991: 54) states that the recipient might feel that s/he must pay back a favour, which would be a burden on the recipient. According to Goldsmith (1992, in Floyd and Ray 2017: 1263), offers of social support – which is a similar concept to attentiveness as mentioned earlier – can threaten a receiver's competence face by suggesting that the receiver is weak or unable to solve his or her problems alone. Likewise, it can threaten the receiver's negative face by invading his or her privacy and imposing unwanted obligations on his or her time and freedom (Floyd and Ray 2017: 1263). In such cases, a potential demonstrator might think that it would be better to leave the other party alone (Fukushima 2015: 278). In other words, type 1 is the kind of attentiveness in which one steps back but still pays attention to the other party, thinking of her/him (see Example [2.21] [the author's own recordings and associated transcriptions]).

JS1 in Example (2.21) is a Japanese university student in her early 20s. After graduating from high school, she spent two years attending a so-called *yobikou* ('prep school'), as she was not successful in passing the entrance examinations for university.

(2.21)

1   JS1:   *Saisho no koro tte iu no wa hinpan ni daigaku haitta tomodachi tomo*
             最初の頃っていうのは頻繁に大学入った友達とも

2   *renraku tottetan desu kedo (.) kou (.) dandan renraku shinaku natte itte (.)*
             連絡取ってたんですけど、こうだんだん連絡しなくなっていって

             At an earlier stage {of my prep school days}, with my friends {from my high school days} who entered universities, I contacted frequently. However, our contact has gradually decreased.

3   *Watashi ga shingaku suru no ni (.)*

4   *yamanashi iku koto ni nari mashi ta tte houkoku shita toki ni (.)*
             私が「進学するのに山梨行くことになりました」って報告した時に

             In order to enter a university, I was moving to Yamanashi {the name of a prefecture in Japan}, I told them.

5   *zutto shinpai shitetanda kedo (.) douiu taimingu de renraku shite iika wakaranakatta kara*
             ずっと心配してたんだけど、どういうタイミングで連絡していいか分からなかったから

             Then, they told me that they had been worried about me but didn't know when to contact me.

6   *daigaku seikatsu no hanashi kiite mo kitto benkyou de (.)*
             大学生活の話聞いてもきっと勉強で

7   *kou anmari (.) ii kanjou wo motanai kamo shirenai shi (.) to omotte*
             こうあんまりいい感情を持たないかもしれないしと思って

             Hearing about college life, I may not have felt very good, when I was studying {in order to enter a university}, they thought.

8   *renraku shinakattanda yo ne* ↑(.) *tte iu no wo itte kureru hito toka* (.)
連絡しなかったんだよねっていうのを言ってくれる人とか
That's why they did not contact me. There was a person who said that.

9   *kou sugoi watashi ni taishite ki wo tsukatte kurete ite* (.)
こうすごい私に対して気を遣ってくれていて
They were very attentive to me.

10   *kou renraku wo shinaku natte ita hito ga takusan iru koto ga* (1.0) *wakatta toki*
こう連絡をしなくなっていた人がたくさんいることが分かった時。
I realised that there were many people who did not contact me {as they were concerned about me}.

11   *de* (.) *kou mata daigaku haittara kankei ga*
で、こうまた大学入ったら関係が

12   *koukou jidai no toki to motodoori ni nattari toka* (.) *tte iu toki ni* (.) *sono* (.)
高校時代の時と元通りになったりとかっていう時にその
After I entered university, our relationships turned out to be the same as those as in our high school days.

13   *rounin shiteru aida tte iu no wa* (.) *wakaranaka tta kedo* (.)
浪人してる間っていうのはわからなかったけど
While I studied at a prep school, I didn't understand {why my friends from high school days did not contact me}.

14   *ato kara a* (.) *souiu koto dattan da tte iu no ga ari mashi ta.*
後から「あ、そういうことだったんだ」っていうのがありました。
However, I realised later that {'They were very attentive at that time'}.

Although her friends from high school days thought of JS1, they withheld from contacting her (lines 5–8). They did not tell JS1 about their college life, while she was attending prep school and trying to enter university. Her friends thought that telling her about their college life would hurt her (lines 6–7), as she could not enter university. Her friends were concerned about the state of JS1, and that is why they did not contact her. They stepped back, but they were very attentive to her (line 9). JS1 realised later why her friends did not contact her and that they were attentive (lines 10–14). It can be said that what the friends of JS1 did was type 1 non-demonstrable manifestation of attentiveness.

Type 2 in Stage 4b (the decision not to demonstrate attentiveness) is that attentiveness is not demonstrated, because the potential demonstrator does not want to demonstrate attentiveness. In type 2, it is likely that a potential demonstrator does not have empathy towards a potential recipient. As a consequence, the potential demonstrator does not have the willingness, which is one of the conditions for demonstrating attentiveness. While the potential demonstrator in type 1 is concerned with the other party's well-being, having a politeness concern, one does not index a polite stance in type 2, as type 2 is absence of attentiveness derived from unwillingness, namely, from lack of empathy (Fukushima 2015: 278–279).

It seems that type 2 non-demonstrable manifestation of attentiveness is closely related to disattending, which is what Haugh argues (2015: 268–271). Haugh (2015: 269–270) explains this by giving an example which includes soliciting. Soliciting, which involves a speaker interactionally positioning another participant to pre-emptively initiate an action sequence for which that other person is thus held primarily responsible (Haugh 2015: 262), is very similar to attentiveness. Example (2.22), which is an exchange between sisters Yu and Mei, illustrates disattending. Prior to Example (2.22), Yu was reporting to Mei that Yu and her husband went to see a film, bringing their two young children, which was troublesome.

(2.22)

1   Y: I can't leave her on her own. I originally thought of asking you to help look after her.

2   M: Oh, but did the two of them understand the film?

(adapted from Haugh 2015: 269)[28]

Mei could understand that Yu was soliciting a pre-emptive offer (or attentiveness, in my terms) to look after Yu's children next time. In other words, Mei could understand Yu's intention and could infer her needs. It might have been possible that Mei would demonstrate attentiveness by offering to look after Yu's children on similar occasions in the future. However, instead of doing so, Mei asked whether the children understood the movie (line 2). The answer to this question was obvious: they could not. The conversation subsequently shifted to another topic (Haugh 2015: 270). 'In this way … Mei recognisably disattended that which had been hinted at by Yu, and so implicated, in turn, a refusal to make such a pre-emptive offer' (Haugh 2015: 270). It can be said that Mei's irrelevant response (line 2) is related to type 2 non-demonstrable manifestation of attentiveness, as her response indicates her decision not to demonstrate attentiveness, which derives from unwillingness. Thus, type 2 non-demonstrable manifestation can be manifested linguistically as in Example (2.22) as well as non-linguistically by just doing or saying nothing.

Although the difference between type 1 and type 2 in Stage 4b needs careful consideration, and these types can be researched in future studies, the demonstration of attentiveness (Stage 4a) is the main focus of this volume. This is because the term 'attentiveness' is used primarily for those with pre-emptive responses in this volume.

After attentiveness has been demonstrated (Stage 4a), a recipient evaluates the attentiveness (Stage 5). Appreciation of attentiveness by a recipient indicates a positive evaluation. A negative evaluation may be made when attentiveness does not match a recipient's behavioural expectations, when a recipient feels that attentiveness constituted meddling, or when s/he feels that her/his territory is infringed. A positive evaluation can occasion politeness and a negative one impoliteness. Evaluation may be manifested linguistically (e.g., by uttering words of appreciation), non-linguistically (e.g., by facial expressions indicating appreciation or good feelings, such as smiles) or one can sense it (e.g., the recipient does not say anything, but the demonstrator feels something in the air, especially when the evaluation is negative) (Fukushima 2015: 279).

In Stage 6, the demonstrator may react to the evaluation (Stage 5) (e.g., saying 'Not at all' in response to thanking by the recipient), although it is not always necessary for a demonstrator to say or do anything; and there are cases in which the demonstrator does not react at all. The demonstrator feels good if s/he has received a positive evaluation, or s/he feels bad after having received a negative evaluation. The former case includes feelings of accomplishment or self-respect, and the latter would decrease those feelings (Fukushima 2015: 279).

2.3 Attentiveness and some other similar concepts

In the previous section, I attempted to elucidate attentiveness from various aspects. In order to further the understanding of attentiveness, the present section investigates the relationship between attentiveness and the four concepts of consideration, empathy, altruism and helping behaviour, building on Fukushima (2019). I believe that an investigation of attentiveness in comparison to the four concepts above, which are related to a heart perspective on politeness and interpersonal relationships, would make the features of attentiveness clearer. The data was elicited through focus groups. In Section 2.3.1, the four concepts above are reviewed, and the focus group data and discussion follow.

2.3.1 Consideration, empathy, altruism and helping behaviour

Consideration is one of the key concepts in theorising politeness (see, among others, Sifianou 1992, 2011, 2015; Watts 2003). Haugh (2019) argues that the notion of consideration and related terms such as attentiveness and solicitude have been raised in discussions of politeness not only in English, but also in other languages.[29] This shows a close relation between consideration and attentiveness and indicates that they are related to politeness. What counts as consideration arguably carries different nuances depending on one's language and cultural background (Fukushima and Haugh 2014: 167; Sifianou 1992: 92–93). For example, consideration in New Zealand English is construed as not getting in the way of other people (Haugh 2019). In other words, consideration is the avoidance of imposition. It aligns with Brown and Levinson's (1987) notion of 'negative face', namely, the desire that one's actions be unimpeded by others (Haugh 2019). This may be in accord with Travis' (1997: 144) notion of consideration, that is, '[t]he main focus of *considerate* is not doing something that may harm another. The notion of wanting to do something for the benefit of another is not an essential element of its meaning' (emphasis in original). However, what consideration in Japanese relational networks means may differ from the above, which will be clarified by the data in this section.

What consideration or *hairyo* (see Haugh 2004: 97; 2015: 252; 2016a: 51) means in the literature differs between researchers. Yamaoka, Makihara and Ono (2010: 143) define *hairyo* as linguistic expressions which keep interpersonal relationships as positive as possible in interpersonal communication. Ide and Ueno (2012: 29) consider *hairyo* as linguistic expressions in which a speaker considers the other party or context. In these definitions of *hairyo*, linguistic expressions are the main focus. In contrast, what Miyake (2011) construes is that *hairyo* encompasses more than just linguistic expressions. For Miyake (2011: 4), *hairyo* encompasses both expressions and behaviours which relate to interpersonal relationships and contexts. According to Miyake (2011: 6–7), positive *hairyo gengo koudou* ('linguistic behaviour of consideration') includes attentiveness, empathy and politeness.[30] Here we can see a connection between consideration, attentiveness, empathy and politeness. This is related to Haugh's (2016a) argument on *omoiyari* ('empathy'); that is, *omoiyari* is related to consideration, attentiveness and politeness.

It seems difficult to make a clear distinction between consideration (*hairyo*) and empathy (*omoiyari*). *Omoiyari* is glossed as 'consideration' and 'empathy' in Kádár and Haugh (2013: 190), and *hairyo* as 'consideration' in Haugh (2004: 97; 2015: 252; 2016a: 51). In Pizziconi (2007: 219), *omoiyarinoaru*, which is listed among the top ten terms of evaluative qualifiers of polite behaviour or polite stances, is glossed as 'considerate'. In Haugh (2019), it is reported that one of the Australian speakers of English equates *considerate* with being able to *empathise* with others. These studies show that there are some overlaps in meaning between consideration and empathy. According to Haugh (2016a: 50–51), *omoiyarinoaru* cannot be readily glossed in English without some loss of meaning. Haugh (2016a: 51) argues as follows: in reaching an understanding of the term *omoiyari* and its relationship with *teineina* ('polite'), we must make recourse to a range of other terms such as *ki wo kubaru* ('attentive'), *hairyo ga aru* ('have consideration'), *kigakiku* ('attentive'), *shinsetsuna* ('kind'), *yasashii* ('gentle') and so on. Indeed, it is not easy to gloss *omoiyari* and *hairyo* in English; however, for the sake of this discussion, *omoiyari* is glossed as 'empathy', following Burdelski (2013), Lebra

(1976, 1993), Takada (2013) and Travis (1998), and *hairyo* as 'consideration', following Haugh (2004: 97; 2015: 252; 2016a: 51). Data in this section will reveal some differences between these concepts.

The similarity between consideration and attentiveness can be found in Shinmura (2018) and Pon (1996, 2005). *Hairyo* means *kokoro wo kubaru koto* ('to allocate heart') and *kokoro zukai* ('work of heart') (Shinmura 2018: 2318). *Kokoro kubari* (a noun form of *kokoro wo kubaru*) and *kokoro zukai* can also mean attentiveness (see Section 2.2.1). Pon (2005) uses consideration (*hairyo*) in the same sense as attentiveness (*kikubari*), and consideration and attentiveness are listed under the same category, namely, *kokoro zukai* ('work of heart') to others in Pon (1996: 78).

Some other aspects of *hairyo* ('consideration') can be found in the literature. For Ide and Ueno (2012: 39), the linguistic behaviour of consideration includes the following: repetition of what the other party said, simultaneous utterances, and discourse phenomena, in which one finishes off what the other party has started to say. The last (discourse phenomena) may be related to what Mizutani (1993) termed *kyowa* (lit. 'mutual utterance'). According to Mizutani (1993: 6), it is often the case that the Japanese leave sentences unsaid, and the other party completes them. The Japanese do not feel discomfort in completing the other party's sentences (Mizutani 1993: 7). Rather, it is considered to be good, as it gives the other party an opportunity to complete the utterance, and completing one's own sentences is unpleasant, sounding stiff (Mizutani 1993: 7). It is also noteworthy that some Japanese researchers (e.g., Jinnai 2006; Sugito and Ozaki 2006) include a concept similar to positive politeness in Brown and Levinson's (1978, 1987) terms (i.e., to reduce the distance between a speaker and the other party) in *hairyo*. According to Jinnai (2016: 115), *shin bokashi hyoogen* ('new expressions of obscuring') functions to increase the affinity towards the other party, emerging as *aite ni chikazuku hairyo* ('consideration to get closer to the other party'). Thus, this kind of consideration can be considered to be similar to positive politeness, which contradicts the notion of consideration in New Zealand English as mentioned earlier (namely, negative politeness).

Another concept which is investigated in relation to attentiveness in this section is empathy (see also Section 2.2.2.). Empathy is to think of others from the bottom of one's heart, and expressing empathy implies a sincere concern for the other party. Lebra (1993: 72) argues that '[t]he most direct expression for empathy is to become another's *mi* (*aite no mi ni naru*)', which means to stand in someone else's shoes. Empathy is other-oriented, and it is closely related to interpersonal relationships, as noted in Section 2.2.2. Empathy is an affective aspect of human beings. It is considered that empathy motivates willingness to demonstrate attentiveness (see Section 2.2.2). Thus, it can be said that empathy is closely related to attentiveness.

It is not only the difference between empathy and consideration which is not always clear, but also that between empathy and attentiveness. For example, the following definitions of empathy (*omoiyari*) seem to include an element of attentiveness in my view. '*Omoiyari* refers to the ability and willingness to feel what others are feeling, to vicariously experience the pleasure or pain that they are undergoing, and to help them satisfy their wishes' (Lebra 1976: 38). Wierzbicka's (1997: 275) definition of *omoiyari* is as follows: 'an ability to read other people's minds and a willingness to respond to other people's unspoken feelings, wants and needs'. According to Travis (1998: 55), '[o]*moiyari* essentially represents a kind of "intuitive" understanding of the unexpressed feelings, desires and thoughts of others, and doing something for them on the basis of this understanding'. 'To help them satisfy their wishes' in Lebra (1976), 'to respond to other people's unspoken feelings, wants and needs' in Wierzbicka (1997) and 'doing something for them' in Travis (1998) are behaviours which can also be construed as demonstrations of attentiveness (see Section 2.2.2).

We also investigate altruism in this section. According to Leech (2014: 22), '[a]ltruism is generally considered to refer to actions that are beneficial to some other individual(s), but not to the actor himself or herself'. Batson (2011: 20) defines altruism as 'a motivational state with the ultimate goal of increasing another's welfare', and Cohen (1978: 81) defines it as 'an act or desire to offer something gratuitously to another person or group because he, she, they, or it needs it or wants it'. For Takemura (1991: 86), altruism is a psychological trait, which shows empathy to others voluntarily without expecting any reward from others. Empathic concern[31] produces altruistic motivation (Batson 2011: 11). The decision of helping or not depends primarily on whether you feel empathy for the person and secondarily on the costs and rewards (Batson 2010). There are also cases in which people help others regardless of the costs; that is, people are motivated purely by altruistic concerns if they have a high degree of empathy, according to the empathy-altruism hypothesis (see, e.g., Aronson, Wilson and Akert 2013: 307). As we can see from these definitions, altruism is closely related to empathy.

Altruism is related also to the understanding of politeness. 'The origin of politeness probably goes back to *cooperation* and *altruism* (or unselfishness), which have been observed as functional forces not only in social groups of homo sapiens but of other species as well' (Leech 2014: 21; emphasis in the original). Drawing on Schwartz (2007), Kádár (2017: 41) argues that '[i]t is relevant to note that the values of politeness and altruism are not clearly separable, as both of them are universal moral values'.

Altruism also seems to include some element of self-sacrifice. For example, Leech (2014: 4) uses the term 'unselfishly' in defining altruism: 'someone does or says something *unselfishly*, for the sake of some other person(s) – to extend a helping hand to them'[32] (Leech 2014: 4; emphasis added). To extend a helping hand may be called helping behaviour in social psychology, which is another concept investigated in this section.

Furuhata (1994: 22) defines helping behaviour as a typical prosocial behaviour, which influences others in a positive way. Helping behaviour is a voluntary action, directed towards others' benefit or happiness, without intending to seek benefit for oneself, and one who helps others is prepared for a certain degree of self-sacrifice (Matsui 1991: 27; Takagi 1998: 12). A potential demonstrator of helping behaviour recognises that some help is needed and helping behaviour is expected (Daibou 2012: 55). In other words, in the case of helping behaviour, someone (a potential recipient of helping behaviour) is already in a situation that requires some help.[33]

Helping behaviour, prosocial behaviours (acts performed with the goal of benefiting another person) (Aronson et al. 2013: 301) and altruism are sometimes used in a similar sense by some researchers (see, e.g., Furuhata 1994: 22; Nakamura and Takagi 1987: 3; Schwartz 1977: 223; Takagi 1998: 11–12). This may be because both altruism and helping behaviour entail an element of self-sacrifice, as noted above.

2.3.2 Focus group data

Building on Fukushima (2019), this section presents more focus group data (see Morgan 1997; Stewart, Shamdasani and Rook 2007) to further explore emic understandings of the concepts investigated. According to Krueger and Casey (2009: 2), '[a] focus group is a carefully planned series of discussions designed to obtain perceptions on a defined area of interest in a permissive, nonthreatening environment'. The focus group is characterised by homogeneity (Krueger and Casey 2009). In other words, participants have something in common such as (1) an occupation, (2) past use of a programme or service, (3) age, (4) gender or (5) family characteristics (Krueger and Casey 2009: 66–67). In order to secure a permissive and nonthreatening environment and homogeneity among participants, three Japanese participants (JS1, JS2 and JS3), who knew each other and got along well, were chosen as the participants.[34] They were homogeneous in terms of occupation (university students), age (early 20s) and gender (female). As the second and the fifth factors above by Krueger and Casey (2009) were not related to the investigation of the relationship between attentiveness and the four concepts, they were not considered when determining participants. Participants were asked to talk freely on how attentiveness, consideration, empathy, altruism and helping behaviour either differed or were similar to each other. The focus group was audio-recorded and transcribed. (See Appendix 1 for transcription conventions. In the English translation, some words are added in { } for clarification).

Example (2.23) illustrates some differences between attentiveness, consideration and empathy.

(2.23)

1   JS1:   *Watashi wa kikubari to hairyo wa (0.5) nandarou na (1.0) tomodachi kankei*
　　　　　　私は気配りと配慮は何だろうな、友達関係

2   *janaku temo sono (0.8) joushi toka buka no aida demo (0.5) aru mono dakedo*
　　　　　　じゃなくても、その上司とか部下の間でもあるものだけど

　　　　　　I {think} attentiveness and consideration are, how to put it, {demonstrated} not only among friends, but also among bosses and subordinates, but

3   *omoiyari tte iu no wa (.) sono (.) shitashii kankei no naka de (.) kanjouteki ni jibun ga*
　　　　　　思い遣りっていうのは、その親しい関係の中で感情的に自分が

4   *kono hito ni koushite agetai (.) tte iu kimochi no hou ga tsuyoku te (.)*
　　　　　　この人にこうしてあげたいっていう気持ちの方が強くて

　　　　　　in the case of empathy, in close relationships, emotions, that is, the feeling that I want to do something for this person, are strong.

5   *kikubari to hairyo wa sono (.) shakaijin (.) ichi shakaijin to shite koushita hou ga*
　　　　　　気配りと配慮はその社会人、一社会人としてこうした方が

6   *aite no tame ni naru toka (.) konoba dewa kou shinakereba ikenai toka (.)*
　　　　　　相手の為になるとか、この場ではこうしなければいけないとか

7   *souiu haikei ga aruno kana tte iu fuu ni kanji masu.*
　　　　　　そういう背景があるのかなっていうふうに感じます。

　　　　　　As for attentiveness and consideration, there is a certain background, namely that doing something is for the sake of the other party, {considered from the perspective of} a member of society, or that one should do certain things on certain occasions. That's how I feel.

8   JS3:   *(1.0) ○○ san {referring to JS1} ga itta sono (0.5) kanjou (.) omoiyari ni wa (.)*
　　　　　　○○さんが言ったその感情、思い遣りには

9   *sono kanjou ga kakawatteru mitaina (.) souiu no wa watashi mo sou darou na to*
10   *omoi masu.*
　　　　　　その感情が関わってるみたいな、そういうのは私もそうだろうなと思います。

　　　　　　As ○○ said, empathy may be related to emotions, or something like that. I also think that way.

In Example (2.23), it is shown that empathy is more emotion-oriented (lines 4, 8–9) than either attentiveness or consideration. This is in accord, at least in part, with the review in Sections 2.2.2 and 2.3.1. That is, empathy is an affective aspect of human beings, which means that empathy is related to emotions. Furthermore, emotions may be needed to stand in someone else's shoes, which is Lebra's understanding of empathy (1993: 72). By contrast, attentiveness and consideration are demonstrated as not necessarily arising out of emotions, according to JS1 in Example (2.23). As a member of society, one considers what would be good for the other party, taking the situation into account, and then demonstrates consideration or attentiveness as appropriate (lines 5–7).

As one thinks *socially* what would be the best in demonstrating attentiveness and consideration, attentiveness and consideration may be demonstrated not only among friends, but also among bosses and subordinates (line 2). By contrast, empathy is demonstrated to those who are close (line 3). In Fukushima (2019), participants stated that empathy was demonstrated to those they were close to, whereas the recipients of attentiveness and consideration may not be as close as those who received empathy. Bosses and subordinates (line 2) are concrete examples of recipients of attentiveness and consideration, who are not necessarily very close. Indeed, attentiveness is demonstrated in every degree of familiarity between demonstrator and recipient regardless of status differences, although the frequency of demonstration of attentiveness may differ (see Sections 2.2.1 and 3.4).

In Fukushima (2019), it is shown that attentiveness differs from consideration. That is, consideration is demonstrated out of a sense of obligation or social pressure, whereas attentiveness is a voluntary action. In Example (2.23), however, attentiveness is considered to be rather similar to consideration in comparison to empathy. JS1 uses an expression, as a member of society (line 5), and states that one should demonstrate consideration or attentiveness, considering the other party or the situation. This may be, in part at least, related to the discussion on attentiveness and social skills, reputation and interpersonal relationships in Section 2.2.1. That is, those who can demonstrate attentiveness as expected in a given society are evaluated positively. Demonstrating attentiveness properly can be considered as a social skill, and that would lead to a good reputation. Attentiveness demonstrated as a member of society may mean something similar to attentiveness demonstrated as expected in a given society. Socially appropriate attentiveness may be something one is expected to do as a member of society. In this respect, attentiveness may be similar to consideration, which is demonstrated out of social pressure, although there are differences between the two concepts as shown in Fukushima (2019).

In Section 2.3.1 we saw that consideration in New Zealand English means not getting in the way of other people, which is the avoidance of imposition (Haugh 2019), and that the notion of wanting to do something for the benefit of another is not an essential element of the meaning of consideration (Travis 1997: 144). However, in the Japanese data above it is shown that it is taken for granted that consideration means doing something for others. In other words, consideration in the Japanese data is an active behaviour, rather than one which simply avoids acts which impose upon others. Although some Japanese researchers define consideration solely in terms of linguistic expressions, as noted in Section 2.3.1, the participants in Example (2.23) did not touch upon this aspect. For the participants, it seems that consideration is expressed by behaviours rather than linguistic expressions (see also lines 1–2 in Example [2.26]).

In Section 2.3.1, it was noted that there are some overlaps of meaning between consideration, empathy and attentiveness. Example (2.23), however, shows that empathy is different from consideration or attentiveness. Example (2.24) further illustrates that empathy differs from the latter two.

(2.24)

1   JS3:   *Kikubari to hairyo wa (.) docchi ka to iu to (.) aite no mi ni naru to iu yori wa*
気配りと配慮はどっちかというと、相手の身になるというよりは

2   *sono sakki* ○○ *san* {referring to JS1} *ga itta mitai ni (.) shakaiteki ni kangaete toka*
そのさっき○○さんが言ったみたいに社会的に考えてとか

Attentiveness and consideration are not to stand in someone else's shoes, but they are rather derived from thinking socially, as ○○ said earlier, or something like that.

3   *risei* (0.5) *risei* ↑ (0.8) *kou joukyou toka kara handan shite* (0.5)
理性、理性、こう状況とかから判断して

Out of reason or rationality, or judging from a situation,

4   *koushitara iinja nai ka toka* (0.5) *nanika koudou wo okosu no ga*
こうしたらいいんじゃないかとか、何か行動を起こすのが

one thinks that it would be good to do a certain thing, or something like that. Then, one would do something.

5   *kikubari (.) to hairyo kana tte omoi masu.*
気配りと配慮かなって思います。

That's attentiveness or consideration, I think.

It is shown in Example (2.23) that empathy is derived from emotions, and that in the case of empathy someone is prepared to do things for people that they feel close to. By contrast, Example (2.24) shows that reason is the motivation behind demonstrating attentiveness and consideration (line 3), which is related to the statement by JS1 (as a member of society) in Example (2.23) (line 5). In other words, one uses reason to determine what kind of attentiveness or consideration one should demonstrate, according to what is socially appropriate. If one does not demonstrate appropriate attentiveness, for example, one may be evaluated negatively as *ki ga kikanai* ('not attentive').

Example (2.25) further exemplifies that empathy differs from attentiveness and consideration.

(2.25)

1 JS2: *Kikubari to hairyo ni tsuite nan desu kedo hh (.) aite ga iru tte iu joutai de*
気配りと配慮についてなんですけど、相手がいるっていう状態で

2 *(2.0) sono (0.5) koudou wo suru toiu ka (1.0) to iu inshou wo watashi wa uke masu.*
その行動をするというか、という印象を私は受けます。

Concerning attentiveness and consideration, my impression is that we can only demonstrate {attentiveness or consideration} when the other party is actually present.

3 *Omoiyari: wa (.) aite ga inai (1.5) nante iu (0.5) me no mae ni aite ga inakute mo.*
思い遣りは相手がいない、何て言う、目の前に相手がいなくても。

{We could demonstrate} empathy, how to put it, even when the other party is not in front of a demonstrator.

JS2's contention in Example (2.25) is that one demonstrates attentiveness and consideration towards someone who is actually in front of the demonstrator (lines 1–2), whereas one can demonstrate empathy even when the other party is not in sight (line 3). This may be related to the original meaning of *omoiyari* ('empathy'), namely, to make *kokoro* ('heart') work towards something or someone from afar (Yuuki 1991: 62), as noted in Section 2.2.2.

It was shown in Fukushima (2019) that altruism and helping behaviour were different from attentiveness, consideration and empathy. Examples (2.26) and (2.27) further illustrate this.

(2.26)

1 JS1: *Nanka kikubari toka (.) hairyo tte ittara (.) sono*
何か気配りとか配慮って言ったら、その

Well, attentiveness and consideration are

2 JS3: *(0.8) koudou [koui.*
行動、行為。

behaviours, actions.

3   JS1:   [*Un un.*

    うんうん。

    Yeah, yeah.

4   *Dakedo shugi tte iwareta ra*

    だけど主義って言われたら

    However, when we hear principles {altruism}

5   JS3:   (0.5) [*Shugi dayo ne hh*

    主義だよね。

    It is principles {altruism}, isn't it?

6   JS2:   [*Souiu hito desu tte koto*

    そういう人ですってこと

    Does that mean that someone is that kind of person?

7   JS1:   *Sou.*

    そう。

    Yeah.

8   JS3:   *Shisou no koto [dayo ne.*

    思想のことだよね。

    It's about thought, isn't it?

9   JS1:   [*Sono (0.5) kono joukyou ni oite kono kikubari wo shiyou toka kono*

10   *omoiyari wo shiyou janakute (.) itsudemo dokodemo hh jibun wa*

11   *ritashugi mitaina.*

    その、この状況においてこの気配りをしようとか、この思い遣りを
    しようじゃなくて、いつでもどこでも自分は利他主義みたいな。

    Well, it is different from demonstrating attentiveness or empathy in a certain situation, but more as if one has {the spirit of} altruism all the time, or something like that.

12   JS3:   *Aa (.) hito to nari (0.5) [no setsumei mitaina.*

    あぁ、人となりの説明みたいな。

    Oh, is that a kind of an explanation of personality, or something like that?

13   JS1:   [*Sou sou sou sou.*

    そうそうそうそう。

    Yeah, yeah, yeah, yeah.

14   JS2:   *Un un un.*

    うんうんうん。

    Yeah, yeah, yeah.

15   S1:   *Nani mo haikei kankei naku (.) itsudemo jibun no jiku ga aru no kana hh*
何も背景関係なくいつでも自分の軸があるのかな。

Does one always have her/his own moral compass, irrelevant of background?

16   JS3:   (1.0) *Demo nanka sono (0.5) souiu koui wo okonau hito jitai ni foukasu shiteru (.)*

17   [*kanji (.) ritashugi.*
でも何かその、そういう行為を行う人自体にフォーカスしてる感じ。
利他主義。

Well, something like that, altruism seems to be focused on people themselves who demonstrate certain behaviours.

18   JS1:   [*Un un. Tashikani.*
うんうん。確かに。

Yeah, yeah. Certainly.

19   JS3:   (1.5) *Kikubari hairyo omoiyari wa sono okonau koudou ni foukasu (0.5) shiteru ki ga*

20   *suru kedo (.) ritashugi wa (0.5) sono*
気配り、配慮、思い遣りはその行う行動にフォーカスしてる気がするけど、利他主義はその

I feel that behaviour is focused on in terms of attentiveness, consideration and empathy, but altruism is

21   JS1:   (0.8) *Hito no tokusei tte iu ka.*
人の特性っていうか。

about someone's personality, or something like that.

(2.27)

1   JS3:   *Ritashugi tte iu to (.) jibun wo (.) sashioite mo (.) hoka no hito no tame ni nani ka (.)*
利他主義って言うと、自分を差し置いても他の人の為に何か

2   *shiyou (.) tte iu (.) kokoroiki ga kanji rarerun desu kedo (.)*
しようっていう心意気が感じられるんですけど

As for altruism, we can feel some kind of spirit, that is, one would try to do anything for other people, even sacrificing oneself.

3   *kikubari hairyo omoiyari wa soko made ikanai kana tte iu kanji ga.*
気配り、配慮、思い遣りはそこまでいかないかなっていう感じが。

However, one does not go that far in demonstrating attentiveness, consideration and empathy.

In Example (2.26), it is shown that altruism differs from attentiveness, consideration and empathy in that the former is more focused on an individual's personality or character (lines 6, 12 and 21), whereas in the case of attentiveness, consideration and empathy, the focus is on behaviour instead (line 19). Another outstanding feature of altruism shown in Example (2.27) is that there is a determination to help others, whatever the consequences (lines 1–2), which is not necessarily the case with attentiveness, consideration and empathy (line 3). The understanding of altruism by JS3 (line 1) in Example (2.27) ('one would try to do anything for other people, even sacrificing oneself') is, at least in part, consistent with the literature reviewed in Section 2.3.1, that is, someone does or says something *unselfishly*, for the sake of some other person(s) (Leech 2014). However, what seems to differ from the review is that the participants in Examples (2.26) and (2.27) take altruism as part of someone's personality rather than it being 'a motivational state with the ultimate goal of increasing another's welfare' (Batson 2011) or 'an act or desire to offer something gratuitously to another person' (Cohen 1978). In other words, the interpretation of altruism by participants focuses on people who would do anything for other people, even sacrificing themselves. What the Japanese participants in this section construe to be altruism may be influenced by the Japanese translation of 'altruism', namely, *ritashugi* (lit. 'principles of benefiting others').

In Example (2.28), an understanding of helping behaviour by a participant is presented.

(2.28)

1	JS1:	*Aite ga (.) motometeru ka motomete nai ka de ittara (.) enjokoui no hou ga (.)*
		相手が求めてるか求めてないかで言ったら、援助行為の方が

2   *sore wo shite morawa nakereba naranai joukyou nano kana tte iu fuu ni omoi masu.*
それをしてもらわなければならない状況なのかなっていうふうに思います。

In terms of whether the other party needs {help} or not, one is in a state in which that {act of helping} needs to be done in the case of helping behaviour {in comparison to attentiveness or consideration}, I think.

JS1's understanding of helping behaviour in Example (2.28) coincides with the review in Section 2.3.1; that is, help is needed in helping behaviour (e.g., Daibou 2012).

2.3.3 Discussion

Building on Fukushima (2019), this section has further investigated the interrelationship between attentiveness and the four concepts, namely, consideration, empathy, altruism and helping behaviour, as it is believed that investigating the similarities or differences between attentiveness and the concepts above would make the characteristics of attentiveness clearer. Although some focus group data confirmed earlier research findings, other data showed nuanced differences among these concepts, which were not necessarily found in the previous literature.

Participants stated that empathy is more emotion-oriented than attentiveness and consideration. This can also be deduced from who is selected to be a recipient of these concepts. Although empathy is demonstrated to those who are close to the demonstrators (Fukushima 2019), attentiveness or consideration may be demonstrated not only among friends, but also among bosses and subordinates, as shown in Example (2.23). On a related note, the motives behind demonstrations of empathy, attentiveness and consideration differ. Whereas demonstration of empathy is driven by emotions, reason motivates someone to demonstrate consideration or attentiveness. However, this does not necessarily mean that attentiveness does not entail any emotional feelings. It is shown in Fukushima (2019) that attentiveness involves gentleness. Moreover, the demonstration of attentiveness is motivated by empathy, as noted in Section 2.2.2. In other words, both attentiveness and empathy are based on affection for others and on the heart perspective (see Fukushima 2019). What participants wanted to say in this section may be that consideration or attentiveness require more reasoning than does empathy, as attentiveness and consideration both require socially appropriate and expected levels of response, and failure to act appropriately can adversely affect one's reputation. What is socially appropriate or expected may differ culturally. We will discuss the issue of culture in the next chapter.

It was shown in Fukushima (2019) that attentiveness, consideration and empathy are different from altruism and helping behaviour. In this section, some differences between these two groups have further emerged. For example, altruism is more focused on individual character and personality, whereas in attentiveness, consideration and empathy the focus is on behaviour. However, as noted earlier, those who cannot demonstrate appropriate attentiveness may be evaluated negatively, which can be considered as a feature or reputation of people. In other words, people's features or reputations are influenced or sometimes determined by their behaviour.

Another difference is that altruism requires some kind of strong determination to help others, which is not the case with attentiveness, consideration and empathy. This is, at least in part, consistent with the review in Section 2.3.1. As for the difference between helping behaviour and attentiveness, consideration and empathy, help is definitely needed in helping behaviour, or someone is already in a state in which they need help, whereas it may not necessarily be the case in consideration, empathy or attentiveness.

Some understanding of the relationships between attentiveness and the above-mentioned four concepts was investigated through the lens of emic understandings in this section. Emic understandings are sometimes loosely equated with first-order politeness (see, e.g., Eelen 2001: 78). Haugh (2007c: 305) suggests that 'politeness research may be better served by revisiting the first-order and second-order politeness distinction as outlined by Eelen (2001) in order to build a more solid foundation for theorizing about (im)politeness' (see also Haugh 2012). To this end, Haugh (2007c: 306–307) argues the importance of *interactionally achieved* politeness. '(Im)politeness is ... conceptualized as being conjointly co-constituted in a collaborative, non-summative manner through interaction by participants' (Haugh 2007c: 306). It can be said that the understandings of the relationship between attentiveness and the four concepts obtained from focus groups in this section were 'interactionally achieved', which is important in understanding im/politeness.

If consideration or *hairyo* entails the elements of simultaneous utterances (Ide and Ueno 2012) and discourse phenomena such as *kyowa* ('mutual utterances') (Mizutani 1993), as noted in Section 2.3.1, consideration was observed while participants engaged in the conversation. Simultaneous utterances can be considered as overlaps, which appeared in Example (2.26) in lines 2 and 3 by JS3 and JS1, lines 5 and 6 by JS3 and JS2, lines 8 and 9 by JS 3 and JS1, lines 12 and 13 by JS3 and JS1, and lines 17 and 18 by JS3 and JS1, and mutual utterances appeared in lines 1 and 2 by JS1 and JS3, and lines 20 and 21 by JS3 and JS1. Participants seemed to *consider* each other and co-constituted the differences or similarities of the concepts investigated.

As noted in Section 2.3.1, some Japanese researchers include a concept similar to positive politeness in consideration. In the focus group data, consideration of this type could be found. For example, *mitaina* ('or something like that'; see n. 12) in Example (2.23) line 9 and in Example (2.26) lines 11 and 12, and *toka* ('or something like that') in Example (2.24) lines 2, 3 and 4 and in Example (2.26) lines 1 and 9 are new expressions of obscuring, which is argued by Jinnai (2006). The reason why this type of consideration (consideration to get closer to the other party) was found in the focus group data may be that participants were close friends, and they tried to further reduce the distance between them or to strengthen solidarity, although this needs further scrutiny.

The concepts examined in this section include those which have been researched separately in different disciplines (e.g., consideration in pragmatics, empathy in anthropology, psychology, psychiatry, medicine and nursing science [see Section 2.2.2] and altruism and helping behaviour in social psychology). In this section, these concepts were investigated regardless of discipline. Thus, it can be said that an interdisciplinary perspective has been taken. The importance of interdisciplinarity is well acknowledged in the field (see, e.g., Haugh 2018: 153; Locher 2015: 7–8; Norrick and Haugh 2015). Further research taking an interdisciplinary perspective will reveal a deeper understanding of attentiveness, as attentiveness is related not only to pragmatics, but also to some other disciplines. Moreover, pragmatics itself has 'the multi-faceted nature' (Locher and Graham 2010: 1), and 'pragmatics is significantly informed by a range of academic disciplines' (Cummings 2005: 1). These arguments are related to the integrative pragmatics approach developed by Culpeper and Haugh (2014) and are similar in that '[i]n many respects, pragmatics can now be conceptualised as lying at the intersection of linguistics, psychology and sociology' (Haugh and Culpeper 2018: 219). Indeed, Haugh and Culpeper (2018: 220) take pragmatics as an interdisciplinary program.

2.4 Conclusion

In this chapter, an attempt has been made to clarify the concept of attentiveness. Section 2.2 examined attentiveness from various perspectives. Attentiveness was investigated in relation to im/politeness, morality and moral order, *ki* ('spirit'), linguistic and non-linguistic aspects, social competence, reputation and interpersonal relationships. Relationships between the demonstrator and the recipient of attentiveness and the intentionality of a potential recipient of attentiveness were also investigated. Different kinds of attentiveness, namely, genuine attentiveness, reflexive attentiveness and business-oriented attentiveness, were explained with some data. The conditions needed for attentiveness to arise, namely, anticipatory inference and empathy, were examined. The processes of attentiveness which lead up to demonstration and evaluation of attentiveness were explained.

In Section 2.3, attentiveness was further examined, taking an interdisciplinary perspective. The relationship between attentiveness and some other related concepts, namely, consideration, empathy, altruism and helping behaviour, was investigated with the aid of focus groups. Taking the importance of interdisciplinarity in the field into account, all of these concepts, which have been researched in different disciplines, were examined in relation to attentiveness. The results from the focus groups show some nuanced differences between these concepts.

What attentiveness means may vary cross-culturally. In the following chapter, therefore, we turn to an examination of attentiveness from a cultural perspective, more specifically, cross-cultural and cross-generational comparisons of attentiveness, including the demonstration and evaluation of attentiveness.

CHAPTER 3

Cross-cultural and cross-generational comparisons of attentiveness

3.1 Introduction

Attentiveness may be demonstrated or evaluated differently by people of different cultural backgrounds. Even though someone might demonstrate attentiveness, thinking of the well-being of the other party, it could be sometimes construed as offensive, intrusive, meddlesome and so on. In the previous chapter, we saw the example of a Japanese cabin attendant bringing a mask to a Japanese passenger who sneezed on an aeroplane as an instance of business-oriented attentiveness. The Japanese passenger appreciated that attentiveness greatly. However, a Chinese lady who had lived in the United States for more than 20 years and who was among the audience of Fukushima (2014) stated that that would be an offence to her, because it would suggest that she was spreading germs around. This shows that the same attentiveness can be evaluated differently by people of different cultural backgrounds. With the above in mind, this chapter explores attentiveness cross-culturally as well as cross-generationally.

Before cross-cultural[1] and cross-generational comparisons of the demonstration and evaluation of attentiveness are made, some issues on culture which are relevant to this chapter are considered in Section 3.2. After that, three data-driven studies, one of them focusing on the demonstration of attentiveness (Section 3.4) and two on the evaluation of attentiveness (Sections 3.3. and 3.5), are presented.

We will focus on evaluation of attentiveness as it is closely linked to interpersonal relationships and it aligns with the recent trend in im/politeness research. In the course of the development of im/politeness research, especially in a discursive or postmodern approach,[2] several important issues have been raised. One of them is the attention to evaluation (see, e.g., Bousfield 2007a, 2007b; Bousfield and Locher 2008; Culpeper 1996, 2003, 2005; Eelen 2001; Haugh 2007c: 302; Locher and Bousfield 2008; see also Davies 2018, who argues for heterogeneity within evaluation). According to Locher (2006: 253), the discursive approach to politeness recognises the evaluative and norm-oriented character of politeness by claiming that politeness belongs to the interpersonal level of linguistic interaction. Eelen considers the evaluative role of the hearer as fundamental and notes that '[i]n everyday practice (im)politeness occurs not so much when the speaker produces behaviour but rather when the hearer evaluates that behaviour' (Eelen 2001: 109). Eelen further contends that 'the very essence of (im)politeness lies in the evaluative moment' (2001: 109). Furthermore, some researchers (see, e.g., Haugh 2007c: 313; Mills 2003; Spencer-Oatey 2005b: 97) argue that politeness is not behaviour per se but an evaluation of behaviour. Research on a hearer's evaluation of im/politeness is important, as 'the final decision as to whether something is perceived as polite or impolite lies in H's interpretation, who judges the relational aspect of an utterance with respect to H's own norms (frames, appropriateness, expectations, personal style, etc.)' (Locher 2004: 90). Sun (2018: 266) argues that the evaluation of politeness behaviour can be as important as its utterance. Despite its importance, evaluation has been rather neglected in previous studies (see, e.g., Eelen 2001: 245–246; Hickey and Stewart 2005b: 7). The investigation of attentiveness evaluation in this chapter will fill the gap in the field.

Evaluations are based on the moral order,[3] or '"seen but unnoticed", expected, background features of everyday scenes' (Garfinkel 1967: 36) (see Section 2.2.1). According to Caffi (2015: 20), Garfinkel's (1967) concept is interestingly recalled by Fukushima and Haugh (2014: 166) in dealing with emic understandings of the moral order that relate to evaluations of im/politeness. Through the lens of the evaluation of attentiveness in this chapter, emic understandings of the moral order will be further investigated. The moral order may differ among different groups (see Spencer-Oatey and Kádár 2016: 81). Thus, what we need to note when investigating attentiveness in this chapter is that participants of different cultural backgrounds may not necessarily share the same moral grounds (see Section 3.2).

We also need to keep in mind that the notion of culture is determined not only by national levels,[4] although this does not mean that we should exclude national levels (which are still very important aspects) from the discussion of culture and the investigation of im/politeness and attentiveness in relation to culture. Cultural differences are not only due to national differences, but are also due to some other differences, including generation, region, gender, religion, social class, profession, educational level, political beliefs/boundaries, language and so on (see, e.g., Eelen 2001: 160; Hofstede 1991: 10–18) (see Section 3.2.1). Even one family or an individual may have a different 'culture' from another, which suggests an intra-cultural variability. Indeed, 'in every single culture there is variation as to what is understood as im/polite by specific individuals in specific situations'

(Sifianou and Garcés-Conejos Blitvich 2017: 589). Differences in culture, the interpersonal relationships between a demonstrator and a recipient of attentiveness and any emotional feelings between them may influence the demonstration or the evaluation of attentiveness. As it is beyond the scope of this chapter to take up all of these, the variables of nation and generation are incorporated in the investigation, a cross-cultural[5] and a cross-generational comparison of attentiveness being made.

As for the different national backgrounds, the UK, Japan and the United States were chosen. In Brown and Levinson's (1987) classification, the cultures in the UK and Japan belong to negative politeness cultures, and the culture in the United States to a positive politeness culture. Also, the UK and the United States are often considered to be individualist cultures, whereas Japan is a collectivist culture, although there are some differing views on these classifications (see Section 3.2.2).

With regards to a cross-generational comparison, Japanese people from two generations were chosen. A cross-generational comparison of attentiveness is included, because of the following reasons. A generation or an age group is one of the factors which constitutes the heterogeneity within the same cultural group. Moreover, not many studies have investigated generational differences in politeness research so far (but see, e.g., Bella 2009; He 2012; Sarkhosh and Alizadeh 2017; Sifianou and Tzanne 2010). Indeed, Murphy (2010: 13) argues that research on language and age has not been explored to the same extent as other sociolinguistic variables. Likewise, Mills (2017: 91) argues that factors such as age are elided with other factors when politeness is focused on.

Section 3.3 investigates the evaluation of attentiveness cross-culturally (between British and Japanese university students). Data is elicited through questionnaires. The research questions are as follows:

1. Are there any differences between the British and Japanese participants in their evaluation of attentiveness?
2. Are there any differences between the British and Japanese participants in rating the degree of imposition required to demonstrate attentiveness?
3. Are there any differences between the British and Japanese participants in their reasons for their evaluation of attentiveness?

As the results of Section 3.3 do not show many differences between the participants, different groups of the participants were chosen (the gender was also controlled) to compare the demonstration and the evaluation of attentiveness cross-culturally and cross-generationally in Sections 3.4 and 3.5. The same situations are used in these two sections, although the situations are presented from different perspectives. While the focus in Section 3.4 is on whether the demonstration of attentiveness is chosen or not, the evaluation of attentiveness is the main focus in Section 3.5, attentiveness being already presented in the situations.

The data in Sections 3.4 and 3.5 was elicited through questionnaires and interviews. As the number of the participants in the interviews was relatively small, it is not intended to draw any generalised conclusion from only the interview data. The interview data can be used to verify the questionnaire data, although we would not be able to completely deny some differences or similarities found in the interview data by different groups of participants. The interview data also tells us some concrete ideas concerning the demonstration and the evaluation of attentiveness, which cannot be obtained just from the questionnaire data.

In Section 3.4, the demonstration of attentiveness is investigated cross-culturally (between Japanese and American participants) and cross-generationally (between the two different generations of the Japanese participants). The research questions are as follows:

1. Are there any differences among the participants in their demonstration of attentiveness?
2. Are there any differences among the participants in their reasons for demonstrating or not demonstrating attentiveness?
3. Are there any differences among the participants in rating the degree of imposition required to demonstrate attentiveness?
4. Is there any relationship between the demonstration of attentiveness and the degree of imposition required to demonstrate attentiveness?
5. In which relationship (between a demonstrator and a recipient of attentiveness) is attentiveness demonstrated?

In Section 3.5, the evaluation of attentiveness is compared cross-culturally and cross-generationally, using the same participants as in Section 3.4. The research questions are as follows:

1. Are there any differences among the participants in their evaluation of attentiveness?
2. Are there any differences among the participants in their reasons for the evaluation of attentiveness?
3. Are there any differences among the participants in rating the degree of imposition required to demonstrate attentiveness?
4. Is there any correlation between the degree of imposition required to demonstrate attentiveness and the evaluation of attentiveness?

3.2 Culture

3.2.1 Some issues on culture

Culture is elusive in nature. Thus, it is difficult to define what culture is (see, e.g., Culpeper 2011b: 12; Spencer-Oatey 2008: 3; Spencer-Oatey and Franklin 2009: 13). As Scollon, Scollon and Jones (2012: 3) point out, the biggest problem with the word 'culture' is that nobody seems to know exactly what it means, or rather, that it means very different things to different people (see also Bond, Žegarac and Spencer-Oatey 2000: 52–54). Culture is a notion that is often used though seldom explicated to any great extent (Eelen 2001: 158). Haugh (2010: 141) raises some key issues in im/politeness research and one of them is the way in which culture itself has been conceptualised. Haugh (2010: 141) questions 'how to define culture in the face of the inherent variability and argumentivity of perceptions of im/politeness that can arise even in intra-cultural interactions – let alone intercultural interactions'.

'Culture' has been variously used and variously defined, as shown in Bargiela-Chiappini (2010: 310), namely that the 157 definitions of 'culture' provided in earlier compilations have doubled in number recently. Spencer-Oatey (2008: 3), for example, defines 'culture' as 'a fuzzy set of attitudes, beliefs, behavioural conventions, and basic assumptions and values that are shared by a group of people, and that influence each member's behaviour and each member's interpretations of the "meaning" of other people's behaviour'. Hofstede (1980: 21) treats culture as 'the collective programming of the mind which distinguishes the members of one human group from another' and defines it as 'the interactive aggregate of common characteristics that influence a human group's response to its environment'.

According to Haugh and Kádár (2017: 604), '[c]ulture is commonly used to refer to any set of persons who can be classed or categorised as having some kind of association through shared beliefs, values and practices, that is, shared ways of doing things as well as shared ways of interpreting or thinking about things in the world (Scollon and Scollon 1995; Spencer-Oatey 2000)'. For Haugh and Kádár (2017: 604–605) '[c]ulture is … both multilayered, involving various social groupings ranging from family or other communal living groups to communities of practices through to diffuse relational networks, and multifaceted, involving recurrent ways of doing, perceiving and evaluating and so on at all levels of social life'.

Culture offers the moral grounds for making evaluations. Without recourse to recurrent, 'seen but unnoticed' ways of going about our everyday lives (Garfinkel

1967), there are no grounds upon which participants may evaluate the talk and conduct of others (and ourselves) as 'good', 'bad', 'appropriate', 'inappropriate', 'polite', 'impolite' and so on (Haugh 2013; Haugh and Kádár 2017: 605). Haugh and Kádár (2017: 605) rightly argue as follows concerning the moral grounds in intercultural communication: the complication in the case of *inter*cultural encounters is that the moral grounds for such evaluations cannot be readily presumed by participants, but must inevitably be negotiated across multiple perspectives.

Haugh (2011: 260) sees the moral dimension of im/politeness as a significant element in a theory of politeness at the social level, and an aid in exploring its interconnections between the individual and the social levels of politeness (Sifianou and Garcés-Conejos Blitvich 2017: 583). According to Mills (2017: 48), 'Kádár and Haugh (2013) characterise this moral order as relatively homogeneous, static and fixed, and do not spell out what the moral order associated with any particular language consists of'. In my view, moral order may change diachronically; however, it is agreed upon among people in a community of practice or any sub-group of a culture for a certain length of time.

Spencer-Oatey and Franklin (2009: 15) summarise important characteristics of culture as follows: (1) culture is manifested through different types of regularities, some of which are more explicit than others; (2) culture is associated with social groups, but no two individuals[6] within a group share exactly the same cultural characteristics; (3) culture affects people's behaviour[7] and interpretations of behaviour; and (4) culture is acquired and/or constructed through interaction with others.

In sum, culture is an abstract entity. Although it is difficult to grasp what culture is, we, people, constitute it in a way. Society consists of people, namely, many individuals. Each individual has feelings, emotions, rationale, sense of justice, values and so on. Every individual evaluates something good, bad, polite, impolite, rude and so on. Our evaluation is based on moral order, which is constituted by recurrent acts and has become normative or expected behaviour. In other words, certain people constitute a certain 'culture', whose members agree upon many things. People evaluate utterances or behaviours according to the norms of appropriateness[8] for a given group or community. The aggregate of these may constitute a culture. Žegarac (2008: 51) lends support for this, at least in part, saying that a culture cannot exist without some cultural representations being in the brains/minds of individuals.

In what follows, social groups, heterogeneity, regularities and evaluations are discussed. While social groups constitute a culture and are related to the heterogeneity of a culture, regularities and evaluations are related to moral order, expectations and norms. However, these cannot be neatly separated from each other, as they are inter-related.

Social groups and heterogeneity

Mills (2009: 1056) argues the importance of heterogeneity within cultural groups, saying that '[r]ather than assuming that cultures and language groups are homogeneous in their usage, we need to be aware of the heterogeneity within cultural groups and it is from this variation that language change in relation to impoliteness norms occurs'. Likewise, Grainger and Mills (2016: 16–19) advocate that cultures are not homogeneous, but they should be seen as being a dynamic and heterogeneous grouping of values, beliefs and ideologies. According to Mills (2015: 133), '[c]onventional linguistic approaches to politeness and culture have tended to assume that different cultures, for example, Arab cultures or English culture, are fairly homogeneous'. This may partly derive from viewing culture on a national level. There are other constituents of culture than just nation. Indeed, Spencer-Oatey and Kádár (2016: 74) argue that 'the notion of "culture" relates not only to national culture, but also to the cultures of all kinds of other groupings, including ethnic, minority, and regional groups, as well as communities of practice'.

In relation to the discussion above, Holliday (1999) argues that there is a need to distinguish between two paradigms of culture: large culture and small culture,[9] the former signifying ethnic, national or international and the latter any cohesive social grouping (Holliday 1999: 237). According to Hofstede (1991: 10–18), the layers of culture are made up of a national level, a regional and/or ethnic and/ or religious and/or linguistic affiliation level, a gender level, a generation level, a social-class level[10] and an organisational or corporate level (for those who are employed). Similarly, Eelen (2001: 160–165) mentions that culture is defined in terms of language, speech community, ethnic group, (geo-)political boundaries, religion, social class and historical-temporal dimension. Depending on these, there can be diversities (or heterogeneity) within a culture.

The heterogeneity of culture or intra-cultural variability may also derive from other factors, such as elite values. Mills (2015: 133) regards culture as being a fairly heterogeneous grouping of values, beliefs and ideologies which are associated with a particular elite group.[11] Elite values may not be foregrounded in particular individuals or situations (Grainger and Mills 2016: 26). Mills (2017) argues that 'elite norms' are focused on when politeness is discussed and that 'class' plays an important role in understanding im/politeness.[12] The differences between working-class and middle-class behaviour[13] and norms within UK society, which were pointed out by Mills (2004), illustrate the heterogeneity in one culture.

Mills (2003) also sheds light on not only elite values and class, but also gender. Mills (2003) argues that politeness is associated with the speech norms at a stereotypical level of middle-class white women and is thus already gendered in English (Mills and Kádár 2011: 32). Likewise, Haugh (2011: 254) contends that norms of politeness (and impoliteness) vary within societies or cultures, across different communities of practices (CoPs),[14] classes, regions and according to gender and age among other things. These suggest that one culture is not necessarily homogeneous and that various sub-groups, which may sometimes differ from each other, co-exist within a culture. It is also worth noting that all people are simultaneously members of a number of different groups and categories, such as gender, ethnic, generational, national and professional groups (Spencer-Oatey and Franklin 2009: 46). Some of these are foregrounded, depending on the situation.

Lim and Ahn (2015: 70) argue that a culture is a field in which different attributes coexist and dialectically interact with each other to reach an optimal relationship for a society at a given time. Furthermore, Sifianou and Garcés-Conejos Blitvich (2017: 589), who also agree that cultures are not homogeneous, point out that cultures and even subcultures are not only heterogeneous, but also unbounded entities. As one of the explanations for this, Sifianou and Garcés-Conejos Blitvich (2017: 589) cite Coupland's (2010: 6) statement, that '[c]ultures diffuse and flow into each other'. Moreover, globalisation, which entails mobility for various reasons and increasing numbers of various kinds of interactions both traditional and novel, particularly given the development of technologically mediated means of communication, makes cultures 'diffuse and flow into each other' (Sifianou and Garcés-Conejos Blitvich 2017: 589). Indeed, globalisation is one of the factors to influence the heterogeneity of culture, but its definition is not always clear. According to Garrett (2010: 447), '"globalization" is often viewed as a "catchword" … whose meaning is vague and elusive, and which is consequently open to variable interpretations'. For Sifianou (2013: 87), 'globalisation is supposed to refer to the acceleration of processes of interconnectedness in every aspect of social life, most evidently in pervasive cultural symbols…' (see also Turner and Holton 2016 for the definition of globalisation, and Sifianou and Garcés-Conejos Blitvich 2018 for globalisation and im/politeness). The argument so far shows the heterogeneity of culture, which can be against the notion that the concept of 'culture' is often complicit with nationalism (see Lempert 2012: 194).

The heterogeneity of culture can be viewed also from the perspective that culture is not static (see, e.g., Lim and Ahn 2015; Matsumoto 2002). As Culpeper and Haugh (2014: 207) rightly point out, cultures continually experience diachronic as well as synchronic change (see also Spencer-Oatey 2005a: 342). One example may be Lakoff's (2005) view on American culture, which has changed from being a respect-based culture to becoming a camaraderie culture. Another example is the view on Japanese culture. According to Yamaguchi (1994: 184), Japanese culture has become more individualistic due to economic growth (see Section 3.2.2). Likewise, Hofstede (1991: 77) points out that Japan has experienced a shift towards individualism because of economic development, although he acknowledges that Japan still retains distinctive collectivist elements in the spheres of family, school and work. Similarly, Japanese culture is a moderately individualistic culture (Gudykunst, Yoon and Nishida 1987: 295) as well as moderately collectivistic (Gudykunst et al. 1987: 297).

It can be said that culture is in a continuous flux, as culture is subject to ideological challenges and changes (Kádár and Bargiela-Chiappini 2011: 5). Some changes are partly due to diachronic changes, as noted above, and also to generation (see, e.g., Hofstede 1991: 10–18; Eelen 2001: 160–165), which is taken up in this chapter. Some generational differences in a culture can be seen in the following. For example, Mills and Kádár (2011: 33) state that older people often tend to see the changes that they perceive to be occurring in society in a negative way. Indeed, the older Japanese and Taiwanese participants in Fukushima and Haugh (2014) bemoaned the way in which attentiveness and empathy were practised less by younger Japanese and Taiwanese. People of different generations may not only have different perspectives on changes in culture, but their behaviour may also differ. Mills (2017: 91) argues that '[o]lder people tend to behave according to a set of beliefs about politeness norms which are not shared by younger people'.

Generation and some other variables which were mentioned earlier, for example, region, gender, class and so on, constitute subgroups in a culture. It is important to note that these subgroups are not subordinate to a national cultural group (see Grainger and Mills 2016: 16). The heterogeneity of culture derives from all these groups.

Regularities and evaluations

On the one hand, I agree with the view above, which regards culture as heterogeneous. On the other hand, we may not be able to deny completely that there are some similar traits or tendencies in one culture, which differentiate one culture from another. In Haugh and Kádár's (2017: 603) words, 'there are regularities in how members *do* and *mean* things in interaction, that is, the ways in which we accomplish and make sense of the social actions, meanings, activities and so on that constitute our daily interactions'. And according to these regularities, members evaluate social actions, activities, meanings and so on (Haugh and Kádár 2017: 603). Haugh and Kádár (2017: 603) stress the importance of studying such regularities at multiple levels. Multiple levels may include factors such as age, gender, region and so on, not only a speech community or a nation from which people come from (see the above-mentioned discussion on social groups). The heterogeneity of culture is influenced by these factors, as mentioned earlier, but there may be some regularities accrued to each factor.

The regularities may be rephrased as the shared set of values, which may partly reflect what Eelen (2001: 165) calls 'homogeneous culture'. By homogeneous culture Eelen (2001: 165) means that 'cultures are by definition internally homogeneous – at least as far as politeness is concerned – because they are the level on which the politeness system is shared'. Eelen (2001: 165) further argues that 'this is not contradicted by the existence of systematic variability, as this kind of variability is system-internal'.[15] In a similar vein, Marra (2015: 377) claims that 'there seems to be an underlying assumption that there is an identifiable "culture" within a speech community. This suggests at least some degree of homogeneity within a group and tends towards culture being conceptualised as a largely fixed social category (albeit with a degree of flexibility as recognised through the discursive approach).' Indeed, a culture involves a social group (such as a nation, ethnic group, profession, generation, etc.) whose members *share* (and presume that they share) *similar* cultural representations held by a significant proportion of the group's members (Žegarac 2008: 51).

The discussion so far may be related to regularity and variability[16] argued by Spencer-Oatey (2005a: 339–342). Spencer-Oatey (2005a: 339) argues that culture is concerned with regularities within a social group, but these regularities do not preclude variability. On the contrary, regularity and variability go hand in hand (Spencer-Oatey 2005a: 339). The variability of culture is also reflected in the changes that can occur over time (Spencer-Oatey 2005a: 342). This is in line with the aforementioned discussion that culture is not static and continually changes both diachronically and synchronically.

3.2.2 Some tendencies in cultures

According to Mills (2017: 30–35), cultures are often split into certain tendencies, such as collectivist and individualist (see, e.g., Hofstede 1980, 1991, 2001; Schwartz 1990, 1994; Triandis 1994; Triandis and Gelfand 2012), positive politeness and negative politeness (Brown and Levinson 1978, 1987) and discernment and volition cultures (Ide 1989). These may be related to the discussion on regularities in the previous sub-section. In what follows, these tendencies are briefly reviewed.

Collectivist and individualist cultures

Hofstede (1980, 1991, 2001) may be one of the most famous scholars with regard to collectivist/individualist cultures and collectivism/individualism. Hofstede defines individualism and collectivism as follows (see also Hofstede 2001: 225):

> Individualism pertains to societies in which the ties between individuals are loose; everyone is expected to look after himself or herself and his or her immediate family. Collectivism as its opposite pertains to societies in which people from birth onwards are integrated into strong, cohesive ingroups, which throughout people's lifetime continue to protect them in exchange for unquestioning loyalty.
>
> (Hofstede 1991: 51)

Collectivist cultures are those where the group is seen to be at the fore and the individual is not seen to be of the greatest value (Mills 2017: 30). This may lead to an emphasis on 'adhering to cultural norms and harmony' (Mills 2017: 30) in collectivist cultures. In individualist cultures, the freedom of the individual from the constraints of the group is paramount (Grainger and Mills 2016: 25). Whereas collectivist cultures are seen as more conservative socially, individualist cultures are seen as more liberal (Mills 2017: 30).

In order to identify the degree of individualism in society, Hofstede (1991) asked 117,000 IBM employees in 50 countries and 3 regions their 'work goal' items.[17] Based on that result, the 50 nations and 3 regions were ranked according to individualism index values (IDV) (Hofstede 1991: 53). Among them, the IDV score for Japan, for example, was 46, with a score rank of 22/23, the IDV score of the UK was 89 (the score rank being 3) and that of USA was 91 (the score rank being 1). These results indicate that American and British cultures belong to individualist cultures, whereas Japan is considered to belong to a more collectivist culture.

According to Markus and Kitayama (1991), in collectivist cultures the self is interdependent with some groups, whereas in individualist cultures the self is independent of groups. Markus and Kitayama (1991: 246) argue that '[t]he sense of individuality that accompanies an interdependent self includes an *attentiveness* and responsiveness to others that one either explicitly or implicitly assumes will be reciprocated by these others, as well as the willful management of one's otherfocused feelings and desires so as to maintain and further the reciprocal interpersonal relationship' (emphasis added), and that '[w]ith an independent construal of the self, others are less centrally implicated in one's current self-definition or identity'. Whereas attending to the self, the appreciation of one's difference from others, and the importance of asserting the self are stressed in American culture, attending to and fitting in with others and the importance of harmonious interdependence with them are emphasised in Japanese culture (Markus and Kitayama 1991: 224).

As noted above, independence and interdependence are the key concepts in individualistic cultures and in collectivistic[18] cultures respectively. Gudykunst et al. explain this further:

> As members of individualistic cultures are socialised into their culture,
> they learn the major values of their culture (e.g., independence, achieve-
> ment) and acquire preferred ways for how members of the culture are
> expected to view themselves (e.g., as unique persons). Members of col-
> lectivistic cultures learn different major values (e.g., harmony, solidarity)
> and acquire different preferred ways to conceive of themselves (e.g., as
> interconnected with others).
>
> (Gudykunst et al. 1996: 512–513)

It is worth noting Gudykunst et al.'s further contention that members of individualistic and collectivistic cultures do not just learn one set of values or just one way
to conceive of themselves. As individualism and collectivism exist in all cultures,
members of individualistic cultures learn some collectivistic values and acquire
views of themselves as interconnected with others, and members of collectivistic cultures learn some individualistic values and acquire views of themselves as
unique persons (Gudykunst et al. 1996: 513). According to Grainger, Mills and
Sibanda (2010: 2161), group face (which is related to collectivist cultures) and
individual face (which is related to individualist cultures) cannot be said to be
mutually exclusive, and neither the interdependent and the independent self can
be said to exist separately. In a similar vein, Mills argues the co-existence of collectivist and individualist features in a culture:

> While it is possible to recognise broadly speaking, tendencies in particular
> cultures towards collectivism or individualism, what is striking about all
> cultural groups is that all societies display both collectivist and individu-
> alist tendencies, and all individuals in interaction tend to display both of
> these tendencies, negotiating the demands of what they see as social forces
> against what they see as their individual needs and aims.
>
> (Mills 2017: 30)

Mills takes Arab and English cultures as examples to show how the features of
collectivist and individualist cultures coexist:

> [W]hile Arab cultures are often characterised as tending towards collec-
> tivist values, individuals nevertheless strive for their individual rights and
> necessarily act as autonomous beings. And while English culture tends to
> be characterised as foregrounding individualist values, individuals never-
> theless recognise the importance of their allegiance to social groups such
> as the family and adjust their behaviour and values to what they see as the
> values of those groups.
>
> (Mills 2017: 30)

Humans will always orient both their own individual needs and those of the group to which they belong. It is also worth noting that '[t]he values which we are describing when we describe a culture as collectivist or individualist are an ideological representation of the values which are assumed to be those of the elite, and while these values may have an influence on individuals within that culture, we need to see that they are only tendencies' (Mills 2017: 30–31).

The following study further illustrates the co-existence of collectivism and individualism. Zhang and Wu (2018) analysed postings of eight of the most-followed Twitter and Sina Weibo celebrities from the USA (an individualist culture) and China (a collectivist culture). Zhang and Wu (2018) found that celebrities in the USA and China displayed a converging trend in their cultural practices as seen in their largely overlapping acts of rapport management on social media. Nonetheless, evidence still exists for the orthodox conceptualisation of individualism-versus collectivism-oriented cultures in shaping differential behaviour (Zhang and Wu 2018: 197). This suggests, at least in part, that collectivist and individualist features co-exist in cultures, although some preferred orientations still exist in the respective cultures.

The United States and Japan have often been compared from the aspect of culture and communication styles (see, e.g., Brown, Hayashi and Yamamoto 2012; Gudykunst 1993; Ogawa and Gudykunst 1999–2000; Yamada 1997). According to Gudykunst and San Antonio (1993: 30), most scholars agree that the United States is an individualistic culture and Japan is a collectivistic culture. American society has been claimed to be an individualistic society and an individual's dignity is highly valued (Uchida 2011: 52). Independence dominates over dependence in the United States, whereas interdependence is stronger than individuality in Japan (e.g., Markus and Kitayama 1991; Yamada 1997: 18–20). These cultural values and assumptions have been claimed to influence communication styles (see, e.g., Fukushima 2000: 116–121)[19] and politeness norms (see, e.g., Ogiermann 2009: 25). According to Triandis and Gelfand (2012: 509), language and communication in individualistic cultures is direct and emphasises the individual, whereas in collectivistic cultures it is more indirect and de-emphasises the individual. Similarly, Ting-Toomey (1999: 103) argues that in individualistic cultures, people tend to encounter more situations that emphasise the preferential use of direct talk, person-oriented verbal interaction, verbal self-enhancement and talkativeness. In contrast, in collectivistic cultures, people tend to encounter more situations that emphasise the preferential use of indirect talk, status-oriented verbal interaction, verbal self-effacement and silence (Ting-Toomey 1999: 103). According to Clancy (1986: 213), it is widely recognised that the communicative style of the Japanese is intuitive and indirect, especially compared with that of Americans. Indeed, there are many studies which characterise Japanese communication as indirect (e.g., Naotsuka et al. 1981; Tsujimura 1987; Watanabe 2005: 229). In fact, Tsujimura (1987: 116–125) states that *ishin-denshin* (communication without language), taciturnity and its social causes, indirect communication and respect for reverberation, and *kuuki*[20] (the function of mood or atmospheric constraints) are the four main characteristics of the Japanese way of communication, as noted in Section 2.2.1.

Explicit communication is assumed to be necessary in the United States, whereas implicit communication is preferred in Japan (see, e.g., Gudykunst 1993; Okabe 1983: 35, 38–39; Yamada 1997: 18–20). These are sometimes referred to as low-context and high-context communication (Hall 1976) respectively[21] (see also Hofstede 1991: 60; Lempert 2012: 193–194; Scollon et al. 2012: 40–42). This means that Japanese is heavily dependent on context, whereas English is not as dependent on it, according to Akasu and Asano (1993: 111).

Lebra (1976: 46) argues that '[c]onsideration of the echo effect in social interaction, which is apt to result in social fusion, brings us to the priority that the Japanese attach to implicit, nonverbal, intuitive communication over an explicit, verbal, rational exchange of information'. Furthermore, Lebra (1976: 46–47) states that 'the Japanese find esthetic refinement and sophistication in a person who sends nonverbal, indirect, implicit, subtle messages. Such a "sophisticated" form of communication is made possible by the empathy between the sender and receiver of the message.' This suggests that implicit communication is possible by empathy. In a similar vein, Clancy (1990: 27) argues that the Japanese intuitive and indirect communication style is based on cultural values that emphasise *omoiyari* ('empathy'). In intuitive and indirect communication, anticipatory inference is also necessary (see Section 2.2.2).

Concerning the importance of inference in Japanese communication, Miyake (2011: iv–vi) gives the following example. Miyake had a car accident in Los Angeles and an ambulance came. When an ambulance attendant asked her, 'Are you all right?', she answered, 'I'm all right', and the attendant and ambulance drove away. Miyake was shocked. She later realised that 'I'm all right' in Japanese (*daijyoubu*) was used when one expected the other party to infer the situation (Miyake 2011: vi). In the incident above, Miyake expected or believed that the ambulance attendant would bring her to hospital, inferring that she was not all right, when she said, 'I'm all right.'[22]

As mentioned previously, one culture can contain both collectivist and individualist aspects.[23] Different generations in one culture may have different orientations towards collectivism and individualism. Take Japanese culture, for example. It is often said that Japanese culture is a collectivist culture (see Yamaguchi 1994: 175). However, Yamaguchi (1994) contends that Japanese culture has gained some individualist features because of the economic success after World War II (see also Brown et al. 2012: 257; Takano and Osaka 1999). Socioeconomic status influences a culture not only synchronically, but also diachronically. According to Yamaguchi (1994: 184), the effects of affluence would likely be most prominent among younger Japanese, because they did not experience the poverty that previous generations endured. Yamaguchi (1994: 184) also points out that education in Japan has changed drastically since World War II, from a totalitarian system to a more democratic system in which students are allowed to behave more individualistically. Yamaguchi's (1994) argument above, which indicates that social and political changes[24] influence the traits of a culture, shows that Japanese people of different generations may differ in the perception of collectivist features, namely that older Japanese people may still have collectivist features whereas younger Japanese people may not necessarily retain them. In other words, the collectivism score is positively correlated with their age (Yamaguchi 1994: 184).

Positive politeness and negative politeness cultures

Brown and Levinson (1978, 1987) argue that cultures tend towards either positive politeness or negative politeness, the gist of which is as follows. In positive politeness cultures, solidarity and camaraderie are important, and social closeness among individuals is stressed. Thus, it is 'approach-based'. Bald-on-record and positive politeness strategies are preferred in positive politeness cultures. In negative politeness cultures, importance is placed on power and distance, and deference and respect characterise interactions. Thus, it is 'avoidance-based'. Negative politeness and off-record politeness strategies are preferred in negative politeness cultures.[25] American or Australian cultures, for instance, are categorised as positive cultures, whereas Japanese and British cultures are categorised as negative politeness cultures, according to Brown and Levinson (1978, 1987). Reflecting these features of cultures, Mills (2017: 32) states how people in these cultures interact with each other. That is, people in positive politeness cultures strike up conversations fairly easily with strangers and even impose on them for small social favours, whereas people apologise more in negative politeness cultures and do not tend to impose on, or even talk to, strangers.

The distinction between positive politeness and negative politeness cultures proposed by Brown and Levinson (1987) has received some criticisms 'on the grounds that it is impossible to categorise whole social groups according to the politeness strategies they prefer' (Sifianou and Garcés-Conejos Blitvich 2017: 575). No society is completely uniform in its politeness orientation (e.g., Sifianou 1992: 39–40, 47–48, 81). For example, Fukushima (2000: 192–195) acknowledged that Japanese culture was not always characterised by negative politeness culture, as proposed by Brown and Levinson (1987). In Japanese culture, not only negative politeness strategies and off-record strategies are used as claimed by Brown and Levinson (1987), but also bald-on-record strategies are used to show solidarity (Fukushima 2000: 194–195).

We can observe some decrease in the negative politeness orientation in Japanese culture, especially among young Japanese people. Such tendency can be found, for example, in the use of address terms, which are important for expressing interpersonal relationships and are closely linked with cultural values (see He and Ren 2016). Negative politeness orientation is often associated with formality. The formal address term for professors (they are sometimes called *kyoujyu* 'professors', too.) or lecturers at universities and teachers at all levels of schools is *sensei* (lit. 'teacher') in Japanese, which shows some respect and a power relationship. *Sensei* plus family name has been widely used. However, some students these days do not use *sensei*, but use *san* (Mr, Mrs, Miss, Ms), which can be used for anybody and does not necessarily show any power difference. Shinichiro Okamoto (2016: 20) reports that he felt resistance when his students addressed him using *san*. I too feel uncomfortable, when I am addressed with *san* instead of *sensei* by my students. I asked my students whether that was a 'norm' for them. Some of the students answered that they had addressed their high school teachers with *san*. So, it is natural for them to use *san* when addressing professors at universities. They do not mean to be impolite to professors, but it seems that they do not have any qualms in using *san*. This may be somewhat related to the changes of address terms in Chinese noted by He and Ren (2016). According to He and Ren (2016: 175–177), (1) linguistic factors, (2) sociocultural changes, (3) globalisation and language contact and (4) new technologies (particularly mass media, social media and the Internet) influence the changes of address terms. They argue that '[p]articularly in informal contexts, inferiors tend to weaken the superior's higher professional ranking and employ more intimate address terms. On the other hand, superiors may not want to highlight their official ranking either. This trend indicates that contemporary Chinese culture is increasingly oriented towards positive politeness' (He and Ren 2016: 176). Although Japanese culture has not experienced sociocultural changes recently, such as the Cultural Revolution (1966–1976) in China, it may be said that there are also some positive politeness orientations (not only negative politeness orientations) in Japanese culture. This shows that it is difficult (or sometimes dangerous) to characterise a certain culture as being either a positive or a negative politeness culture. For example, American culture (western USA) is characterised as a positive politeness culture by Brown and Levinson (1987: 245), but it is a distancing one (or negative politeness culture in Brown and Levinson's terms) when compared to Spanish culture (Barros García and Terkourafi 2014).

Sifianou and Garcés-Conejos Blitvich (2017: 576) point out the different orientation of culture, depending on the social class to which one belongs; that is, upper classes having a negative politeness ethos and lower classes a positive politeness ethos (see Brown and Levinson 1987: 245; Mills 2004). Different orientation of culture may also depend on urban or rural areas. The former may have more negative politeness orientation than the latter, and the latter more positive politeness orientation than the former. These arguments may be, in part, in accord with Grainger and Mills' (2016: 27) statement, namely that cultures cannot be categorised as simply positive or negative politeness cultures, and with Mills and Kádár's (2011: 27) argument, namely that each group does make use of both types of politeness (positive and negative) to a greater or lesser extent.[26] We should also take note that these norms are not ones which are accepted by all people within a cultural group; they are often the norms of the elite, which are contested by subgroups, as Kádár and Mills (2011) and Mills (2017: 33) show (see the earlier discussion on social groups and heterogeneity).

Another issue we need to think about concerning positive and negative politeness cultures is whether societies as a whole can be seen as in fact tending to be concerned with social distance simply because deference is conventionalised within the language (Mills and Kádár 2011: 27). Mills and Kádár argue that deference in many Asian cultures is conventionalised, just as indirectness is conventionalised in British English. Thus, what is meant by 'deference' or 'indirectness' in one culture may not necessarily mean the same in another culture. In relation to this, Mills and Kádár (2011: 24) argue that positive and negative politeness features do not have the same function or meaning in different cultures (see, e.g., Gu 1990). In a similar vein, Sifianou and Garcés-Conejos Blitvich (2017: 577) argue that being classified into the same politeness orientation does not necessarily mean to 'exhibit identical preferences of linguistic or non-linguistic behaviour, since societies develop under different socio-historical circumstances'.

Sifianou and Garcés-Conejos Blitvich (2017: 577) rightly contend that positive and negative politeness strategies should be used with caution as broad approximations and in the knowledge that no society is completely uniform in its politeness orientation. Although there are certain tendencies which can be described as positive politeness or negative politeness cultures, 'such distinctions should not be understood as absolute dichotomies but as useful abstractions which can help explain specific orientations or tendencies', as Sifianou and Garcés-Conejos Blitvich (2017: 577) argue. Furthermore, I agree with the view that positive politeness and negative politeness cultures may need to be reconceptualised as scalar rather than dichotomous distinctions (Garcés-Conejos Blitvich 2010), as positive politeness and negative politeness orientations interact or tangle in intricate ways in our cultures, including sub-cultures.

Discernment and volition cultures

Ide (1989) proposed the distinction between discernment and volition. Matsumoto (1989) claimed that Japanese politeness is centred on discernment. According to Ide

(1989: 230), to behave according to *wakimae* is to show verbally and non-verbally one's sense of place or role in a given situation according to social conventions. Ide (1989) claimed that the closest equivalent term for *wakimae* in English is 'discernment' (see also Hill, Ide, Ikuta, Kawasaki and Ogino 1986: 347–348), and that the choice of linguistic forms or expressions in which the distinction between the ranks of the roles of the speaker, the referent and the addressee are systematically encoded will be called the discernment aspect of linguistic politeness (Ide 1989: 230). She focused on the use of honorifics in Japanese and showed that the use of polite forms or plain forms is determined by the situations and variables (e.g., power and social distance) of an addressee. In contrast to the discernment aspect, 'the aspect of politeness which allows the speaker a considerably active choice, according to the speaker's intention from a relatively wider range of possibilities' is called the 'volitional' aspect (Hill et al. 1986: 348). Ide (1989) described these two styles of politeness as being related to Eastern and Western cultures respectively. It is pointed out, however, that the polarisation of volition-discernment is problematic (see Kádár and Mills 2013) and that the use of Japanese honorifics is not as simple as being determined by an awareness of one's position in the social group (Pizziconi 2011; see also Haugh 2005 and Section 4.3). Moreover, it is not possible to distinguish clearly enough between the usages of politeness that are motivated by social pressures (discernment cultures) and those that are chosen by the individuals (volition cultures), as social pressures are negotiated by individuals within particular communities of practice, rather than by individuals and society set in opposition to one another (Grainger and Mills 2016: 22). Some problems were raised on discernment and volition cultures as shown above (see also Section 4.3.1); and discernment and volition cultures are not as widely used and discussed as positive politeness and negative politeness cultures or collectivist and individualist cultures. Thus, they are not included in the discussion in subsequent sections.

3.3 Evaluation of attentiveness: A cross-cultural (Japanese–British) comparison

This section compares the evaluation of attentiveness by Japanese participants with that by British participants.

3.3.1 Data and methodology

Participants

All the participants were university students in order to guarantee uniformity among the participants and comparability between them.[27] They were 74 British (18 males and 56 females; mean age: 23.0) and 138 Japanese (29 males and 109 females; mean age: 19.7) undergraduates.[28] Participants were selected from those who live in their own culture, as people who live in foreign cultures may have different cultural values from those who live in their home country, being influenced by the culture in which they live.

Research instrument

A questionnaire was prepared to elicit evaluation data on attentiveness. The situations in the questionnaire were chosen carefully from ones which actually occurred. Situations with both high and low degrees of imposition required to demonstrate attentiveness were included. Different degrees of intrusion into the private territory of a recipient of attentiveness, which may influence the evaluation of attentiveness, were also taken into account when selecting the situations. Examples of linguistically as well as non-linguistically demonstrated attentiveness (see Section 2.2.1) were included in the situations, because non-linguistically manifested politeness has been rather neglected in the field, despite its importance (see, e.g., Sifianou and Garcés-Conejos Blitvich 2017: 583; Sifianou and Tzanne 2010), as noted in Section 1. The questionnaire was prepared both in English and in Japanese so that the participants could answer in their own mother tongue.

The social distance between demonstrator and recipient of attentiveness in this section was close in all the situations. This is because the social distance between them was small in most of the naturally occurring situations. Furthermore, social distance may influence evaluation of attentiveness. Indeed, Sifianou (1997b: 68) explains how social distance influences evaluation of attentiveness.[29] According to Sifianou (1997b: 68), 'when there is social distance, doing things for others without being requested to could be perceived as an imposition, since these actions may require reimbursement'.

The situations used in the instrument include the following (alphabetical letters were used to identify the individuals in the situations to avoid gender influence and any influence personal names might have on the participants):

Situation 1

You've got flu and have been in bed. You live alone in your flat. You have already told your close friend, G, that you had flu. G lives far away from your flat (it takes about an hour by car). While you were in bed, G came to your flat with some food one evening.

Situation 2

You and your classmate, H, take the same lecture. The lecture dragged on. You had to leave, because you had a part-time job. The next day when you met H, H said to you as follows and gave you a handout.

H: Yesterday after you left, the lecturer gave us a handout. You haven't got one, have you?

Situation 3

You were going to take notes at a lecture, but you realise that you haven't got a pen. Your close friend, I, who was next to you, said to you as follows.

I: You haven't got any pen? You can use this.

Situation 4

You live with your parents. Books were scattered around in your room. You were thinking of sorting them out, but you went to the university to attend a lecture without doing so, as it takes a long time. When you came home, your mother, J, said to you as follows.

J: I've sorted out your books in your room.

Situation 5

You had lunch with your close friend, K, in a cafeteria. After eating, K cleared away K's and your dishes.

Situation 6

You are going to graduate from the university soon. You wanted to travel before graduation, and you went to the USA. When you returned from the trip, there was a note from your close friend, L, saying that L has cooked dinner for you. There were many good dishes in the refrigerator. You left the key of your flat with L. L lives close by.

After the description of the situations, the following was given in each situation: (1) a five-point Likert scale[30] for evaluation of attentiveness by a demonstrator, 1 being a very positive evaluation and 5 being a very negative evaluation, (2) a space to write down the reasons for the evaluation (the participants could write any reason) and (3) a five-point Likert scale to rate the degree of imposition required to demonstrate attentiveness, 1 being a very small imposition and 5 being a very big imposition.

Procedure

The questionnaire was distributed to each participant in their own mother tongue. The participants were asked to evaluate six attentiveness situations and to respond according to a five-point Likert scale. In addition, they were asked to give reasons for their evaluations. The participants were also asked to rate the degree of imposition required to demonstrate attentiveness on a five-point Likert scale.

3.3.2 Data analysis

The procedure for the data analysis was as follows:

1. A three-way ANOVA (nationalities [2] × gender [2] × situations [6]) was conducted in order to investigate whether there were any differences in the evaluation

of attentiveness among the participants across the different situations.

2. A three-way ANOVA (nationalities [2] × gender [2] × situations [6]) was conducted in order to investigate whether there were any differences in the evaluation of the degree of imposition required to demonstrate attentiveness among the participants across the different situations.

3. The reasons for the evaluation of attentiveness provided by the participants were examined.

3.3.3 Results and discussion

The results of the first analysis (a three-way ANOVA) showed that the main effect of the situation factor was significant ($df = 5/1045$, $F = 59.854$, $p < .0001$). The interaction between the situation factor and the nationality factor was significant ($df = 5/1045$, $F = 6.687$, $p < .0001$). Since the interaction was significant, post hoc tests (unpaired t-tests for the comparison of nationalities in each situation) were conducted. The results showed that there were significant differences in Situations 2 ($df = 211$, $t = 3.943$, $p < .001$), 3 ($df = 211$, $t = 4.135$, $p < .0001$), 4 ($df = 211$, $t = 3.074$, $p < .001$) and 6 ($df = 211$, $t = 2.889$, $p < .01$) among the participants in the evaluation of attentiveness. The mean scores of the evaluation of attentiveness in each situation by the British and Japanese participants are presented in Table 3.1.

Table 3.1: Mean scores for the evaluation of attentiveness by British and Japanese participants

Situation	British participants		Japanese participants	
	M	*SD*	*M*	*SD*
1. Bringing food	1.2	.58	1.4	.74
2. Taking a handout*	1.7	.91	1.3	.57
3. Lending a pen*	1.5	.72	1.2	.50
4. Sorting out the books**	2.7	1.27	3.2	1.20
5. Clearing away the dishes	1.7	.81	1.8	1.16
6. Cooking dinner**	1.9	1.12	2.4	1.30

1 = most positive evaluation; 5 = most negative evaluation; *M* = mean score; *SD* = standard deviation
*There was a significant difference at the .001 level ($p < .001$).
**There was a significant difference at the .01 level ($p < .01$).

As shown in Table 3.1, the mean scores evaluated by the British participants were significantly higher than those by the Japanese participants in Situation 2 (a handout) (British: 1.7; Japanese: 1.3) and in Situation 3 (a pen) (British: 1.5; Japanese: 1.2). The mean scores evaluated by the Japanese participants were significantly higher than those by the British participants in Situation 4 (books) (Japanese: 3.2; British: 2.7) and in Situation 6 (dinner) (Japanese: 2.4; British: 1.9). As

1 indicates a very positive evaluation and 5 represents a very negative evaluation on the Likert scale in the questionnaire, these results mean that the Japanese participants evaluated attentiveness more positively than the British participants in Situations 2 and 3, and that the British participants evaluated attentiveness more positively than the Japanese participants in Situations 4 and 6.

The results of the second analysis (a three-way ANOVA) showed that the main effect of the situation factor was significant ($df = 5/1045$, $F = 163.056$, $p < .0001$). However, there was no main effect from the nationality factor or the gender factor, and no significant interactions were found.[31] There were no significant differences between the British and Japanese participants in the rating of the degree of imposition required to demonstrate attentiveness. The mean scores of the degree of imposition required to demonstrate attentiveness in each situation are presented in Table 3.2.

Table 3.2: Mean scores for the degree of imposition required to demonstrate attentiveness by British and Japanese participants

Situation	British participants		Japanese participants	
	M	*SD*	*M*	*SD*
1. Bringing food	3.8	1.22	4.0	1.00
2. Taking a handout	1.8	.99	2.1	1.01
3. Lending a pen	1.6	1.06	1.8	.98
4. Sorting out the books	3.4	.79	3.6	1.05
5. Clearing away the dishes	2.4	.94	2.5	1.15
6. Cooking dinner	3.6	.97	3.8	1.15

1 = small imposition; 5 = large imposition; *M* = mean score; *SD* = standard deviation

As for the reasons for their evaluation of attentiveness, there were no major differences between the British and Japanese participants in Situations 2 (handout) and 3 (pen), although there were significant differences in the evaluation of attentiveness in these situations. Both groups of participants 'appreciated attentiveness' (Situation 2: British: 83.7%; Japanese: 91%; Situation 3: British: 87.9%; Japanese: 94.7%).

The British participants evaluated attentiveness in Situation 4 (books) more positively than the Japanese participants. More British participants (41.5%) 'appreciated attentiveness' than Japanese participants (27.5%).

Although there was a significant difference in the evaluation of attentiveness in Situation 6 (dinner), both the British (74.6%) and Japanese (54.5%) participants 'appreciated the attentiveness'. Among the negative reasons provided by the participants, 'being intrusive' was given most frequently both by the Japanese (29.5%) and British participants (19%). There were no British participants who stated other negative reasons, but some Japanese participants stated the following reasons: 'feeling it as a burden' (6%), 'the demonstrator does not have to do that' (3%) and 'faulting/criticizing the recipient (incapability)' (0.8%).

In Situations 1 (food) and 5 (dishes), there were no significant differences between the British and Japanese participants in the evaluation of attentiveness. In these situations, most British (Situation 1: 91.2%; Situation 5: 52.6%) and Japanese participants (Situation 1: 89.6%; Situation 5: 68.5%) 'appreciated the attentiveness'. In Situation 5, both groups of participants wrote that 'there was no obligation on the demonstrator', although the number of Japanese participants who gave this reason was small in comparison to that of the British participants (British: 29.8%; Japanese: 1.6%). Only British participants (5.3%) wrote that 'it was with a low degree of imposition on the demonstrator'. Both groups of the participants wrote that 'I wanted to do that myself' (Japanese: 13.4%; British: 3.5%). Only Japanese participants (9.4%) wrote that 'I felt it as a burden'.

In sum, there were no major differences between the British and Japanese participants in the reason for positive evaluation ('appreciating attentiveness'), which was expected in a way, as positive evaluation of attentiveness derives mainly from appreciation of attentiveness. However, some differences between the two groups of participants were found in their reasons for negative evaluation. While both groups of participants wrote 'being intrusive', only the Japanese participants wrote 'feeling it as a burden'. The Japanese participants gave this reason in Situations 1 (food), 4 (handout), 5 (dishes) and 6 (dinner), although the number of participants who gave this reason was relatively small (Situation 1: 4.4%; Situation 4: 0.8%; Situation 5: 9.4%; Situation 6: 6%) (These situations were evaluated as having a higher degree of imposition than Situations 2 and 3).[32] This may be related to reimbursement, as discussed earlier. That is, a recipient feels that s/he has to reimburse the attentiveness s/he has received. The Japanese participants may have felt that they had to reimburse the attentiveness, because the degree of imposition required to demonstrate attentiveness was high. As mentioned earlier, a recipient of attentiveness feels that s/he has to reimburse the attentiveness when there is social distance between demonstrator and recipient, according to Sifianou (1997b). However, the results of the present section show that the high degree of imposition required to demonstrate attentiveness can be a factor which makes a recipient feel that s/he has to reimburse the attentiveness.

The previously mentioned reimbursement may be related to a custom of *okaeshi* (lit. 'returning') in Japan. That is, when somebody receives a gift, s/he is expected to give a gift in return. This applies not only to such material things as gifts, but also to what somebody does for somebody else. This may also apply to the case of attentiveness. A recipient of attentiveness may feel that s/he has to do something in return, having felt a burden when attentiveness was demonstrated.

The idea behind *okaeshi* may be the fact that a recipient wants to pay the debt back, that is, *okaeshi* is a means to redress a debt–credit imbalance. This may be related to what Ohashi (2008, 2010, 2013) argues, namely that caring for the debt–credit equilibrium is a significant politeness phenomenon in Japan, and to Lebra's (1976) description of Japanese culture, namely, *on*-reciprocity. According to Lebra (1976: 91), an *on* ('favour') relationship, once generated by giving and receiving a benefit, compels the receiver-debtor to repay *on* in order to restore balance (see also the discussion on reciprocity in relation to reflexive attentiveness in Section 2.2.1). The recipient of attentiveness may have felt a debt, but s/he could not redress the debt, therefore feeling a burden. This reason, feeling a burden, may be one of the factors which led the British and Japanese participants to different evaluations of attentiveness.

There may be some other reasons/factors which influenced the evaluation of attentiveness and which sometimes made the British and Japanese participants evaluate attentiveness differently. 'Intrusion on private territory' may be one of them. In Situations 4 (books) and 6 (dinner), the demonstrator of attentiveness came into the private territory of the recipient when the recipient was not there. In other words, the degree of intrusion into private territory is relatively high in these two situations, compared with other situations. It was anticipated that the British participants would evaluate attentiveness in these situations more negatively than their Japanese counterparts, because 'the English seem to place a higher value on privacy and individuality' (Sifianou 1992: 41). The results here, however, show that the Japanese participants seemed to have been offended by the intrusion into their private territory more than the British participants. The changes in the living (housing) situations in Japan may have something to do with this result. That is, in a traditional Japanese house, there are many common rooms which parents and children share. For example, a traditional Japanese room with *tatami* ('straw mats') can function as a living room during the daytime and as a bedroom at night, with parents and children sleeping in the same room. On the other hand, in a modern Japanese house, there are individual rooms, and children have their own rooms, which is not very different from Western housing. Most of the Japanese participants in this study may have grown up in such a modern Japanese house. Although different degrees of intrusion were taken into account in this section, the participants were not asked to rate the degree of intrusion. Therefore, the correlation between the evaluation of attentiveness and the degree of intrusion could not be clearly investigated. This can be incorporated into future studies.

The degree of necessity may be another factor, which is related to the evaluation of attentiveness. In Situation 1 (food), the recipient needed what the demonstrator did for her/him. There was no significant difference between the British and

Japanese participants in their evaluation of attentiveness, and both the British and Japanese participants appreciated the attentiveness. In some way, the degree of necessity may relate to how much the recipient anticipates the attentiveness. There are occasions in which the recipient expects the other party to demonstrate attentiveness, and there are occasions in which s/he does not expect attentiveness at all (see the discussion on the intentionality of a potential recipient of attentiveness in Section 2.2.1). There may be cases in which a recipient evaluates attentiveness positively when attentiveness is demonstrated as the recipient had expected. In other words, positive evaluation of attentiveness derives from one's expectation, which is related to necessity. This seems to resonate with the following explanation of politeness:

> Politeness … always arises relative to some kind of situation-specific social norms. These norms are essentially expectations about what people *should* show they think of others, or what people *should* show they think of themselves. In other words, these social norms are expectations in the sense of *thinking something is necessary*. In this way, whether a particular behaviour is regarded as polite or not, depends on its perception relative to what one thinks is necessary for people to show they think of someone else, or think of themselves. (emphasis in original)

> (Haugh 2003: 399)

It may also be said that a positive evaluation of attentiveness, which is related to necessity, would lead to politeness.

In this section, the evaluation of attentiveness by British and Japanese university students was investigated. In the next section, the demonstration of attentiveness is investigated cross-culturally (between Japanese and American participants) and cross-generationally (between Japanese people of two generations).

3.4 Demonstration of attentiveness: Cross-cultural (Japanese–American) and cross-generational (among the Japanese) comparisons

This section compares the demonstration of attentiveness among Japanese and American participants, and that among Japanese participants of two different generations.

3.4.1 Data and methodology

Questionnaires were used to elicit quantitative data, and interviews were conducted to obtain qualitative insights. Interview data can also be expected to verify questionnaire data.[33]

Participants

Participants were all females in order to avoid gender difference, as gender may be a factor which would influence the demonstration of attentiveness. The participants consist of university students and adults who are considered to belong to the educated middle class. As gender, educational level and social class were controlled, it is believed that we can focus on the differences or similarities between the demonstration of attentiveness by people of different national backgrounds and different generations.

Questionnaire

Two hundred and eighty people served as the participants, and they consisted of the following three groups:

1. 156 Japanese university students[34] (JS hereafter) (age range: 18–28; mean age: 20.2);
2. 92 Japanese parents[35] (JP hereafter) (age range: 36–76; mean age: 51.5);
3. 32 American university students[36] (AS hereafter) (age range: 19–23; mean age: 20.7).

Interview

Eighteen participants (six participants for each group, namely, Japanese students, Japanese parents and American students) served as the participants for the interviews. Their age range and the mean age of the participants were similar to those of the participants for the questionnaires: Japanese students (age range: 20–22; mean age: 20.5), Japanese parents (age range: 48–55; mean age: 51.33), and American students (age range: 20–23; mean age: 21.66).

Research instrument (questionnaire)

A multiple-choice questionnaire was used as the research instrument. The questionnaire in this section tries to clarify the participants' norms on attentiveness, the participants choosing what they believe to be appropriate in each situation. In other words, they make metapragmatic judgments on the demonstration of attentiveness. According to Kasper (2000: 330), '[m]ultiple choice is a versatile questionnaire format which can elicit information on production, comprehension, and metapragmatic judgements'. Therefore, a multiple-choice questionnaire suits the aim of this section.

There is another reason why a multiple-choice questionnaire was used. It is important to think about the burden on participants when distributing questionnaires. When the burden on the participants is very heavy (e.g., time-consuming), the participants may not write appropriate answers, and consequently the data elicited may not be reliable.

Multiple-choice responses require that subjects evaluate a very small number of presented alternatives against their memory structures of compatible events, a much less demanding task than having to conduct a free memory search and make an appropriate selection from a wide array of possible solutions.

(Kasper 2000: 330–331)

A multiple-choice questionnaire, therefore, does not give the participants a heavy burden; and reliability of the data can be ensured.

A rating-scale questionnaire was used to ask the participants to evaluate the degree of imposition required to demonstrate attentiveness. A five-point Likert scale was chosen as in Section 3.3.[37] Six situations in the questionnaire were taken from those which occurred in actual students' and parents' lives. The situations that would be applicable to both students and parents were chosen. A few amendments were made so that the situations would suit both students and parents.[38] The situations used in the questionnaire included the ones with linguistic cues (Situations 2 and 4) and non-linguistic cues (Situations 1, 3, 5 and 6), as attentiveness can be demonstrated in response to both linguistic and non-linguistic cues (see Section 2.2.1).

In order to investigate in which relationship (between a demonstrator and a recipient) attentiveness is demonstrated, the relationship varies from very familiar to not familiar at all: (1) very familiar (a close friend/close colleague in Situation 2); (2) familiar (friends/colleagues in Situations 3 and 4; a professor/boss in Situation 5); (3) not very familiar (an acquaintance in Situation 1); and (4) not familiar at all (a stranger in Situation 6).

The situations are as follows (alphabetical letters were used to identify the individuals to avoid gender influence and any influence personal names might have on the participants; the text in parentheses were for the parents' questionnaire):

Situation 1

You are sitting on a train. There are many standing passengers, but there is a vacancy in a priority seat[39] in the same car. At the next station, your acquaintance, A, gets on the train. A is carrying a lot of baggage. You do not have any heavy baggage.

Situation 2

You and your close friend (colleague), B, have gone for lunch in the canteen (at a restaurant near the company). B says that B has carelessly left her wallet at home. B lives near the campus (the company).

Situation 3

You are in a big city and have stopped at a big bookstore, X. You happen to find a book, Y, which your seminar friend (colleague), C, has been looking for for her thesis (project). The book, Y, is not available at local bookstores. It costs $50.

Situation 4

You hear that your colleague at your part-time job (company), D, has to suddenly take five days leave, because of a funeral service. According to the work schedule, you do not work on the days of D's leave.

Situation 5

You have attended a lecture at the university (a project meeting at a company). There were presentations from every group in the class (every project group). There has been a huge amount of papers submitted to a professor (a section chief) from every group. You do not have any urgent appointment after the class (meeting).

Situation 6

When you are walking in a train station, you notice that somebody has just dropped her/his rail pass.

In each situation, there were three questions: Question 1 (whether you would demonstrate attentiveness or not), Question 2 (the reason for Question 1) and Question 3 (how you would rate the degree of imposition required to demonstrate attentiveness). Multiple choices were given for Questions 1 and 2. Constructing the multiple choices for Question 1, the possibilities of responding to off-record requests in Fukushima (2000: 91–92)[40] were taken into consideration. The choices for Question 1 include the following: (1) the participant would demonstrate attentiveness; (2) the participant would suggest or say something which may be useful for the other party; (3) the participant would not do or say anything; and (4) other. Below are the examples from Situations 1 (seat) and 4 (work schedule):

Situation 1

Question 1. What would you do in this situation?

(1) You offer A a seat. Or you hold A's baggage.

(2) You tell A that there is a vacancy in a priority seat.

(3) You keep reading your book.

(4) Other (write what):

Situation 4

Question 1. What would you do in this situation?

(1) You suggest that you can work on the days of D's leave instead of D.

(2) You suggest that some other colleagues work on the days of D's leave.

(3) You do not say anything.

(4) Other (write what):

The multiple choices in Question 2 (the reasons for the choice in Question 1) include the following: (1) the participant wants to be of some help to the other party; (2) the participant thinks it would be alright to just give the other party the information, or they thought it was a matter for the other party; (3) it was troublesome; and (4) other.[41] Below is an example from Situation 4 (work schedule):

Question 2. Why did you choose the above?

(1) You wanted to be of help to D.

(2) It was D's matter.

(3) It would be troublesome.

(4) Other (write what):

A five-point Likert scale, 1 being 'the attentiveness does not require of the demonstrator any imposition' and 5 being 'the attentiveness requires of the demonstrator a high degree of imposition' was given for Question 3. Below is an example from Situation 4 (work schedule):

Question 3. How much imposition would it cause you if, instead of D, you worked on the days of D's leave? Circle a number on the scale, 1 being 'no imposition', and 5 being 'high imposition'. (A five-point Likert scale is given.)

Procedure

Questionnaire

The questionnaire was distributed to each participant in their own mother tongue. In each situation the participants were asked to choose one of the multiple choices in Questions 1 and 2: (1) what they would do under certain situations (whether they would demonstrate attentiveness or not) and (2) why they would do so. And then they were asked to rate the degree of imposition required to demonstrate attentiveness on a five-point Likert scale in Question 3. The participants were asked to fill in the questionnaire anonymously in order to obtain honest judgments. If the participants had been asked to give their names, they may have been tempted to present a good image to others and might have selected different choices compared with their natural inclination. This is what Kádár and Haugh (2013: 31) call the possible influence of 'social desirability effects': informants wanting to be seen to be saying the 'right' thing or wanting to think of themselves as the kind of person who says the 'right' thing. Anonymity can avoid this kind of problem.

Interview

The participants were asked to state what they would do and why in each situation, after reading six situations which were the same as those in the questionnaire. Interviews were conducted in the mother tongue of each participant. Each interview lasted approximately 15 minutes.

3.4.2 Data analysis

Questionnaire

The data analysis procedure was as follows:

1. In order to answer research Questions 1 ('Are there any differences among the participants in their demonstration of attentiveness?') and 2 ('Are there any differences among the participants in their reasons for demonstrating or not demonstrating attentiveness?'), the choices for Question 1 and those for Question 2 were added up.
2. In order to answer research Question 3 ('Are there any differences among the participants in rating the degree of imposition required to demonstrate attentiveness?'), a one-way ANOVA (participants) was conducted.
3. In order to answer research Question 4 ('Is there any relationship between the demonstration of attentiveness and the degree of imposition required to demonstrate attentiveness?'), two different forms of ANOVA were conducted. A two-way ANOVA (participants × participants' choices) was conducted in Situations 1, 3, 4 and 5, and a one-way ANOVA (participants) was conducted in Situations 2 and 6.[42]
4. In order to answer research Question 5 ('In which relationship between a demonstrator and a recipient is attentiveness demonstrated?'), the relationship between the demonstrator and the recipient of attentiveness was identified.

Interviews

All the interviews were audio-recorded and transcribed.

3.4.3 Results and discussion

Questionnaire

There were no major differences in the demonstration of attentiveness among the participants, except for Situation 5 (papers) (see Table 3.3). Some other choices (Choice 4)[43] varied in each situation.

Table 3.3: Demonstration of attentiveness by Japanese and American participants

Situation	Participants	Choice 1 (%)	Choice 2 (%)	Choice 3 (%)	Choice 4 (%)
Situation 1 (seat)	JS	80.8	12.8	3.8	2.6
	JP	88.0	6.5	2.2	3.3
	AS	81.3	12.5	3.1	3.1
Situation 2 (lunch)	JS	96.1	1.3	0.6	1.9
	JP	94.6	1.1	0	4.3
	AS	90.6	0	0	9.4
Situation 3 (book)	JS	1.9	62.8	1.3	34.0
	JP	16.3	60.9	1.1	21.7
	AS	6.3	65.6	0	28.1
Situation 4 (work schedule)	JS	56.2	3.2	25.6	18.6
	JP	50.0	1.1	26.0	22.8
	AS	50.0	6.3	28.1	15.6
Situation 5 (papers)	JS	55.1	1.9	39.1	3.8
	JP	91.3	0	6.5	2.2
	AS	46.9	0	50.0	3.1
Situation 6 (rail pass)	JS	92.3	5.8	0.6	1.3
	JP	87.0	12.0	1.1	0
	AS	96.9	0	3.1	0

Choice 1: The participants would demonstrate attentiveness.
Choice 2: The participants would suggest or say something which may be useful for the other party.
Choice 3: The participants would not do or say anything.
Choice 4: Other
JS: Japanese students; JP: Japanese parents; AS: American students

As for the reasons for demonstrating or not demonstrating attentiveness, most of the participants selected Choice 1 (they want to be of some help to the other party) (see Table 3.4). There were various reasons in Choice 4 (other).[44]

With respect to the degree of imposition required to demonstrate attentiveness, there were significant differences among the participants in Situations 1, 3 and 5 (see Table 3.5) according to the results of ANOVA.[45] In Situation 1 (seat), the score by Japanese students was significantly higher than that by Japanese parents and American students. In Situation 3 (book), the score by Japanese students was significantly higher than that by Japanese parents. In Situation 5 (papers), the score by Japanese students was significantly higher than that by Japanese parents.

As for the relationship between the demonstration of attentiveness and the degree of imposition required to demonstrate attentiveness, there were significant differences in Situations 1, 3, 4 and 5, according to the results of ANOVA.[46] In Situation 1 (seat), there was a relationship between the demonstration of attentiveness and the degree of imposition required to demonstrate attentiveness only

Table 3.4: Reasons for the demonstration of attentiveness by Japanese and American participants

Situation	Participants	Choice 1 (%)	Choice 2 (%)	Choice 3 (%)	Choice 4 (%)
Situation 1 (seat)	JS	67.9	7.1	3.2	21.8
	JP	77.2	7.6	2.2	13.0
	AS	78.1	6.3	3.1	12.5
Situation 2 (lunch)	JS	63.5	1.9	10.9	23.7
	JP	67.4	0	9.8	22.8
	AS	75.0	0	6.3	18.8
Situation 3 (book)	JS	60.9	17.9	0.6	20.5
	JP	65.2	17.4	0	17.4
	AS	71.9	18.8	3.1	6.3
Situation 4 (work schedule)	JS	43.6	5.8	19.2	31.4
	JP	44.6	15.2	8.7	31.5
	AS	56.3	9.4	9.4	25.0
Situation 5 (papers)	JS	51.2	7.1	20.5	21.2
	JP	70.7	1.1	5.4	22.8
	AS	43.8	18.8	12.5	25.0
Situation 6 (rail pass)	JS	78.2	4.5	1.9	15.4
	JP	73.9	13.0	2.2	10.9
	AS	93.8	0	3.1	3.1

Choice 1: The participants wanted to be of some help to the other party.
Choice 2: The participants thought it would be all right to just give the other party the information, or they thought it was a matter for the other party.
Choice 3: It was troublesome.
Choice 4: Other
JS: Japanese students; JP: Japanese parents; AS: American students

Table 3.5: Mean scores for the degree of imposition required to demonstrate attentiveness by Japanese and American participants

Situation	Japanese students		Japanese parents		American students	
	M	*SD*	*M*	*SD*	*M*	*SD*
1. Seat*	1.935	.948	1.597	.865	1.437	.618
2. Lunch	1.666	.939	1.532	.895	1.906	.962
3. Book*	2.929	1.349	2.347	1.378	2.656	1.334
4. Work schedule	2.967	1.177	2.619	1.221	2.906	1.058
5. Papers*	2.128	1.19	1.739	1.077	1.937	1.134
6. Rail pass	1.692	1.000	1.75	1.105	1.5	.879

*There was a significant difference at the .01 level ($p < 0.01$).
1 = small imposition; 5 = large imposition; *M* = mean score; *SD* = standard deviation

among Japanese parents. Japanese parents who selected Choice 3 (to keep reading a book) tended to rate a higher degree of imposition than those who selected Choice 1 (demonstration of attentiveness). In Situation 3 (book), those who selected Choice 2 (giving information about the book) tended to rate a higher degree of imposition than those who selected Choice 1. In Situations 4 (work schedule) and 5 (papers), those who selected Choice 3 (saying nothing) tended to rate higher scores for imposition than those who selected Choice 1.

As far as the relationship between the demonstrator and the recipient of attentiveness is concerned, the demonstration of attentiveness was chosen in situations in which a demonstrator and a recipient of attentiveness were very familiar with each other (Situation 2: a close friend/colleague), familiar (Situation 4: a friend/colleague), not very familiar (Situation 1: an acquaintance) and not familiar at all (Situation 6: a stranger). This shows that attentiveness is demonstrated whatever the relationship between the demonstrator and the recipient is.

Having the above results in mind, a detailed discussion is given next. Most of the participants selected Choice 1 (demonstration of attentiveness) most frequently in Situations 1 (seat), 2 (lunch), 4 (work schedule) and 6 (rail pass) (see Table 3.3). This suggests that the desire to help someone who is in trouble (see Section 2.3) would not differ among the participants, although some cross-cultural differences in reason emerged (see the discussion below).

In Situation 3 (book), most of the participants selected Choice 2 (giving information about the book) most frequently. In Situation 3, the degree of imposition required to demonstrate attentiveness is rather high compared to that in other situations (see Table 3.5). This may be because it would cost the demonstrator $50 if she were to buy the book. When the degree of imposition is high, the recipient may feel that it has caused the demonstrator a burden. This can be deduced also from the fact that there was a correlation between the demonstration of attentiveness and the degree of imposition required to demonstrate attentiveness. Indeed, a Japanese student wrote in Choice 4 (other) that it would be a burden on the recipient.

The most frequently selected choice in Situation 4 (work schedule) by all three groups of participants was Choice 1 (demonstration of attentiveness), as noted above. It can be detected from the reasons that some attentiveness is reflexive, as some participants (JS, JP and AS) wrote in Choice 4 (other) that 'I want to work, because I can get extra pay' (see also interview data below). Choice 3 (saying nothing) was selected next frequently after Choice 1 by all three groups of participants. Selection of Choice 3 is associated with a high degree of imposition (see Table 3.5), as there was a correlation between the demonstration of attentiveness and the degree of imposition required to demonstrate attentiveness. These results may also be because the recipient (D) had to be responsible for her leave as well as the owner of the shop or company where D works. Indeed, some participants (JS, JP and AS) wrote in Choice 4 (other) as follows: 'It is up to the company to assign people to cover D's job'. Therefore, her colleague may have remained silent (Choice 3).

In Situation 5 (papers), the most frequent choices varied among the participants, Japanese students and Japanese parents preferring Choice 1 (demonstration of attentiveness) (55.1% and 91.3%, respectively) and American students preferring Choice 3 (50.0%). Although the most frequent choice by Japanese students and Japanese parents was Choice 1, the percentage differed greatly. And Japanese students selected Choice 3 (say nothing) (39.1%) far more frequently than Japanese parents (6.5%). These results can be regarded as a generational difference as well as a cross-cultural difference. Japanese parents selected to demonstrate attentiveness, because demonstrating attentiveness to their superiors was natural for them, which can be detected from the reasons in Choice 4 (see also interview data). The power difference between demonstrator and recipient (subordinate and boss) may have influenced the high frequency of the selection of demonstrating attentiveness by the Japanese parents (see the discussion on relationships between demonstrator and recipient of attentiveness in Section 2.2.1).

The score for the degree of imposition required to demonstrate attentiveness in Situation 5 by Japanese students (2.128) was significantly higher than that by Japanese parents (1.739) (see Table 3.5). And there was a relationship between the demonstration of attentiveness and the degree of imposition required to demonstrate attentiveness in this situation. Therefore, it can be said that the degree of imposition was one of the factors which led the participants to select different choices. Japanese parents, who rated the degree of imposition lower than Japanese students, selected Choice 1 (demonstration of attentiveness) more frequently than Japanese students.

With regard to the results in Situation 5, it can be said that Japanese parents could infer the needs of a recipient, while some Japanese and American students may not have been able to do that. The following reason given by the students (both Japanese and American) shows this: 'I probably would not think about it unless they asked'. The following reason, given only by American students, indicates that they did not even admit the necessity of inferring the needs of the other party: 'If the professor needed help, he would ask'.

Another factor which is required for attentiveness to arise is a potential demonstrator's willingness (see Section 2.2.2). Even when one infers the other party's wishes and admits the necessity of demonstrating attentiveness, attentiveness does not arise unless a potential demonstrator is willing to demonstrate attentiveness. In Situation 5 (papers), Japanese students who selected Choice 3 (saying nothing) in Question 1 selected Choice 3 (It was troublesome) in Question 2 as the reason. This implies that they did not have the willingness to demonstrate attentiveness.

It is noteworthy that some reasons provided by Japanese participants in Choice 4 (other) could not be found among American participants; for example: 'I feel bad, only I remain seated' from a Japanese student, and 'It depends on whether A is older or younger than me' from a Japanese parent in Situation 1 (seat); 'It is mutual' (*otagai sama*) from a Japanese student and a Japanese parent in Situations 2 (lunch) and 4 (work schedule); 'It would be a burden on a recipient' (*ki wo tsukawa seru*)[47] from a Japanese student in Situation 3 (book).

Interview

Overall, the results of the interview data (the author's own recordings and associated transcriptions) did not differ very much from those of the questionnaire data. That is, there were no major differences among the three groups of participants except for Situation 5 (papers). The participants would demonstrate attentiveness because they want to be of some help to the other party in most situations (Situations 1, 2, 4 and 6). In Situation 3 (book), most of the participants would contact their friend, C, and would buy the book, if necessary, or give C information about the book. In Situation 5 (papers), what they would do and why they would do so varied among the participants. Next, the more detailed results of each situation are presented.

In Situation 1 (seat), four Japanese students (see Example [3.1]), five Japanese parents and four American students stated that they would offer their seat, and two Japanese students and one Japanese parent would carry A's baggage (see Example [3.2]). These could be considered as equivalent to Choice 1 (demonstration of attentiveness) in the questionnaire. They thought it would be a lot of trouble for A to carry heavy baggage. By offering their seat, they could be of help to the other party. A slight difference was found in the American student's data (see Example [3.3]). She would offer her seat if the other party looked tired.

(3.1)

1   JS2:   *Seki wo yuzuri masu. (.) Omosou na nimotsu wo motte (.) tatte iruno wa taihen*

2   *dakara.*

          席を譲ります。重そうな荷物を持って立っているのは大変だから。

          I would offer my seat. It would be troublesome to stand, carrying heavy baggage.

(3.2)

1   JP1:   *Jibun ga koshi wo itamete iru kara (.) nimotsu wo hiza no ue ni oki masu.*

          自分が腰を痛めているから荷物を膝の上に置きます。

          As I have a pain in the back, I would carry A's baggage on my lap.

(3.3)

1   AS3:   If they were like super tired from hanging on the baggage, (.) I would of course give

2   my seat.

Two American students would let A be seated in a priority seat, which differed from the Japanese participants (see Examples [3.4] and [3.5]).

(3.4)

1   AS4:   They can sit there until elderly people come. (.) If an elderly person comes, you have

2   to move.

(3.5)

1   AS5:   I would probably have A sit in a priority seat. (.) There is no one that needs the seat at

2   the moment. (.) Then it's fine. There is an empty seat. (.) If someone comes, who

3   needs a seat, I'll tell them, (.) 'Get off.'

In Situation 2 (lunch), all of the Japanese students said that they would lend money, as it takes time to go back home (see Example [3.6]), or it does not cost a lot to pay for lunch, which means there is a low degree of imposition required to demonstrate attentiveness, coinciding with the questionnaire data (see Example [3.7]).

(3.6)

1   JS3:   *Ohiru yasumi ichijikan mo nai node* (.) *iki kaeri taihen nanode* (.) *okane wo kashi*

2   *masu.*

            お昼休み一時間もないので、行き帰り大変なのでお金を貸します。

            As a lunch break is less than an hour and it would be a trouble to go back and forth, I will lend B some money.

(3.7)

1   JS4:   *Gakushoku no ohiru 500 yen shinai. (.) Dakara futan ja nai.*

            学食のお昼500円しない。だから負担じゃない。

            As lunch in a canteen costs less than 500 yen, it is not a huge burden.

Three Japanese parents said that they would lend money. The reasons varied: a demonstrator would demonstrate attentiveness because of interpersonal relationships (see Example [3.8]), or because of time (see Example [3.9]). In Example (3.10), the demonstrator would expect the other party to pay for her if she were in a similar situation.

(3.8)

1   JP3:   *B san wa (.) shitashii douryou.*
Bさんは親しい同僚。
B is a close colleague.

(3.9)

1   JP4:   *Kaisha ni made (.) tori ni iku jikan (.) mottainai.*
会社にまで取りに行く時間もったいない。
It would be a waste of time to go back to the company {to fetch money}.

(3.10)

1   JP6:   *Moshi jibun ga onaji tachiba nara (.) tatekaete morau.*
もし自分が同じ立場なら、立て替えてもらう。
If I were in the same situation, I would get B to lend the lunch money.

Three other Japanese parents would just pay for lunch (i.e., they do not expect B to pay them back). The reasons are based on the interpersonal relationships between the demonstrator and the recipient of attentiveness (see Examples [3.11] and [3.12]), and the demonstrator feels sorry for the other party (see Example [3.13]).

(3.11)

1   JP2:   *B san niwa (.) higoro (.) o sewa ni natte iru node.*
Bさんには日頃お世話になっているので。
B always supports me.

(3.12)

1   JP1:   *Itsumo B san towa (.) shitashiku shite iru node.*
いつもBさんとは親しくしているので。
I always have a close relationship with B.

(3.13)

1   JP5:   *Wazawaza (.) kaisha ni modora seru nomo (.) kinodoku dakara.*
わざわざ会社に戻らせるのも気の毒だから。
I would feel sorry, if I were to let B go back to the company all the way.

In English, there may be no exact equivalent to *o sewa ni natte iru* (*sewa* literally means 'care') in Example (3.11), which can mean that one is helped, supported and cared about by the other party. In a way, this shows interdependent relationships, which are related to collectivist features. It contains some kind of gratitude to the other party, too. In this sense, it may mean 'thanks to someone'. It is also used as an idiomatic expression. For example, the phrase *o sewa ni natte ori masu* is often used at the beginning of a business letter/email[48] or in answering the phone at a business in Japan, although the other party does not necessarily help, support or care about that person. In Example (3.11), this phrase means that the colleague always supports JP2 and cares about her. Thus, she would demonstrate attentiveness in return. Here we can see some kind of reciprocity. Although reciprocity was discussed in relation to reflexive attentiveness in Section 2.2.1, the attentiveness JP2 demonstrates is not necessarily reflexive attentiveness, which is for the benefit of the demonstrator. Reciprocity here would rather function as motivation for demonstrating attentiveness.

All the American students stated that they would pay for lunch, but there were differences whether they would expect B to pay them back or not (see Examples [3.14] and [3.15]).

(3.14)

1	AS3:	I'll just pay. (.) I'll treat you. My heart is bigger than yours. (.) I'm a student and I'm
2		broke. (.) Usually, when I go out to eat, it costs 20 dollars. But the lunch costs 5
3		dollars. (.) It's a small meal. I'll pay.

(3.15)

1	AS4:	Don't worry about it. (.) I'll just pay for it, and you can just pay me back when we get
2		back to your place. (.) I don't wanna interrupt us eating, (.) 'cause like we've just got
3		there, and I'm probably hungry, and I just like, (.) just wanna eat food.

Whereas Example (3.14) shows that the demonstrator will treat the other party to lunch, Example (3.15) indicates that the demonstrator wants the money back later. Moreover, Example (3.15) shows the demonstrator's desire to eat lunch immediately, which is for her own sake rather than thinking of the other party. This kind of reason was not found in the Japanese data, which can be considered as a cross-cultural difference.

In Situation 3 (book), all of the Japanese students said that they would contact C (either by email or telephone). If C still needed it, they would buy the book (see Example [3.16]).

(3.16)

1	JP3:	*C san ni meeru de renraku wo totte (.) mada C san no temoto ni nakereba kau.* (0.4)
		Cさんにメールで連絡を取って、まだ Cさんの手元になければ買う。
2		*Jimoto no shoten niwa naishi (.) sotsuron niwa hitsuyou. (.) C san no yaku ni tachi tai.*

地元の書店にはないし、卒論には必要。Cさんの役に立ちたい。

I'll contact C by email. If C does not have the book, I will buy it. That book is not available at the local bookstore and C needs that book for her thesis. I want to be of help to C.

All the Japanese parents and American students commented that they would contact C. It depends on the situation whether they would buy the book or not, namely whether C wants it (see Example [3.17]), whether C pays her back or not (see Example [3.18]) or whether C can go to the bookstore or not (see Example [3.19]).

(3.17)

1 JP4: *C san ni denwa shite (.) hoshii to iu node areba (.) katte iki masu. (0.5)*
Cさんに電話して、欲しいというのであれば買っていきます。

2 *Douryou nanode (.) shinrai no okeru aidagara dakara. (.)*
同僚なので信頼の置ける間柄だから。

3 *Denwa ga tsunagara nakattara (.) atta toiu houkoku wo (.) kaette kara shi masu.*
電話が繋がらなかったら、あったという報告を帰ってからします。

I'll call C and if C wants it, I will buy it. As C is my colleague, I can trust her. If I cannot contact C by phone, I will tell C that I found the book, upon returning.

(3.18)

1 AS2: I first call them and say, (.) 'I found this book. (.) It's 50 bucks. Do you want it?', (.)
2 implying she has to pay me back. (.) If she says, '50 bucks? No, I'd find it online.' (.)
3 Then, OK, never mind.

(3.19)

1 AS5: It would depend on if the person could go to the bookstore by themselves, and I would
2 (.) I feel like either I would tell them that it's there (.) so that they could go get it, (.) or
3 if it's really far away, (.) and it's just easier for me to get it for them, (.) I would get it
4 for them.

There was another American student, who would buy the book without any condition, after contacting C (see Example [3.20]).

(3.20)

1 AS6: I would call first. (.) I would buy it. I'm very (.) Books are very important. So, (.) I can
2 understand the situation. I would be (.) I feel like (.) I would be thankful. I have a lot
3 of overseas friends. (.) They can't get books easily. I would mail them a book, even
4 though they are overseas. (.) I'm used to doing this kind of thing.

In Situation 4 (work schedule), all the Japanese students stated that they would stand in for D, but the reasons varied (see Examples [3.21], [3.22] and [3.23]).

(3.21)

1   JS3:   *Yotei nai node hima. (.) Ie no koto (.) taihen nanode (.) tasuke tai.*

予定ないので暇。家のこと大変なので助けたい。

As I do not have any plan, I have time. D has difficulty, because of the situation at home. So, I want to help D.

(3.22)

1   JS2:   *Jibun ga komatta toki ni (.) tasukete moraeru.*

自分が困った時に助けてもらえる。

I'd be helped when I am in need.

(3.23)

1   JS1:   *Otagai sama dato omou.*

お互い様だと思う。

I think it is mutual.

Example (3.21) shows the demonstrator's desire to help D, which can be considered as genuine attentiveness, whereas Example (3.22) indicates reflexive attentiveness (see Section 2.2.1). Example (3.22) is similar to Example (2.12) in that she demonstrates attentiveness as she expects the recipient to reciprocate the favour in the future when she is in need. Example (3.23) indicates mutuality, which is related to interdependence.

All the Japanese parents said that they would stand in for D (see Example [3.24]).

(3.24)

1   JP2:   *Chouji wa sakete toure nai. (.) Kawari ni dekiru koto nanode (.) yasumi wo henjyou shi*

2   *masu. (0.5)*

弔事は避けて通れない。代わりにできることなので休みを返上します。

One cannot avoid a funeral service. As I can stand in for D, I would give up my days off {and come to work}.

3   *Jissai ni (.) konomae (.) kouiu koto ga arima shita. (0.3)*

実際にこの前こういう事がありました。

Actually, there was a similar case recently.

4   *Doyoubi wa (.) touban de (.) koutai de shukkin shi masu. (0.4)*

土曜日は当番で交代で出勤します。

On Saturdays we work on a shift.

5   *Senjitsu ie dewa (.) tambo no shitaku ga atta kedo (.) houji toiu hito no kawari ni (.)*

6   *shigoto ni dema shita.*

先日家では田んぼの支度があったけど、法事という人の代わりに仕
事に出ました。

The other day we had to prepare the rice field at home. But there was somebody {who
could not work} because of a memorial service. So, I came to work, standing in for her.

In Example (3.24), JP2 would demonstrate attentiveness, standing in for D, as a
memorial service is something which one cannot avoid. The reason why D cannot
come to work outweighed JP2's work at home, namely, preparing the rice field.

Half of the Japanese parents stated mutuality as a reason for standing in for D
(see Example [3.25]), as discussed earlier.

(3.25)

1   JP4:   *Otagai sama nanode.*

お互い様なので。

It is mutual.

Most of the American students said that they would cover for D, but the reasons
varied (see Examples [3.26] and [3.27]).

(3.26)

1   AS3:   Hey, (.) I'm covering your hours so I would take their hours and their money.

(3.27)

1   AS2:   Actually, (.) firstly, I'll wait if anyone else would take place. (0.6) Secondly, check

2   whether I can be paid extra. (.) I'll negotiate with another co-worker. (.) I'd separate

3   the days with another colleague. (.) You take two. I take three. You're just doing a

4   favor, so you don't want to sacrifice your time, (.) but you still want to help. (0.5) It's

5   something unexpected. (.) I want to go to Disneyworld. It's not like that. (.) It's a

6   serious topic. So, (.) try to help that person as much as possible.

In Example (3.26), the demonstrator would cover the work because she can get
money, which is for her own sake. As mentioned earlier, this reason was found
also in the questionnaire data. This reason may be similar to Example (3.15) in
that the demonstrator thinks of herself rather than the other party. Although AS2
in Example (3.27) also wants the money, she considers that it is because of the
funeral service ('a serious topic' and 'unexpected' in her words), which differs
from having fun (going to Disneyworld). In other words, AS2 thinks that the
reason for taking the days off is legitimate. In Example (3.27) there are some other
aspects. AS2 does not want to sacrifice her time that much, but she wants to help
D. This is why she would like to share the workload with another colleague. It can

be said that the reason why one might demonstrate attentiveness may not always be straightforward. Various factors can motivate a demonstrator to demonstrate attentiveness, although the demonstrator may not be always aware of all of them.

There was one American student who said she would not work (see Example [3.28]).

(3.28)

1	AS6:	I don't know. (.) I won't work. (.) Even though they are my friends. (.) Because it's
2		work. To me, I have to balance work and school. I don't know. (.) There are also other
3		people. They can take the job, too. (.) It's not a big deal. Unless the person personally
4		asks me to take over the job, I won't work. That's the work. (.) I prioritise school over
5		work.

Although a funeral service was something 'unexpected and serious' for AS2 in Example (3.27), 'it's not a big deal' for AS6 in Example (3.28). She will not work, as she prioritises school over work. This shows that AS5 cares most about herself.

In Situation 5 (papers), four Japanese students would help their professor bring the papers to the professor's office, because it would be a lot of trouble for the professor to carry a huge amount of papers. Two other Japanese students stated that it would depend on the relationship between the professor and the demonstrator. One of them stated further that it is natural to demonstrate attentiveness, as the professor always cares about her (see Example [3.29]).

(3.29)

1 JS3: *Sensei to no kankei ni mo yori masu. (.)*
先生との関係にもよります。

It also depends on the relationship between the professor {and me}.

2 *Zemi no sensei ya (.) shitashii sensei dattara kenkyuushitsu ni motte iki masu. (0.2)*
ゼミの先生や親しい先生だったら、研究室に持って行きます。

If the professor is the one from the seminar {which I belong to}, or I feel close to the professor, I would carry papers to the professor's office.

3 *Fudan kara o sewa ni natte iru node atarimae. (.)*
普段からお世話になっているので当たり前。

It is natural, because the professor always supports me and cares about me.

4 *Shitashiku nakereba (.) koe wo kake masen.*
親しくなければ声をかけません。

If I do not feel close to the professor, I would not mention anything.

Example (3.29) shows some features of reciprocity. As the professor always supports her and cares about her (*o sewa ni natte iru*, line 3), she wants to return the favour by bringing the papers to the professor's office. She does not want to seek for any benefit by doing so. Thus, this may be different from reflexive attentiveness, although it involves reciprocity. As shown in Example (3.11), reciprocity functions as motivation for demonstrating attentiveness here.

All the Japanese parents would help their boss carry the papers, as they think it is natural to work for the boss (see Example [3.30]), which confirms the questionnaire data.

(3.30)

1   JP2:   *Jyoushi ni motte itte yoika (.) ukagai wo tatete (.) motte iki masu. (.)*
上司に持って行ってよいか伺いを立てて持って行きます。
I would ask my boss if I could carry the papers. Then, I would carry the papers.

2   *Tsutome to shite wa (.) jyoushi no tame ni suru no wa touzen.*
勤めとしては上司の為にするのは当然。
As a part of the work, it is natural to help the boss.

Four American students said that they would help the professor, but the reasons varied (see Examples [3.31] and [3.32]).

(3.31)

1   AS1:   It's not a big deal to help. (.) It would take a minute or two to help. (.) If it would take
2   three, four hours …

(3.32)

1   AS2:   He's grading. (.) I want to make good impression.

Example (3.31) indicates that helping the professor would not involve too much imposition. It may be that the demonstrator would just help the professor (genuine attentiveness). However, in Example (3.32) the demonstrator would like to get a good grade, which is why she would demonstrate attentiveness. Thus, it is considered as reflexive attentiveness, as it is for the demonstrator's benefit.

There were two American students who would not help the professor (see Example [3.33]).

(3.33)

1   AS2:   He knows it's coming. (.) I'm not a TA or anything. (.) There's nothing to do with me,
2   whether or not he has a lot of papers. (.) UCLA is a big university. It's their job. (.)
3   I'm not a TA. (.) I won't be helping.

According to AS2 in Example (3.33), the professor should be responsible for her/his job, and helping the professor is a job for a teaching assistant (TA). As AS2 is not a TA, she thinks 'there's nothing to do with her', which may indicate independence.

This section has investigated the demonstration of attentiveness by Japanese parents, Japanese students and American students. The next section compares the evaluation of attentiveness by the same three groups of participants as in this section.

3.5 Evaluation of attentiveness: Cross-cultural (Japanese–American) and cross-generational (among the Japanese) comparisons

This section investigates the evaluation of attentiveness by Japanese and American participants and that by Japanese participants of two different generations.

3.5.1 Data and methodology

The data were elicited through questionnaires with six situations to obtain quantitative data, and interviews were conducted using the same six situations to obtain qualitative data. The correlation between the degree of imposition required to demonstrate attentiveness and the evaluation of attentiveness is also investigated in this section.

Participants

Participants (both for questionnaire and interview) are the same as those in Section 3.4.

Research instrument (questionnaire)

Six situations (the same as those in Section 3.4) were presented. What differs from Section 3.4 is that attentiveness was already demonstrated in each situation. In order to investigate whether the familiarity between the demonstrator and the recipient of attentiveness influences the evaluation of attentiveness,[49] the familiarity between them varied. The situations are as follows (alphabetical letters were used to identify the individuals to avoid gender influence and any influence personal names might have on the participants; the text in parentheses were for the parents' questionnaire) .

Situation 1

You get on a train. You carry a lot of baggage. There are many standing passengers, but there is a vacancy in a priority seat in the same car. Your acquaintance, A, is sitting on the train, reading a book. A does not have any heavy baggage.

A offers you a seat. How would you evaluate that?

Situation 2

You and your close friend (colleague), B, have gone for lunch in the canteen (at a restaurant near the company). You have carelessly left your wallet at home. You live near the campus (the company).

B pays for your lunch. How would you evaluate that?

Situation 3

You are looking for a book, Y, for your thesis (project). C, your seminar friend (colleague), is in a big city and has stopped at a big bookstore, X. C happens to find the book, Y. It costs $50. The book, Y, is not available at local bookstores.

C buys you the book, Y. How would you evaluate that?

Situation 4

You have to suddenly take five days leave, because of a funeral service. According to the work schedule, your colleague at your part-time job (company), D, does not work on the days of your leave.

You find that D would work for you. How would you evaluate that?

Situation 5

You are a professor at the university (a section chief in a company). There were presentations from every group in the class (every project group). There has been a huge amount of papers submitted to you from every group.

One of your students (subordinates) helps you carry the papers to your office. How would you evaluate that?

Situation 6

When you are walking in a train station, it seems that you have dropped your rail pass.

Someone hands you the rail pass. How would you evaluate that?

In each situation, a five-point Likert scale was given for the evaluation of attentiveness, 1 being 'very appreciative' and 5 being 'not at all appreciative'. Multiple choices were given for the reasons for the evaluation of attentiveness, which are based on the results in Section 3.3. In Section 3.3, the participants stated any reason for their evaluation of attentiveness. Those reasons could be classified into positive (e.g., they appreciated attentiveness) and negative reasons (e.g., being intrusive; feeling it as a burden). The multiple choices for the reasons for the evaluation in this section, therefore, included the following: (1) 'I needed that' or 'that was helpful'; (2) 'I felt it as a burden' or 'it was imposing'; and (3) 'other'.[50] The degree of imposition required to demonstrate attentiveness may influence the evaluation of attentiveness. Thus, situations with both high and low degrees of imposition were included. However, the perception of the degree of imposition may differ individually or culturally. The participants, therefore, were asked to evaluate the degree of imposition required to demonstrate attentiveness in the questionnaire.

Procedure

Questionnaire

The questionnaire was distributed to each participant in their own mother tongue. In each situation, the participants were asked (1) to evaluate attentiveness on a five-point Likert scale, 1 being 'they appreciate the attentiveness very much' and 5 being 'they do not appreciate the attentiveness at all';[51] (2) to select a reason for their evaluation of attentiveness from the three reasons given ([1] 'I needed that' or 'that was helpful'; [2] 'I felt it as a burden' or 'it was imposing'; and [3] 'other'); and (3) to evaluate the degree of imposition required to demonstrate attentiveness on a five-point Likert scale, 1 being 'a small imposition' and 5 being 'a large imposition'.

Interview

After reading the situations and the attentiveness demonstrated in each situation, the participants were asked to state how they would evaluate the attentiveness. Interviews were conducted in each participant's mother tongue. Each interview lasted approximately 15 minutes.

3.5.2 Data analysis

Questionnaire

The data analysis procedure was as follows:

1. In order to answer research Question 1 ('Are there any differences among the participants in their evaluation of attentiveness?'), a one-way ANOVA (participants) was conducted. The mean scores of the evaluation of attentiveness were also calculated.
2. In order to answer research Question 2 ('Are there any differences among the participants in their reasons for the evaluation of attentiveness?'), the participants' choices were added up.
3. In order to answer research Question 3 ('Are there any differences among the participants in rating the degree of imposition required to demonstrate attentiveness?'), a one-way ANOVA (participants) was conducted. The mean scores of the degree of imposition required to demonstrate attentiveness were also calculated.

4. In order to answer research Question 4 ('Is there any correlation between the degree of imposition required to demonstrate attentiveness and the evaluation of attentiveness?'), a Pearson correlation coefficient was calculated.

Interview

All the interviews were audio-recorded and transcribed.

3.5.3 Results and discussion

Questionnaire

There were significant differences among the participants in the evaluation of attentiveness in Situations 5 (papers) and 6 (rail pass), according to the results of the first analysis.[52] In Situation 5, the score by American students (1.875) was significantly higher than that by Japanese parents (1.413) and that by Japanese students (1.301). In Situation 6, too, the score by American students (1.312) was significantly higher than that by Japanese parents (1.086) and that by Japanese students (1.057).[53] As 1 on a five-point scale was 'they appreciate the attentiveness very much' and 5 was 'they do not appreciate the attentiveness at all', these results mean that in both Situations 5 and 6, American students made the most negative evaluation of attentiveness; and Japanese students appreciated the attentiveness most (see Table 3.6).

Table 3.6: Mean scores for the evaluation of attentiveness by Japanese and American participants

Situation	Japanese students		Japanese parents		American students	
	M	*SD*	*M*	*SD*	*M*	*SD*
1. Seat	1.455	.837	1.5	.777	1.593	.756
2. Lunch	1.352	.689	1.304	.588	1.468	.915
3. Book	1.685	.962	1.673	.840	1.718	1.142
4. Work schedule	1.301	.656	1.423	.801	1.406	.910
5. Papers*	1.301	.636	1.413	.743	1.875	1.099
6. Rail pass*	1.057	.363	1.086	.028	1.312	.820

*There was a significant difference at the .01 level ($p < .01$).
1 = They appreciate the attentiveness very much; 5 = They do not appreciate the attentiveness at all; *M* = mean score; *SD* = standard deviation.

As regards the reasons for the evaluation of attentiveness, there were no major differences among the three groups of participants, most participants having selected Choice 1 ('I needed that' or 'that was helpful') most frequently in all of the situations. A closer look at the results, however, tells us that there were some differences in percentage among the participants. Although American students selected Choice 1 most frequently (68.8%) in Situation 5 (papers), their percentage was lower than the Japanese participants (JS: 92.3%; JP: 87.0%). American students also selected Choice 2 ('I felt it as a burden' or 'it was imposing') (15.6%) and Choice 3 ('other') (15.6%) in Situation 5. From these results it can be said that the American students placed an importance on independence. 'One is independent, and one, therefore, is responsible for her/himself' is one of the features of individualist cultures (see Section 3.2). Attentiveness may sometimes mean that one cannot pursue some acts by themselves, which insinuates that one cannot act independently. This may have led to more selections of Choice 2 by American participants than by Japanese participants. American participants wrote that 'A professor should be aware that a lot of papers would be turned in, so he should have brought something to carry them with' (Situation 5), which may be related to the idea that one needs to be responsible for oneself (see also the discussion in Section 3.4).

Some other differences between the Japanese and American participants could be found in the reasons. For example, 'it is mutual' (*otagaisama*) was found in the reasons for Choice 3 ('other')[54] only by Japanese participants. The idea behind *otagaisama*, or mutuality, is to help others when you can and be helped by others when you are in need. This may accord with some features of collectivist cultures, that is, 'one depends on the others or the group s/he belongs to' (see Section 3.2) to a certain extent. Mutuality was considered to be important by the Japanese participants also in the demonstration of attentiveness, as shown in Section 3.4.

Not only differences, but also some similarities among the participants were found in the reasons for the evaluation of attentiveness. In Situations 1 (seat) and 2 (lunch), some participants (American students in Situation 1 and Japanese parents and American students in Situation 2) wrote that 'attentiveness was expected' in Choice 3 ('other') (see the discussion below). In these situations, there were no significant differences in the evaluation of attentiveness (see Table 3.6).

As for the degree of imposition required to demonstrate attentiveness, there were significant differences in evaluating the degree of imposition among the participants in Situations 1 (seat), 3 (book) and 5 (papers), according to the results of the third analysis (ANOVA).[55] In Situation 1, the mean score by Japanese students (1.935) was significantly higher than that by Japanese parents (1.597) and that by American students (1.437) (1 signifies a low degree of imposition and 5 a high degree of imposition). In Situation 3, the mean score by Japanese students (2.929) was significantly higher than that by Japanese parents (2.347). In Situation 5, the mean score by Japanese students (2.128) was significantly higher than that by Japanese parents (1.739).

With respect to the correlation between the degree of imposition required to demonstrate attentiveness and the evaluation of attentiveness, there were significant correlations between them in Situations 2 (lunch) and 3 (book) by the Japanese students, and in Situations 1 (seat), 3 (book), 4 (work) and 5 (papers) by the Japanese parents (see Table 3.7).

Table 3.7: Correlation between the degree of imposition required to demonstrate attentiveness and the evaluation of attentiveness by Japanese and American participants (Pearson correlation coefficients)

Situation	Japanese students	Japanese parents	American students
1. Seat	0.159	0.270*	−0.228
2. Lunch	0.402*	0.252	0.051
3. Book	0.326*	0.545*	−0.002
4. Work	−0.021	0.492*	0.208
5. Papers	−0.026	0.369*	0.278
6. Rail pass	−0.004	0.210	−0.089

* There was a significant difference at the .01 level ($p < 0.01$)

Among the situations which showed significant differences for the evaluation of attentiveness (namely, Situations 5 and 6; see Table 3.6), there was a significant correlation between the degree of imposition required to demonstrate attentiveness and the evaluation of attentiveness by the Japanese parents in Situation 5 (papers). The Japanese parents evaluated attentiveness in Situation 5 (papers) as 1.413 (1 signified that they appreciated the attentiveness very much and 5 signified that they did not appreciate the attentiveness at all) and rated the degree of imposition required to demonstrate attentiveness as 1.739. From these results it can be said that they evaluated attentiveness positively, because the degree of imposition was low.

Interview

In the interview data (the author's own recordings and associated transcriptions), major differences among the three groups of participants in the evaluation of attentiveness were not found except for in Situations 3 (book) and 5 (papers). In these situations, two American students evaluated attentiveness negatively, whereas the other participants evaluated attentiveness positively. In the other four situations, all three groups of participants evaluated attentiveness positively. Some examples are presented for each situation to show some of the differences as well as some of the similarities among the participants.

In Situation 1 (seat), all of the three groups of participants evaluated attentiveness positively (see Examples [3.34], [3.35] and [3.36]).

(3.34)

1   JS2:   *Arigatai.*

        有り難い。

        Thankful.

(3.35)

1   JP1:   *Tasuka tta kara.*
             助かったから。
             It was helpful.

(3.36)

1   AS1:   This person is considering.

AS1 in Example (3.36) touched upon the demonstrator's personality. AS1 thinks that the demonstrator of attentiveness is considering, as she made a positive evaluation of the attentiveness demonstrated. This may be related to the discussion on attentiveness and social skills, reputation and interpersonal relationships in Section 2.2.1.

In Situation 2 (lunch), all of the participants evaluated attentiveness positively, as the demonstrator helped the recipient (see Example [3.37]).

(3.37)

1   JP5:   *Komatte ite (.) tasuke te kure ta kara.*
             困っていて助けてくれたから。
             She helped me, when I was in need.

Although they are thankful, the participants felt indebtedness at the same time as shown in Example (3.38). This tendency could be found in all three groups of participants.

(3.38)

1   AS1:   Yeah, I'd be very thankful, (.) but feel I'm in debt. (.) I should treat you next time.

Example (3.38) indicates that the recipient of attentiveness would like to pay the debt back, which is similar to *okaeshi* ('returning'). As noted in Section 3.3, Ohashi (2013 and elsewhere) argues that the debt–credit equilibrium is a significant politeness phenomenon in Japanese. Example (3.38) suggests that AS1 also had a concept similar to *okaeshi*, and that *okaeshi* is not unique to Japanese culture. This is also related to reciprocity, as noted in Section 2.2.1. We cannot draw any generalised conclusion from this data alone, and further scrutiny is needed.

In Situation 3 (book), the Japanese students and Japanese parents evaluated attentiveness positively (see Examples [3.39] and [3.40]), whereas two of the American students evaluated it negatively (see Examples [3.41] and [3.42]).

(3.39)

1   JS2:   *Yuujin ga (.) watashi no sagashite iru hon wo (.) oboete ite kure te (.)*
             友人が私の捜している本を覚えていてくれて

My friend remembered the book which I had been looking for.

2   *nedan takai shi (.) jibun no youji de itte iru noni (.) kasabaru hon wo (.)*

3   *motte kaette kure ta node (.) kansha no doai wa ookii.*

値段高いし、自分の用事で行っているのにかさばる本を

持って帰ってくれたので、感謝の度合いは大きい。

It was expensive. She brought me back a bulky book, although she went {to a big city}
for her own business. Therefore, I appreciate her a lot.

(3.40)

1   JP1:   *Hitsuyou na hon dato iu koto wo shitte ite (.)*

必要な本だということを知っていて

She knew that it was the book I needed.

2   *sore wo sacchi shite (.) katte kite kure ta node (.) arigatai.*

それを察知して買って来てくれたので、有り難い。

She inferred that and bought it for me. Therefore, I am thankful.

In Example (3.40), the recipient of attentiveness made a positive evaluation, not
only because the demonstrator bought the book, but also because she inferred the
recipient's needs. Here we can see the importance of inference (see the discussion
below).

(3.41)

1   AS4:   C is so nice. (.) That was ridiculous. (.) C didn't have to buy me the book. Especially

2   it's like $50. (.) That would be hella-helpful. (.) Just telling me where the book was

3   would be helpful. (.) Super nice 'cause it's expensive, and the fact that they remember

4   it was just ridiculous.

(3.42)

1   AS5:   He was thoughtful but rude, kind but dumb. (.) He should have asked. (.) Considerate

2   but inconsiderate. (.) He's a good guy, but he was thinking about himself. (.) He wants

3   to feel good by helping.

The negative evaluation by the American student in Example (3.41) included 'super
nice', which may correspond to the notion of 'over-polite' argued by Watts (2005:
xliii–xliv). The negative evaluation in Example (3.42) in some respects includes an
element of reflexive attentiveness, as it suggests that the demonstrator would like
to be praised because s/he demonstrated attentiveness. This is an instance in which
the demonstrator of reflexive attentiveness could be evaluated negatively.

In Situation 4 (work schedule), all the participants evaluated attentiveness positively (see Examples [3.43], [3.44] and [3.45]).

(3.43)

1   JS4:   *Yasumi no hi nanoni (.) kyuuna youji (.) watashi no tame ni (0.3) yasumi wo kezutte*

2   *kure te (.) arubaito wo shite kure te (.) ureshii.*

休みの日なのに急な用事、私の為に休みを削ってくれてアルバイトをしてくれて嬉しい。

Although she was supposed to take days off, she worked part time for me, cutting down her holidays, because of my sudden duty. I am happy.

(3.44)

1   JP5:   *Yasumu kotoni natte ita noni (.) watashi no jyoukyou wo kangaete (.) kinmu shite*

2   *kure ta koto (.) arigatai.*

休む事になっていたのに私の状況を考えて勤務してくれたこと有り難い。

She was supposed to take days off, but she worked, considering my situation. Therefore, I'm grateful.

(3.45)

1   AS2:   I am really grateful to D.

Some participants said that they felt guilty or they felt like they owed D in Situation 4. This kind of statement was found in all of the three groups of participants (see Example [3.46]).

(3.46)

1   AS4:   I would feel real guilty. (.) That's 5 days. (.) That's a lot. I owe them. (.) I have to

2   make them up somehow.

In Example (3.46), we can see that the recipient of attentiveness feels in debt and wants to pay that back, which can be regarded as reciprocity, as was found in Situation 2 (see Example [3.38]).

In Situation 5 (papers), most of the participants evaluated attentiveness positively (see Examples [3.47], [3.48] and [3.49]), although two American students evaluated it negatively (see Examples [3.50] and [3.51]).

(3.47)

1   JP4:   *Boudai na ryou ni kizuite kure ta koto to (.)*

膨大な量に気付いてくれた事と

She realised that I had a huge amount {of papers}.

2   *youji ga atta kamo shire nai noni (.)*

用事があったかもしれないのに

Although she may have had her own duties,

3   *shiryou wo hakonde kure ta node* (.) *ureshii.*

資料を運んでくれたので嬉しい。

she carried them. Therefore, I am grateful.

(3.48)

1   JP1:   *Boudai na shiryou wo motsu nowa taihen nanode* (.)

膨大な資料を持つのは大変なので

It is a lot of work to carry a huge amount {of papers}.

2   *motte moraete* (.) *ureshiku omoi masu.*

持ってもらって嬉しく思います。

I am thankful, because she carried them.

(3.49)

1   AS1:   The student is really nice. (.) Like he really notices.

(3.50)

1   AS5:   Bribing him by helping him. (.) He wants a better grade.

(3.51)

1   AS2:   A little weird to me. (.) At UCLA there's a TA. (.) TA would definitely help.

AS1 in Example (3.49) made a positive evaluation, touching upon the personality of the demonstrator, which resonates with Example (3.36). AS1 made a positive evaluation, because the demonstrator noticed the other party's needs (see the discussion on inference below). The negative evaluation shown in Example (3.50) indicates that reflexive attentiveness can be evaluated negatively (see also Example [3.42]). In Example (3.50), demonstrating attentiveness may trigger a better grade, which is for the benefit of the demonstrator. Example (3.51) shows that helping the professor is a job for a teaching assistant. Thus, it is weird for AS2 to help the professor. This accords with the data for the demonstration of attentiveness (see Example [3.33]).

In Situation 6 (rail pass), all of the participants evaluated attentiveness positively (see Examples [3.52], [3.53] and [3.54]).

(3.52)

1   JS6:   *Teiki takai shi* (.) *naito komaru.*

定期高いし、ないと困る。

A pass costs a lot and I would be in trouble if I lost it.

2   *Sugoku kansha.*

すごく感謝。

I am really thankful.

(3.53)

1   JP2:   *Arigatai. (.) Tanin ga oshiete kudasa tta. (.)*

有り難い。他人が教えて下さった。

Thankful. Someone I don't know let me know.

2   *Hirotte watashite kudasa tta. (.) Mizushirazu no watashi ni.*

拾って渡して下さった。見ず知らずの私に。

S/he has picked it up and handed it to me. To me, who is a total stranger.

(3.54)

1   AS1:   I would think, oh, (.) such a nice person. Like, (.) of course, that's something that

2   people should do, (.) but in reality people don't so. (.) So, it would be really nice to

3   see someone (.) like actually do that. (.) Thanks, so helpful.

Discussion based on questionnaire and interview data

It was anticipated that there would be cross-cultural differences among the participants in the evaluation of attentiveness. That is, Japanese participants would evaluate attentiveness more positively than American participants. This assumption derives from some literature (see Section 3.2). For example, Markus and Kitayama (1991: 224) argue as follows: Whereas attending to the self, the appreciation of one's difference from others and the importance of asserting the self are stressed in American culture, attending to and fitting in with others and the importance of harmonious interdependence with them are emphasised in Japanese culture. Moreover, attentiveness is closely related to interpersonal reality, which is more cherished in collectivist cultures than in individualist cultures (e.g., Yoshida 1994: 257). Inference, which is needed for attentiveness to arise (see Section 2.2.2), may play a more important role in Japanese culture than in American culture (see Section 3.2).

The results from the questionnaire data show that some cross-cultural differences in the evaluation of attentiveness were found only in Situations 5 (papers) and 6 (rail pass), American participants having evaluated the attentiveness in these situations most negatively. Also, in the interview data, negative evaluations were found only from American participants in Situations 3 (book) and 5 (papers). These results are consistent with the assumption above. In the other four situations, however, there were similarities across the two cultures. In other words, similarities outweighed differences. This may be partly due to the fact that

Japanese culture has gained some individualist features, and this may be also partly because of globalisation (see Section 3.2). That is, Japanese people in contemporary Japan may not be so different from others (e.g., at least the American participants in this section), although further scrutiny is needed. On a related note, it is noteworthy that Sifianou (2013: 87) points out the homogenisation of the world under the influence of the omnipresent American culture as one of the various threats attributed to globalisation.

In the interview data, it was found that inference was a factor, which led to a positive evaluation of attentiveness. For example, one recipient was thankful, because the demonstrator inferred the recipient's need. This was found in the data from all three groups of participants, although not all of them used the term 'inference' (e.g., they used the following: 'inferred' [*sacchi shite* in Situation 3] and 'realised' [*kizuite kure ta* in Situation 5] in the Japanese data, and 'notices' in Situation 5 in the American data; see Examples [3.40], [3.47] and [3.49]). This suggests that inference is important not only in Japanese culture, but also in American culture (at least for some American participants in this section), although more data are definitely needed before this can be confirmed. However, this contradicts some of the results in Section 3.4, that is, some American students did not even admit the necessity of inferring the needs of the other party in Situation 5 (e.g., 'If the professor needed help, he would ask'). It would be interesting to investigate this issue further with more data in future research.

Other cross-cultural and cross-generational similarities were also found. Some reasons written in Choice 3 ('other') in the questionnaire show that attentiveness is positively evaluated by all three groups of participants, when attentiveness was expected, for example, in Situations 1 (seat) and 2 (lunch). The interview data in Situations 1 (seat) and 2 (lunch) also show that, when attentiveness was helpful for the recipient, attentiveness was positively evaluated by all three groups of participants. These results suggest that acting according to the other party's expectation and helping the other party would lead to a positive evaluation of attentiveness. This may be related to the discussion in Section 3.3, that is, the expectation of a potential recipient of attentiveness, which is linked to their needs, influences the evaluation of attentiveness. As no cross-cultural nor cross-generational differences were found in the evaluation of attentiveness in these situations, it can be said that the expectation among the participants did not differ either.

According to the questionnaire data, the Japanese parents felt attentiveness to be a burden in Situation 4 (work schedule). The Japanese parents (14.1%) selected Choice 2 ('I felt it as a burden' or 'it was imposing') as a reason more frequently than other participants (JS: 5.8%; AS: 6.3%). In this situation, the degree of imposition required to demonstrate attentiveness was relatively high (JS: 2.967; JP: 2.619; AS: 1.937), and there was a correlation between the degree of imposition and the evaluation of attentiveness by the Japanese parents (see Table 3.7). In other words, the Japanese parents felt attentiveness to be a burden, because the degree of imposition required to demonstrate attentiveness was high.

Feeling guilt or indebtedness on receiving attentiveness can be regarded as a cross-cultural and cross-generational similarity, as all three groups of participants stated, 'I would feel guilty' or 'I feel indebtedness'. Some people felt indebtedness even when the degree of imposition required to demonstrate attentiveness was not rated as very high (JS: 1.666; JP: 1.532; AS: 1.906) as in Situation 2. In Situation 2, attentiveness was demonstrated by a close friend/colleague. Himeno (2003) claims that the recipient of attentiveness sometimes feels guilty when attentiveness is demonstrated by somebody who is not close. The results in this section, however, show that the recipient of attentiveness feels indebtedness even when attentiveness is demonstrated by someone who is close.

In Situation 6 (rail pass), attentiveness demonstrated by the stranger (the least familiar) was positively evaluated. This shows that familiarity does not seem to have influenced the evaluation of attentiveness, which is contradictory to Himeno's (2003) claim. A pass costs a lot, and the person who lost the pass would be in trouble. Attentiveness in Situation 6 was helpful to the recipient. Thus, whether attentiveness was helpful to the recipient was a more important factor in the evaluation of attentiveness than the familiarity between demonstrator and recipient.

It was anticipated that there would be cross-generational differences between Japanese students and Japanese parents in the evaluation of attentiveness. That is, Japanese parents would evaluate attentiveness more positively than Japanese students, as the collectivist score positively correlates with age (see Section 3.2) and attentiveness may be more highly evaluated in collectivist cultures than in individualist cultures. The Japanese parents, however, did not evaluate attentiveness more positively than the Japanese students in any situation. There were significant differences in the evaluation of attentiveness between the Japanese parents and the Japanese students in Situations 5 (papers) and 6 (rail pass). In these situations, the Japanese students evaluated attentiveness more positively than the Japanese parents, which was contradictory to what was anticipated. This may be because the Japanese parents (mean age: 51.5 [questionnaire]; 51.33 [interview]) were, of course, older than the Japanese students (mean age: 20.2 [questionnaire]; 20.5 [interview]), but they were born long after World War II and educated in a democratic system in which students are allowed to behave more individualistically (Yamaguchi 1994: 184). The Japanese parents in this section may fall into the same category as the younger Japanese, who did not experience the poverty that previous generations endured, as noted by Yamaguchi (1994) (see Section 3.2).

The Japanese parents may not have as many collectivistic features as the older generation (e.g., those who were born and educated before World War II).

The Japanese parents in this section were not as old as those in the study by Hirschon (2001) either. Hirschon (2001: 26) states that giving up seats on public transport facilities (which is the same as in Situation 1) is considered to be an offensive act by some older people, as they feel insulted that they might be considered weak and infirm. The Japanese parents in this section did not evaluate the attentiveness in Situation 1 (seat) negatively. If someone older than the age group of the Japanese parents in this section was given a seat, s/he may evaluate it negatively, as s/he may prefer to deny the fact that s/he is getting old. If the Japanese parents had been older than those in this section, there might have been a cross-generational difference in the evaluation of attentiveness, which can be pursued in future research.

In a study on the conceptualisation of im/politeness in Greek, Sifianou and Tzanne (2010) found no cross-generational differences between the 78 younger informants (aged between 18 and 22) and the 20 older informants (aged between 43 and 60). The informants in Sifianou and Tzanne (2010) were of roughly the same age as those in this section. Even though a cross-generational comparison was not among the main aims of the paper above, Sifianou (pers. com.) suggested that, when acting as informants, the younger members of society may reflect their family's (namely, their ingroup's) views, that is, they may be reproducing what they have been taught. She also added that it may be that there are no substantial differences between the generations to be recorded. This suggestion resonates with Pan and Kádár's (2011) view on Chinese: despite large-scale socio-political changes and apparent changes in politeness norms, in essence there is considerable continuity between the earlier and modern use of language.

Indeed, parents' influence on children can be very strong, and it may take a long time for some cultural traits (both linguistic and non-linguistic) to change. In the meantime, old and new traits co-exist: some old traits may appear resistant to change and dominate over new ones, and in other cases the reverse may be the case. Thus, what is needed is comparisons involving various age groups. In this way, we will be in a better position to judge whether there are generational differences in the evaluation of attentiveness.

3.6 Conclusion

This chapter has drawn attention to attentiveness from a cross-cultural perspective. As culture plays a significant role, some issues concerning culture which are relevant to this chapter were first presented. As discussed in this chapter, cross-cultures include cross-generations. Thus, attentiveness was investigated cross-culturally (between British and Japanese participants and between Japanese and American participants) and cross-generationally (between Japanese of two different generations). Both demonstration and evaluation of attentiveness were examined.

It is sometimes said that Japanese culture is categorised as a collectivist culture, and British and American cultures as individualist cultures (see Section 3.2). According to Markus and Kitayama (1991: 224), many Asian cultures have distinct conceptions of individuality that insist on the fundamental relatedness of individuals to each other, and that the emphasis is on attending to others, fitting in and harmonious interdependence with them. What Markus and Kitayama (1991) mean by 'attending to others' is not exactly the same as the definition of attentiveness in this volume. That is, attentiveness in Markus and Kitayama's (1991) sense does not necessarily include an offer of pre-emptive help to the other party, inferring the needs of the other party. However, 'attending to others', in their terms at least, shows concern for other people, which is necessary to demonstrate attentiveness in my terms, too. Moreover, inference, which is needed to demonstrate attentiveness (see Section 2.2.2), is more valued in collectivist cultures than in individualist cultures, as noted in Section 3.2. This may lead to the assumption that attentiveness is more valued in collectivist cultures than in individualist cultures. Thus, it was anticipated that the Japanese participants would evaluate attentiveness more positively than the British participants (Section 3.3) or the American participants (Section 3.5) and that the Japanese participants would demonstrate attentiveness more frequently than the American participants (Section 3.4). It was also anticipated that the older Japanese would demonstrate attentiveness more frequently than the younger Japanese (Section 3.4) and that the older Japanese would evaluate attentiveness more positively than the younger ones (Section 3.5), as collectivism correlates positively with age (see Section 3.2). However, the results did not show exactly what was anticipated. In what follows, the results of each section are summarised, and some implications are presented.

The results of Section 3.3, which explored the evaluation of attentiveness by the British and Japanese participants, show that only in Situations 2 (handout) and 3 (pen) did the Japanese participants evaluate attentiveness more positively than the British participants, who evaluated attentiveness more positively than the Japanese participants also in two other situations (Situations 4 [books] and 6 [dinner]). The degree of imposition required to demonstrate attentiveness in Situations 2 and 3 was evaluated as lower than in other situations. When the degree of imposition was high, a Japanese recipient felt the attentiveness as a burden. This may be the reason why it was only in situations with a low degree of imposition that the Japanese participants evaluated attentiveness more positively than the British participants did.

The results in Section 3.3 may be partly regarded as heterogeneity of a culture (see Section 3.2). The findings of Section 3.3 suggest that both the old tradition of Japan, which is characterised by collectivist features, and the new trend, which is characterised by individualist features, may co-exist in contemporary Japanese culture. This may resonate, in part at least, with the discussion in Section 3.2 (both collectivist and individualist features co-exist in a culture) and that in Section 3.5 (old and new cultural traits co-exist). It was also found in Fukushima (2004: 378) that the new perspective on Japanese culture is not very different from that on other cultures, in spite of the fact that the uniqueness of Japanese culture has been sometimes emphasised in the literature.

The reason why there were no major differences in the evaluation of attentiveness between the Japanese and British participants in Section 3.3 may also be due to the fact that all of the participants were university students who share a similar culture paradigm,[56] namely, younger generation and university students. This is why attentiveness is further investigated with participants of different generations in the following sections.

In Section 3.4, the demonstration of attentiveness among Japanese students, Japanese parents and American students was compared. The results show that there were no major cross-cultural nor cross-generational differences in the demonstration of attentiveness among the participants. The participants would demonstrate attentiveness in four situations out of the six in the questionnaire, because they wanted to be of help to the other party. There was a relationship between the demonstration of attentiveness and the degree of imposition required to demonstrate attentiveness in four situations. That is, attentiveness is more frequently demonstrated when the degree of imposition is lower. Attentiveness is demonstrated in every degree of familiarity between a demonstrator and a recipient, namely, from very familiar to not very familiar at all.

In Situation 5 (papers), however, a cross-generational as well as a cross-cultural difference in the choice of demonstration of attentiveness was found. While most of the Japanese parents chose to demonstrate attentiveness, barely half of the Japanese and American students selected to demonstrate attentiveness.

In the reasons for the demonstration of attentiveness, some cross-cultural differences were found. Some features of collectivist cultures were found in the reasons given by the Japanese students and those by the Japanese parents (e.g., mutuality, which may indicate interdependence), and some features of individualist cultures were found in the reasons given by American students (e.g., independence), although more data is needed before this can be confirmed.

Section 3.5 attempted to investigate the evaluation of attentiveness cross-culturally and cross-generationally, eliciting data from the same three groups of participants as in Section 3.4. The results show that there were both differences and similarities in the evaluation of attentiveness by the participants. The American students evaluated attentiveness most negatively in Situations 5 (papers) and 6 (rail pass) in the questionnaire; and two American students made negative statements in Situations 3 (book) and 5 (papers) in the interview. These can be regarded as cross-cultural differences. In other situations, however, there were no major differences, most of the participants having evaluated attentiveness positively. Moreover, the Japanese students evaluated attentiveness more positively than the Japanese parents, which was contradictory to the anticipation. It can be inferred from these results that the participants' moral order, which reflects on the evaluation of attentiveness, does not differ very much.

In many cross-cultural studies, cross-cultural differences have been emphasised. Indeed, there were some cross-cultural differences in this chapter, too, and pointing out cross-cultural differences is important. However, similarities, if there are any, should also be noted, since having similarities is significant in cross-cultural studies. This may be related to an argument by Kerkam:

> When theorists analyse languages, especially in relation to politeness and impoliteness, they tend to take an approach which foregrounds difference. Thus, they see languages and cultures as falling into two diametrically opposed categories; they are unable to see languages as being on a cline or being similar in many ways.
>
> (Kerkam 2007, in Mills 2017: 31)

As many factors which may influence the evaluation of attentiveness are intricately entangled, they are not easily tangible. Questionnaire and interview data in this chapter, however, contributed to untangling some factors to a certain extent. Matching to a recipient's expectation, being helpful to a recipient, inferring a recipient's needs were triggers to a positive evaluation; and excessiveness (e.g., being 'super-nice') or the recipient's feeling it as a burden lead to a rather negative evaluation.

It is hoped that a comparison of the evaluation of attentiveness between many more different groups, including more nationalities and generations with many more age differences, or some other variables which could not be included in this chapter, will be conducted in the future so that we would be able to grasp what would influence the evaluation of attentiveness cross-culturally more precisely. If we knew some more of the factors that contribute to a negative evaluation of attentiveness, we would be able to reduce some misunderstandings caused by the different evaluation of attentiveness among people who have different cultural backgrounds. Furthermore, the demonstration and evaluation of attentiveness are two sides of the same coin. If we were able to discern some of the factors of negative evaluation of attentiveness, we may be able to demonstrate attentiveness, avoiding such factors. Then, we may be able to be of some help to the other party by demonstrating attentiveness without making a recipient feel a burden or being meddlesome, for example.

In the next chapter, attentiveness in Japanese relational networks is investigated.

CHAPTER 4

Attentiveness in Japanese relational networks

4.1 Introduction

We have investigated attentiveness cross-culturally and cross-generationally in the previous chapter. In this chapter, we focus on attentiveness in Japanese relational networks. In previous politeness research on Japanese, the variable of generation has not been taken up thoroughly, despite its importance (but see, e.g., Fukushima and Haugh 2014). Thus, it is incorporated in this chapter, and attentiveness is examined cross-generationally.

Politeness, a multifaceted phenomenon, encompasses not only linguistic but also non-linguistic aspects (see, e.g., Fukushima and Sifianou 2017). As noted in Section 2.2.1, non-linguistic aspects of politeness are also very important in im/politeness research (see, e.g., Sifianou and Garcés-Conejos Blitvich 2017: 583). This chapter considers attentiveness both from linguistic and non-linguistic viewpoints.

This chapter investigates attentiveness from the perspective of emic understandings, as they are important in recent im/politeness research (see Section 2.1). Emic understandings of im/politeness (or first-order politeness) are inextricably linked with evaluation,[1] which we investigated in Chapter 3. The basic concept of a discursive approach is to make a difference between the interactant's and the researcher's interpretations of politeness, labelling the former as 'first-order' and the latter as 'second-order' politeness. In order to reach theoretical second-order conclusions by means of objective data analysis, avoiding subjectivity (which researchers inherently possess) and the exclusion of certain views about politeness, a focus on the lay interpretation of politeness is needed (Kádár and Mills 2011: 8). That is, first-order politeness (politeness1) (see, e.g., Terkourafi 2012; Watts, Ide and Ehlich 2005 [1992]; Watts 2003) needs to be focused on so that it would be possible to better theorise second-order politeness (politeness2) (see, e.g., Eelen 2001; Terkourafi 2011a). In a similar vein, Garcés-Conejos Blitvich,

Lorenzo-Dus and Bou-Franch (2010: 691) argue that 'the discursive approach shifts the focus of its research agenda from analysts' interpretation based on models or theories of im-politeness (politeness2) to providing evidence that the participants themselves have evaluated a given behavior as polite or rude (politeness1)'. As Haugh (2010: 140) rightly points out, 'if we as researchers do not consider the evaluations of ordinary speakers of particular interactions as "polite" or "offensive", among other things, then we are neglecting an area of very real concern to such speakers'. Likewise, Locher (2015: 6) argues that 'one of the achievements of what has been termed the "discursive approaches to politeness research" was to again draw attention to the negotiability of the emic understandings of evaluative concepts such as "polite", "impolite", "rude", etc. ....'.

Having the above argument in mind, we explore the emic understandings of attentiveness (*kikubari*) and its related notions, namely, empathy (*omoiyari*)[2] and anticipatory inference (*sasshi*) (see Section 2.2.2) by Japanese participants of two different generations through metapragmatic[3] interviews in Section 4.2. Section 4.2 attempts to examine some cross-generational differences and similarities regarding these three concepts envisaged by the participants. Some aspects of moral order[4] among Japanese of two different generations will be revealed through the emic understandings of the above concepts.

Section 4.3 investigates attentiveness through the conceptualisation of politeness in Japanese cross-generationally. It is well documented that politeness is conceptualised differently across cultures (see, among others, Barros García and Terkourafi 2014; Haugh 2004, 2007a; Haugh and Hinze 2003; Hill et al. 1986; Ide, Hills, Carnes, Ogino and Kawasaki 2005 [1992]; Obana and Tomoda 1994; Pizziconi 2007; Sifianou 1992, 2011, 2015). However, *intra*cultural variation in cross-cultural politeness research is a rather neglected area (Kádár and Haugh 2013: 243; see also Culpeper and Haugh 2014: 297), and attention to the conceptualisation of politeness in different social subgroups within the same culture still seems to be limited (but see Sifianou and Tzanne 2010). Generation constitutes one of the social groups or subgroups, as noted in previous chapters. Thus, the variable of generation is included in the investigation in Section 4.3.

Generation is incorporated also because the results of Fukushima and Sifianou (2017) showed that both Japanese and Greek participants conceptualised politeness fairly similarly, despite the differences in their ethnicity and country of origin. Their conceptualisation differed from traditional ways of viewing politeness, including vertical relations and formalities, for example. Another significant similarity between Japanese and Greek participants was that politeness was often conceptualised as a non-linguistic manifestation, associated with morality and emotions. This aspect has not been thoroughly investigated in previous im/

politeness research, which has concentrated almost exclusively on linguistic performance. One of the reasons why Japanese and Greek participants in Fukushima and Sifianou (2017) appear to conceptualise politeness differently from the previous accounts may lie in the young age of the participants, as they were all university students in their late teens and early twenties. Building on Fukushima and Sifianou (2017), Section 4.3 explores whether a shift in the conceptualisation of politeness is indeed the case, given the young age of the participants, or not.

The meaning of the concept of *teineisa* ('politeness') or *teineina/teinei* ('polite'),[5] which is analogous to politeness in Japanese, may be changing. As it is beyond the scope of Section 4.3 to trace the meaning of politeness historically, Section 4.3 aims to investigate whether there is any change in the conceptualisation of politeness in Japanese relational networks in three decades (the age difference between two groups is about 30 years) (see Section 4.3.2). Attentiveness was one of the major constituents of politeness in Fukushima and Sifianou (2017). Whether this also applies to the Japanese participants of two different generations is investigated in Section 4.3.

Although the participants in Sections 4.2 and 4.3 differ, they are all Japanese females who are considered to belong to the middle class. Gender and class are controlled in order to focus on the variable of generation and to reduce the possible gender- or class-based influences on the data.

4.2 Emic understandings of attentiveness

In this section, we will investigate emic understandings of attentiveness and its related concepts, namely, anticipatory inference and empathy, by Japanese participants from two different age groups.

4.2.1 Data and methodology

In order to tease out the emic understandings of attentiveness, anticipatory inference and empathy by the Japanese, metapragmatic interviews were conducted in the mother tongue (namely, Japanese) of the participants.

Participants

Two groups of Japanese people served as the participants: (1) Japanese university students (JS) (age range: 20–22; mean age: 21.4) and (2) Japanese parents (JP) (age range: 46–60; mean age: 52.6). The participants in the second group were of approximately the same age as the parents of the university students (which is why they are called 'Japanese parents'), but they were not required to be related to the students. They were educated middle-class people. Each group consisted of ten people.

Procedure

The following questions were prepared for the interview:

1. Do you often infer the wishes or needs of the other party? If so, can you give us some examples?
2. Do you think showing empathy to others is important in your culture or in your daily life? If so, to what extent and why? If not, why not?
3. Do you think attentiveness is important in your culture or in your daily life? If so, to what extent and why? If not, why not?

The second part of each question ('If so, …?') was asked after the interviewee answered the first part of the question. Some questions (e.g., 'If not, why not?') were not always asked, depending on the answers given to the first part of each question. All the interviews were audio-recorded and transcribed. As the participants could state whatever they wanted in answering the questions, content analysis (Krippendorff 2013) was applied to the data analysis.

4.2.2 Results and discussion

The results show that there were both cross-generational differences and similarities. The differences emerged as salient in how the participants envisaged empathy. All the Japanese parents stated that showing empathy was important, whereas some Japanese students stated that it could be meddling. As regards the similarities, most of the participants would infer the other party's wishes or needs. The importance of attentiveness could also be regarded as a similarity. More detailed accounts of these results are presented below with some excerpts from the interview data.

Anticipatory inference

With regard to anticipatory inference, most of the participants stated that they would infer the other party's wishes or needs. However, there were some subtle differences between the Japanese participants of two different generations. Whereas all the Japanese parents stated that they would infer the other party's needs, JS2 in Example (4.1) stated that she would not infer the needs of the other party ('I' indicates the interviewer and 'JP2' the interviewee). In the English translations in the following examples, some words are added in { } for clarification, where necessary.

(4.1)

1   I: *Anata wa yoku (.) hoka no hito no youbou ya (.) niizu wo sasshi masu ka.*
          あなたはよく他の人の要望やニーズを察しますか。

          Do you often infer the wishes or needs of the other party?

2   JS2:   *Ee (.) amari sasshi nai hou dato omoi masu.*
えぇ、あまり察しない方だと思います。
Well, I don't think I infer them very often.

However, some Japanese students stated that they would infer the other party's needs (see Example [4.2]).

(4.2)

1   I: *Jaa (.) anata wa yoku (.) hoka no hito no youbou ya niizu wo (.) sasshi masu ka.*
じゃぁ、あなたはよく他の人の要望やニーズを察しますか。
Well, do you often infer the wishes or needs of the other party?

2   JS3:   *Hai (.) sassuru hou dato omoi masu.*
はい、察する方だと思います。
Yes, I think I do.

3   I: *Jaa (.) rei wo agete itadake masu ka.*
じゃぁ例を挙げて頂けますか。
Then, could you give us some examples?

4   JS3:   *Etto (.) tatoeba (0.8) etto (.) tanin (.) tomodachi de attari (.) tanin no (.) tanin ga (.)*
えっと、例えば、えっと他人、友達であったり、他人の、他人が、

5   *eeto (0.7) fudebako wo dashite ite (.) kuroi pen bakkari detekite (.)*
えぇと、筆箱を出していて、黒いペンばっかり出てきて
Well, for example, the other party or a friend takes out her pen case, well, {and} only black pens come out.

6   *hontou wa (.) sensei ga akai chooku de kaita kara (.) hoka no iro de kaete*
本当は先生が赤いチョークで書いたから、他の色で変えて

7   *kakitai noni (.) kuroi pen shika dete konakattara (.) hai (.) tte (.) orenji iro no*
書きたいのに黒いペンしか出てこなかったら、「はい」ってオレンジ色の

8   *pen toka (.) jibun no motte iru mono wo (.) age masu.*
ペンとか、自分の持っているものをあげます。
She wants to write in other colours as the professor wrote with red chalk. If only black pens came out {from her pen case}, I would hand her an orange pen, for instance, whatever I have, saying 'here'.

In Example (4.2), JS3 infers the other party's wants, namely, to write in different colours other than black (lines 6–7), and she states that she would hand the other party a different-coloured pen, which can be regarded as attentiveness (lines 7–8). It seems that anticipatory inference for JS3 includes the demonstration of attentiveness. Example (4.3) shows the understanding of anticipatory inference by a Japanese parent.

(4.3)

1   I: *Yoku (.) hoka no hito no youbou ya (.) niizu wo sasshi masu ka.*
よく他の人の要望やニーズを察しますか。
Do you often infer the wishes or needs of the other party?

2   JP1:   *(3.2) Sassuru hou dato omoi masu ga.*
察する方だと思いますが。
I think I do.

3   I: *Jaa (.) nanika rei wo agete itadaite (.) yoroshii de shou ka.*
じゃぁ何か例を挙げて頂いてよろしいでしょうか。
Well, then, could you cite any examples?

4   JP1:   *(2.0) A (3.4) uun rei wo ageru (1.0) sassuru hou da (.) uun (2.8) hito no jyoutai kana.*
あ、うぅん、例を挙げる、察する方だ、うぅん、人の状態かな。
Well, uh, to cite an example. I infer them, well, the state of people, maybe.

5   *Aa (.) nanika wo kochira kara tanonda toki ni (.) ee (.) ima isogashii jyoutai de*

6   *aru noka toka.*
あぁ、何かをこちらから頼んだ時に、えぇ、今忙しい状態であるのかとか。
Well, when I ask someone something, {I think about the state of people}, well, whether s/he is busy, or something like that.

7   I: *Aa.*
あぁ。
Uhhuh.

8   JP1:   *Hai (.) kono hito wa koremade no shigoto ga (.) dekiruka douka tte iu koto mo (.)*

9   *daitai wakari masu.*
はい。この人はこれまでの仕事ができるかどうかっていうこともだいたい分かります。
Yes, I can almost guess what kind of work s/he can do.

10   I: *Hai.*
はい。
Yes.

11   JP1:   *Hai (.) sono ue de (.) maa ano (.) kakunin wa shimasen keredo (.) koremade wa*

12   *dekiru darou to iu koto de (.) onegai wo suru youna koto wa ari masu.*
はい。その上でまぁあの確認はしませんけれど、これまではできるだろうということで、お願いをするようなことはあります。

Yes. Knowing/inferring the ability of that person, I ask {someone something}, although I do not confirm that.

13   I: *Sore wa riidaa to shite (.) tte iu shigoto gara desu yo ne.*

それはリーダーとしてっていう仕事柄ですよね。

That comes from your position as a leader {JP1 is the chief of a library and she is called a leader}, doesn't it?

14   JP1:   *Sou desu ne (.) hai. Sou desu ne. (.) Hito no shinjyou to shite (.) sou desu ne.*

そうですね、はい。そうですね。人の心情としてそうですね。

That's right. Yes. That's right. That's right, {from the perspective of} people's feelings.

15   *Ano (.) chotto taichou ga warui no kana (.) tte iu nomo daitai wakari masu. (.)*

あのちょっと体調が悪いのかなっていうのも大体分かります。

I can almost tell whether s/he is not in a good physical condition.

16   *Maa (.) jibun ga taichou yokumo nai (1.0) dakara daitai onaji youna katachi de (.)*

17   *maa (.) tsukarete iru toka (.)*

まぁ自分が体調良くもない、だから大体同じような形でまぁ疲れているとか

18   *kyou wa chotto choushi ga ii na (.) tte iu no wa (.) wakari masu ne.*

今日はちょっと調子がいいなっていうのは分かりますね。

Well, I am not in a very good physical condition. That's why I can tell s/he is also tired as I am, or s/he is in a good condition today.

19   I: *Sou iu no wo sasshite (.) maa (.) shigoto no shiji wo soreni oujite suru (.) tte iu koto*

20   *desu ne.*

そういうのを察してまぁ仕事の指示をそれに応じてするってことですね。

You infer that {the other party's condition} and you give {her/him} directions accordingly, do you?

21   JP1:   *Chotto hanashi kakeru toki nimo (.) daitai kou (.) ano (.) isogashiku nai youna*

22   *toki wo erande (.) o hanashi wo shitari (.) to iu koto wa shi masu.*

ちょっと話しかける時にも、大体こうあの忙しくないような
時を選んで、お話をしたりということはします。

Even when I talk to {other librarians} for a second, I try to talk to them when they are not busy.

Example (4.3) shows that JP1 infers the other party's condition, that is, whether someone is busy or in a good physical condition or not (lines 5, 15 and 17–18). She tries to ask someone to do something when the other party is not very busy (lines 21–22). This shows that JP1 (the boss) infers the subordinate's condition so that the other party can do what JP1 asks her/him to do. Moreover, JP1 knows the ability of the other party (lines 8–9), as JP1 has worked as a boss with other librarians for a certain amount of time. JP1 infers the other party's state (e.g., being busy or not) or physical condition, thinking of the other party as well as with regard to the efficiency of the work.

Empathy

Concerning the results for empathy, showing empathy to others was important to almost all of the participants. However, there was a subtle cross-generational difference in the degree of its importance. While all the Japanese parents stated that showing empathy to others was very important, two Japanese students stated that the degree of its importance was about 70% (see Examples [4.4] and [4.5]). Example (4.5) includes the excerpts after JS3 stated that empathy was important.

(4.4)

1   I: *Jaa (.) omoiyari wa anata no bunka ya nichijou seikatsu no naka de (.) juuyou dato*
2   *omoi masu ka.*

じゃぁ思い遣りはあなたの文化や日常生活の中で重要だと思います
か。

Well, do you think empathy is important in your culture or in your ordinary life?

3   JS2:   *Hai (.) juuyou dato omoi masu.*

はい、重要だと思います。

Yes, I think it is important.

4   I: *Dono teido deshou ka. (.) Chotto juuyou ka (.) soretomo sugoku juuyou ka.*

どの程度でしょうか。ちょっと重要か、それともすごく重要か。

To what extent? Is it a little important or very important?

5   JS2:   *(3.0) Sugoku to made wa ikanai desu kedo (.) nanawari gurai juuyou desu.*

すごくとまではいかないですけど7割位重要です。

I do not think it is very important, but it is about 70% important.

6   I: *Hai (.) jaa doushite deshou ka.*

はい、じゃぁどうしてでしょうか。

Yes, why is that?

7   JS2:   *Sono (1.0) osekkai ni nacchau toki mo (.) yappari aruja nai desu ka.*

その、お節介になっちゃう時もやっぱりあるじゃないですか。

Well, there are occasions when it can be meddling, aren't there?

8   *Aite ga nozonde inai noni (.) jibun ga ki wo kikasete (.) kaette ki wo waruku shichau*
9   *baai mo aru node.*

相手が望んでいないのに自分が気を利かせて却って気を悪くしちゃ
う場合もあるので。

The other party, who may not want that, may feel bad when I am attentive.

10   *Souiu fuu na (1.0) ano seki wo yuzuru baai mo (1.0) seki douzo tte itte mo (.)*
そういうふうな、あの席を譲る場合も「席どうぞ」って言っても
When I offered a seat, saying 'Have a seat',

11   *ii desu yo (.) tte kotowarare ta toki ni (.) aa (.) kore tte (.) yokei datta no kana tte*

12   *omottari shite shimau node.*
「いいですよ」って断られた時にあぁ、これって余計だったのかなって
思ったりしてしまうので。
the other party refused that, saying 'No thank you'. At that time, I thought that was
unnecessary.

(4.5)

1   I: *Jaa (.) dono teido juuyou de shou ka.*
じゃぁどの程度重要でしょうか。
Then, to what extent is {empathy} important?

2   JS3:   *Nanajuu paasento teido dato omoi masu.*
70% 程度だと思います。
Well, I think it is about 70% {important}.

3   I: *Naze desu ka.*
何故ですか。
Why is that?

4   JS3:   *Etto (.) yappari omoiyari ga atta hou ga (.) hito tono komyunikeeshon ga sumuuzu ni*
えっと、やっぱり思い遣りがあった方が人とのコミュニケーション
がスムーズに

5   *iku to omou to iuno to (1.0) eeto (.) yahari jibun de nandemo kandemo itte shima tte*
いくと思うというのと、えぇと、やはり自分で何でもかんでも言っ
てしまって

6   *hito ni yatte morau nowa (.) jibun wa ki ga hikeru to omou node.*
人にやってもらうのは自分は気がひけると思うので。
Well, I think we can communicate with each other smoothly with empathy. I would
not feel comfortable if I were to say everything {I wanted} and other people did that
for me.

7   *Omoiyari ga atta hou ga (.) eeto (.) ii to omoi masu.*
思い遣りがあった方が、えぇといいと思います。
I think it is better to have empathy.

8   *Sono mainasu sanjuu paasento wa (.) sokoni tayotte wa ikenai to iu tokoro desu.*

そのマイナス30%はそこに頼ってはいけないという所です。

However, we should not depend on that. That's why it's minus 30%.

JS2 in Example (4.4) stated that showing empathy could sometimes be seen as meddling (line 7), and JS3 in Example (4.5) stated that we should not depend on empathy (line 8). These Japanese students did not necessarily evaluate empathy negatively, as they acknowledged its importance. These statements include doing something for others (e.g., offering a seat; line 10 in Example [4.4]), which can be regarded as attentiveness; and JS2 used the words, *ki wo kikase te* ('attentive') (line 8). It can be said that empathy for these Japanese students includes doing something and being attentive.[6] This shows that the participants did not always distinguish empathy from attentiveness. JS2 pointed out the possibility that the other party may not want the attentiveness, and consequently s/he may feel bad (lines 8–9 in Example [4.4]). That is where the feelings or emotions[7] of meddle-someness emerge on the part of a recipient of attentiveness. On such an occasion, JS2 thought that was unnecessary (lines 11–12 in Example [4.4]). This is why JS2 answered that empathy was about 70% important (line 5 in Example [4.4]).

JS3 did not clearly state that the other party inferred her needs and did something for her, but she mentioned that she would not feel comfortable (or would feel embarrassed) if she said everything (she wanted) and other people did that for her (lines 5–6 in Example [4.5]). In other words, JS3 prefers a communication style with anticipatory inference, and she appreciates when somebody demonstrates attentiveness; that is, when someone infers her needs and does something for her, even when she does not state her desires clearly. The elements of anticipatory inference and attentiveness are included in her comments on empathy. This may resonate with the contention that anticipatory inference is related to empathy, as noted in Section 2.2.1. This also indicates that the three concepts investigated in this section are related to each other. The statement by JS3 also supports earlier views (e.g., Tsujimura 1987) that anticipatory inference is important in Japanese communication.

Although there were some subtle cross-generational differences concerning empathy as noted above, empathy was important for almost all of the Japanese students and Japanese parents (see Examples [4.6] and [4.7]). Examples (4.6) and (4.7) include excerpts after the participants stated that empathy was important.

(4.6)

1   I: *Dono teido juuyou de shou ka.*

どの程度重要でしょうか。

To what extent is {empathy} important?

2   JS10:   (1.9) *Yappa hito wa hitori ja ikite ikenai to omou node*
やっぱ人は一人じゃ生きていけないと思うので
Well, people cannot live alone, I think.

3   (0.6) *yappa* (1.2) *shitashii* (.) *ano kazoku toka no naka demo yahari* (0.9)
やっぱ、親しいあの家族とかの中でもやはり

4   *omoiyari wa* (0.9) *ano* (0.6) *sono ningen kankei wo yoi mono ni shite ikutte iu nomo*
思い遣りはあの、その人間関係を良いものにしていくっていうのも
Well, even among close family members, I think empathy is important, as it makes
our human relationships good.

5   *soudesu shi* (1.2) *hai* (1.2) *kou uun* (.) *sumi yasui kankyou ni surutte iu nomo* (1.4)

6   *taisetsu dato omoi masu.*
そうですし、はい、こう、うぅん住みやすい環境にするっていうの
も、大切だと思います。
I think it is also important to make our environment easy to live in.

(4.7)

1   I: *Naze* (.) *kou omoiyari tte* (.) *juuyou nande shou ka.*
何故、こう思い遣りって重要なんでしょうか。
Why is empathy important?

2   *Maa wakari kitta youna shitsumon kamo shirenai desu kedo* (.) *nanika o hanashi*

3   *itadake masu ka.*
まぁ分かりきったような質問かもしれないですけど、何かお話頂け
ますか。
It may be a self-evident question, but could you tell us something about that?

4   JP10:   *E* (1.0) *omoiyari ga naze hitsuyou ka.* (4.0)
え、思い遣りが何故必要か。
Well, why is empathy important?

5   *E* (.) *yappari omoiyari ga naito* (.) *ningen kankei ga naritata nain ja nai ka* (.) *tte*

6   *omoi masu keredo.*
え、やっぱり思い遣りがないと人間関係が成り立たないんじゃない
かって思いますけれど。
Well, I think we cannot establish human relationships well without empathy.

7   *Yappari* (.) *hito wo omou kokoro desu kara.*
やっぱり人を思う心ですから。
After all,{empathy means having} the heart to think about others.

Both JS10 and JP10 think that empathy is important, as it contributes to
establishing good human relationships (line 4 in Example [4.6] and lines 5–6 in

Example [4.7]). Human relationships (*ningen kankei*) in these examples mean interpersonal relations (see Haugh et al. 2013), which encompass 'mutual social connections amongst people that are mediated by interaction, including power, intimacy, roles, rights and obligations' (Culpeper and Haugh 2014: 197). 'Mutual social connections amongst people' are related to the statement by JS10, namely that people cannot live alone (line 2 in Example [4.6]). Thus, it is important to think of others. Indeed, empathy means 'having the heart to think about others', according to JP10 (line 7 in Example [4.7]). This may imply the importance of the heart perspective in politeness research (see Intachakra 2012), although further investigation is needed.

Empathy is further clarified with some more examples (see Example [4.8]).

(4.8)

1   I: *Omoiyari wa (.) anata no bunka toka nichijyou seikatsu no naka de (.) jyuuyou dato*

2   *omoi masu ka.*

思い遣りはあなたの文化とか日常生活の中で重要だと思いますか。

Do you think empathy is important in your culture or in your daily life?

3   JP9:   *Aa sou desu ne. (.) Hai.*

あぁそうですね。はい。

Well, that's right. Yes.

4   I: *Do no teido desu ka.*

どの程度ですか。

To what extent?

5   JP9:   *Eeto (.) dono teido tte iuno wa (.) eeto*

えぇと、どの程度っていうのは、えぇと

What do you mean by 'to what extent'?

6   I: *Sugoku jyuuyou desu ka.*

すごく重要ですか。

Is {empathy} very important?

7   JP9:   *Aa (.) yappari sou desu ne. (.) Sou desu ne. (.) Omoiyatte sou desu ne (.) koudou suru*

8   *koto wa (.) taisetsu dato omoi masu node.*

あぁ、やっぱりそうですね。そうですね。思いやってそうですね、行動することは大切だと思いますので。

Well, after all, that's right. That's right. I think it is important to act, thinking of {others}.

9   I: *Jaa (.) ano doushite desu ka.*

じゃぁ、あのどうしてですか。

Well, why is that?

10   JP9:   *Yahari (.) omoiyaru tte koto wa (.) aite no tachiba ni mo tatsu (.) tte koto nanode.*
やはり思い遣るってことは相手の立場にも立つってことなので。
Well, to have empathy is to stand in the other party's place.

JP9's understanding of empathy (line 10) coincides with Lebra's (1993: 72) definition of empathy, that is, 'to become another's *mi*', which means 'standing in someone else's shoes'.

   Another Japanese parent thinks that empathy is very important (see Example [4.9]).

(4.9)

1   I: *Omoiyari wa anata no bunka ya nichijyou seikatsu de (.) jyuuyou dato omoi masu ka.*
思い遣りはあなたの文化あるいは日常生活の中で重要だと思いますか。
Do you think empathy is important in your culture or in your daily life?

2   JP5:   *Sou desu ne. (.) Hai.*
そうですね。はい。
That's right. Yes.

3   I: *Jaa (.) dono teido jyuuyou deshou ka.*
じゃぁ、どの程度重要でしょうか。
Well, to what extent is {empathy} important?

4   JP5:   *(2.1) Uun kekkou ookina hijyuu wo shimete iru to omoi masu.*
うぅん、結構大きな比重を占めてると思います。
Well, it accounts for a fairly big proportion, I think.

5   I: *Jaa (.) naze desu ka. (.) Naze tte iu nowa (.) chotto iinikui kamo shire masen kedo.*
じゃぁ、何故ですか。何故っていうのちょっと言いにくいかもしれませんけど。
Well, why is that? It may be difficult to say why, though.

6   JP5:   *Unn (.) tatoeba shinsai ga ari mashi ta yo ne. (.)*
うぅん、例えば震災がありましたよね。
Well, for example, there was an earthquake, wasn't there?

7   *De (.) yappari ima watashi ga ichiban omotte iru nowa (.)*
で、やっぱり今私が一番思ってるのは

8   *ano (.) watashi jishin ga Sendai no shusshin nanode.*
あの私自身が仙台の出身なので。
What I think now most is, well, I myself come from Sendai {the name of a city}.

9   I: *Sou deshi ta yo ne. (.) Goryoushin wa daijyoubu deshi ta ka.*
そうでしたよね。御両親は大丈夫でしたか。

>   That's right. Are your parents all right?
>
> 10   JP5:   *Daijyoubu desu. (.) Hai. De (.) kono aida kisei shite kitan desu kedo (.)*
>   大丈夫です。はい。で、この間帰省してきたんですけど
>   They are all right. Yes. Well, I went back to my hometown recently.
>
> 11   *maa (.) genchi wo mite (.) yappari sono hisai shita hitotachi ni (.)*
>
> 12   *nani ga dekirundarou tte (.) monosugoku atte (.)*
>   まぁ現地を見てやっぱりその被災した人たちに
>   何ができるんだろうってものすごくあって
>   Well, looking at the scene, I wondered a lot what I could do for the disaster victims.
>
> 13   *soreto douji ni (.) ichiban ookikatta noga (.) yappari Fukushima no asoko wa ano:*
>   それと同時に一番大きかったのがやっぱり福島の、あそこはあのー
>   At the same time, what I thought most was about Fukushima {where nuclear power plants were damaged}, well,
>
> 14   *nante iundarou (1.0) fukkou shiyou nimo (.) sono fukkou no kiban jitai ga dame ni*
>
> 15   *nacchateru kara (.)*
>   何て言うんだろう、復興しようにも、その復興の基盤自体が駄目に
>   なっちゃってるから
>   how to put it, the basis of recovery is damaged, even though one tries to recover it.
>
> 16   *yappashi souiu koto wo kangaeru to (.) teiuka ano: souiu hitotachi no kimochi wo*
>
> 17   *omoiyaru tte koto ga (.) mazu zentei jya naikana to (.)*
>   やっぱしそういうことを考えると、ていうかあのー、そういう人達
>   の気持ちを
>   思い遣るってことがまず前提じゃないかなと
>   When I think of that, after all, well, it may be a premise to think of the feelings of those people.
>
> 18   *souiu hisai ni atta hitotachi ga (.) donna omoi wo shiterun darou (.) tte iu koto wo (.)*
>   そういう被災に遭った人達がどんな思いをしてるんだろうっていう
>   ことを
>
> 19   *sono kangaeru (.) tte iu no wa (.) yappari (.) ningen toshite wa (.) kihonteki na sutansu*
>
> 20   *jya naikana (.) to omou node.*
>   その考えるっていうのはやっぱり人間としては基本的なスタンス
>   じゃないかなと思うので。
>   I think it is a basic attitude as human beings, after all, to think how those disaster victims feel.

JP5, who thinks that empathy is very important, refers to the great earthquake which hit Japan on 11 March 2011.[8] JP5 is originally from Sendai (a city in Tohoku, the northern part of Japan; line 8), where there was great damage. Returning to her hometown and encountering the reality of the situation, she thinks of the disaster victims. According to JP5, to think of the feelings of the victims is a basic attitude for human beings (lines 16–20), which confirms Bousfield's (2016) understanding of empathy, that is, our understanding of empathy appears to be one defining common denominator for human responses to external stimuli involving other humans (see Section 2.2.2). It is shown in Example (4.9) that people empathise also with those whom they do not necessarily know personally.

Attentiveness

The participants of both generations stated that attentiveness was important in Japanese relational networks. Thus, a cross-generational similarity was found for the perspective of attentiveness, although there was a subtle difference (see the discussion below). Examples (4.10) and (4.11) show the excerpts after the participants stated that attentiveness was very important.

(4.10)

1   I: *Doushite desu ka.*
どうしてですか。
Why is that?

2   JS1:   (1.0) *Etto yahari sakihodo no omoiyari to onaji youni (.) sono kizukai wo shite (.)*
えっと、やはり先ほどの思い遣りと同じようにその気遣いをして

3   *sarete to iu kankyou no naka de sodatta koto mo aru node (.)*
されてという環境の中で育ったこともあるので
Well, it is the same as empathy. I was brought up in an environment where people demonstrate attentiveness to each other.

4   *yahari (1.0) watashi ga suru koto mo nan desu ka ne (.) nichijou teki dato*
やはり私がすることも何ですかね、日常的だと

5   *omoi masu shi (.) tabun sarenai (.) tte iu koto mo (.) chotto nante iun desu ka ne (.)*

6   *fukai dewa nai keredo* (3.0)
思いますし、多分されないっていうことも、ちょっと、何て言うんですかね、
不快ではないけれど
Well, it is an ordinary thing that I demonstrate attentiveness, I think. Perhaps, if someone does not demonstrate attentiveness, what to say, I would not say I feel unpleasant, but …

7   *sasshite hoshii noni na (.) tte iu toki ni (.) watashi ga mawari ni sasshite morae nai to*
察してほしいのになっていう時に私が周りに察してもらえないと
If I want the other party to infer my needs and people around me do not infer them,

8   *yahari chotto* (2.0) *douiu kibun nan darou* (2.0) *uun* (1.0) *iradachi dewa nai desu kedo*

やはりちょっと、 どういう気分なんだろう、うぅん、 苛立ではない
ですけど

I would feel, well, what kind of feelings do I have, well, it may be a little different from irritation, but

9　　*kizuite hoshii na (.) mitai na fuu ni omotte (.)*
「気づいてほしいな」 みたいなふうに思って

I want someone to infer my needs {be attentive}.

10　　*ma (.) sore wa koutei teki na kanjou dewa nakute (.) hitei teki na kanjou wo*
ま、それは肯定的な感情ではなくて否定的な感情を

11　　*idaku node (.) ningen kankei wo (.) kizukai ga nai to (.) ningen kankei wo ryoukou ni*
抱くので、人間関係を、気遣いがないと人間関係を良好に

12　　*tamotsu ue de wa (.) shougai kana (.) to iu fuu ni omoi masu.*
保つ上では障害かなというふうに思います。

Well, I have negative feelings, not positive ones. So, it would be troublesome to establish good human relationships without attentiveness, I think.

JS1's statement in Example (4.10) suggests that demonstrating attentiveness is in a way taken for granted, as she grew up in an environment where attentiveness was demonstrated (lines 2–4). JS1 has negative feelings when attentiveness is not demonstrated or the other party does not infer her needs (lines 5–10). This means that attentiveness is very important in Japanese relational networks. Moreover, JS1 thinks it would be difficult to maintain good human relationships if there were no attentiveness (lines 11–12).

(4.11)

1　I:　　*Jaa (.) naze desu ka.*
じゃぁ、何故ですか。
Why is that?

2　JP10:　*Naze desu ka (2.0) kikubari ga naito yahari (.) hito to nanika (.) shoutotsu shite*
3　　　　*shimau ki ga shi masu.*
何故ですか。気配りがないとやはり人と何か衝突してしまう気がし
ます。

Why? Without attentiveness we collide with people, I feel.

JP10 in Example (4.11) states that without attentiveness we collide with people (lines 2–3). This suggests that attentiveness is definitely needed in Japanese relational networks. The statement above by JP10 implies that in a way attentiveness plays the role of a lubricant when dealing with people. These statements are related to those on empathy (that is, empathy is important in interpersonal relations). We can see a close link between empathy and attentiveness here. Both

Examples (4.10) and (4.11) are related to interpersonal relations. In other words, attentiveness is important when people deal with others in Japanese relational networks.

Attentiveness entails the elements of empathy and inference for some participants. Inferring the other party's needs is almost identical to attentiveness for JS10 (see Example [4.12], which shows excerpts after JS10 has stated that attentiveness was important).

(4.12)

1   I: *Jaa (.) dono teido daiji deshou ka.*

じゃぁ、どの程度大事でしょうか。

Well, to what extent is {attentiveness} important?

2   JS10:   (1.3) *Dono teido* (1.2) *yappa nihon* (0.8) *nihonjin wa yahari* (0.6) *aite no*

どの程度、やっぱ、日本、日本人はやはり、相手の

3   *tachiba ni tattara* (.) *iwa nakute mo* (0.5) *maa sassuru toka tte iu koto ga* (0.4)

立場に立ったら言わなくても、まぁ察するとかっていうことが

4   *maa (.) kikubari janai kana to omotte (.) sorede (.) naritatteru bubun mo (.)*

5   *iroiro aru to omou node.*

まぁ気配りじゃないかなと思って、それで成り立ってる部分も色々あると思うので。

To what extent? If Japan, or the Japanese people, after all, consider things, standing in the other party's position, even though {the other party} does not say anything, well, to infer {the other party's needs} is attentiveness, I think. That's how {our society} is formed, I think.

For JS10, who thinks that attentiveness is important in Japanese society, attentiveness seems to be understood as a mixture of empathy and anticipatory inference. According to JS10, to stand in the other party's position or *tachiba* (the 'place one stands'; Haugh 2005: 47) and to infer the other party's needs are formative for Japanese society (lines 2–5). This 'standing in the other party's position' may relate to Lebra's (1993: 72) expression for *omoiyari*, namely, 'to become another's *mi*', which is similar to 'to feel what others are feeling' (Lebra 1976: 38) and to stand 'in the place of the other party' (Uchida and Kitayama 2001: 276). The statement by JS10 (lines 2–5) partly coincides with Uchida's (2011: 51) view, namely that Japanese society is formed by depending on empathy. In Example (4.12), we can see an overlap between attentiveness and empathy. Furthermore, it is worth noting that anticipatory inference, which is needed for attentiveness to arise, is included in the understanding of attentiveness by JS10 (line 3–4).

All of the participants think that attentiveness is important. However, there was a subtle cross-generational difference in the degree of its importance (see Example [4.13]).

(4.13)

1   I: *Jaa (.) kikubari wa anata no bunka ya nichijyou seikatsu no naka de (.) jyuuyou dato*

2   *omoi masu ka.*

じゃぁ、気配りはあなたの文化や日常生活の中で重要だと思いますか。

Well, do you think attentiveness is important in your culture or in your daily life?

3   JS3:   *Hai.*

はい。

Yes.

4   I: *Dono teido jyuuyou de shou ka.*

どの程度重要でしょうか。

To what extent is {attentiveness} important?

5   JS3:   *Nanajyuu paasento kurai.*

70 ％くらい。

About 70 %.

6   I: *Naze de shou ka.*

何故でしょうか。

Why is that?

7   JS3:   *Etto (.) ki wo kubarareta hito wa yahari (.) eeto (.) ureshii to omoi masu shi (.)*

えっと、気を配られた人はやはり、えぇと嬉しいと思いますし

Well, one who receives attentiveness feels good, after all, I think.

8   *kikubari shite ageru hito mo (.) warui ki wa shinai to omoi masu.*

気配りをしてあげる人も悪い気はしないと思います。

One who demonstrates attentiveness does not feel bad, I think.

9   *Tada (.) etto (.) ikisugiruto osekkai ni natte shimau koto ga aru node (.) mainasu no*

10   *sanjuu paasento desu.*

ただ、えっと行き過ぎるとお節介になってしまうことがあるので、マイナスの

30％です。

However, well, excessive {attentiveness} can be meddling. That's why it is minus 30%.

JS3 in Example (4.13) stated that attentiveness was about 70% important (line 5), as excessive attentiveness could be seen as meddling (line 9). However, this does not necessarily mean that JS3 has a negative evaluation of attentiveness. As noted in the comments on empathy, JS3 seems to prefer a communication style that includes anticipatory inference and attentiveness (see Example [4.5]).

It does not directly relate to the importance of attentiveness; however, it is worth noting the comments by JS3 (line 8). That is, a demonstrator of attentiveness feels good. This may be linked to the feelings of accomplishment or self-respect of a demonstrator of attentiveness, as noted in Section 2.2.3.

All the Japanese parents stated that attentiveness was very important. JP6, in particular, stressed the importance of attentiveness (see Example [4.14]).

(4.14)

1   I: *Kikubari wa (.) anata no bunka toka (.) nichijou seikatsu no naka de (.) juuyou dato*

2   *omoi masu ka.*

       気配りはあなたの文化とか日常生活の中で重要だと思いますか。

       Is attentiveness important in your culture or in your daily life?

3   JP6: *Kikubari (1.0) juuyou dato omoi masu.*

       気配り、重要だと思います。

       Attentiveness, I think it is important.

4   *Kono (.) kikubari (.) tte iu no wa (.) chotto tonchinkan dato (.) watashi niwa yoku*

5   *etto (.) chikaku ni iru hito ni (1.0) dekite nai ne (.) tte iwareru.*

       この気配りっていうのはちょっととんちんかんだと、私にはよく、えっと近くにいる人にできてないねって言われる。

       If I demonstrate irrelevant attentiveness, someone close to me points that out.

6   I: *Dakara (.) juuyou dato omotteru (.) tte koto desu yo ne.*

       だから、重要だと思ってるってことですよね。

       So, you think attentiveness is important, don't you?

7   JP6: *Aa (.) hai (.) omotte masu (.) omotte masu.*

       あぁはい、思ってます、思ってます。

       Well, yes, I think so. I think so.

8   I: *Jaa (.) dono teido tte yappari (.) nan paasento toka (.) sugoku toka (.) sugoku daiji.*

       じゃぁどの程度って、やっぱり何パーセントとか、すごくとか、すごく大事。

       Then, to what extent, how much percent, {is attentiveness} very, very important?

9   JP6: *Un (.) daiji desu yo ne. (.) Sore dekinakya ningen ja nai tte iu ka. (.) Hahaha (.)*

10   *otona ja nai jan (.) mitaina.*

       うん、大事ですよね。それできなきゃ人間じゃないっていうか。ははは、大人じゃないじゃんみたいな。

       Yeah, it is important. If one cannot do that {demonstrate attentiveness}, one is not a human being {laughter}, or one is not mature, or something like that.

JP6 comments on the importance of demonstrating appropriate or relevant attentiveness (lines 4–5). This suggests that it is important to infer the other party's needs correctly and to demonstrate attentiveness as the other party expects in Japanese relational networks. Moreover, it is worth noting that the ability to demonstrate attentiveness is indispensable for one's maturity, according to JP6 (lines 9–10). The statement by JP6 entails the elements of being really human and morally mature, which coincide with Lebra's (1976: 38) interpretation of empathy. As Lebra (1976) includes an aspect of attentiveness (in my terms) in her definition of empathy, the elements above may also apply to attentiveness; that is, demonstrating attentiveness includes the elements of being human and morally mature. Here there seems to be some kind of connection between attentiveness and morality (see also Section 2.2.1), although further scrutiny is needed.

The next section further investigates attentiveness in Japanese relational networks from the perspective of the conceptualisation of politeness.

4.3 Attentiveness and politeness

In the previous section, we investigated the emic understandings of attentiveness and its related concepts cross-generationally in Japanese relational networks. In this section, we consider attentiveness cross-generationally through the conceptualisation of politeness in Japanese. First, the theoretical background of politeness research is reviewed, and then the data and methodology of this section are presented. Results and discussion follow.

4.3.1 Theoretical background

The definition of *teinei* ('politeness') by Shinmura (2018: 1986) includes *chuui bukaku kokoro ga iki todoku koto* ('attentive') and *teatsuku reigi tadashii koto* ('warm-hearted' and 'good manners') (see also Haugh and Obana 2011: 150). Various aspects which indicate vertical relations were noted in previous research on the conceptualisation of politeness in Japanese, for example, *keii* ('respect') in Ide et al. (2005 [1992]) and Haugh (2004); *jooge kankei* ('vertical relations') in Obana and Tomoda (1994); *enryo* ('restraint') in Obana and Tomoda (1994), Haugh (2004) and Pizziconi (2007); *hikaeme* ('discrete') in Obana and Tomoda (1994): *herikudaru* ('humble') and *kenkyona* ('modest' or 'humble') in Pizziconi (2007). Some other concepts which do not necessarily indicate vertical relations were also noted in the conceptualisation of *teinei* ('politeness') in previous studies, for example, *omoiyari no aru*[9] ('considerate') in Ide et al. (2005 [1992]) and in Pizziconi (2007); *shinsetsu* ('kind') in Haugh (2004) and in Pizziconi (2007); *teatsui* ('warm') in Haugh (2004); and *seijitsu* ('sincere') in Pizziconi (2007).

Ide et al. (2005 [1992]) also included *tekisetsuna* ('appropriate') in their research on the concept of politeness. They link that to *wakimae* ('discernment'), which was also noted in Obana and Tomoda (1994) and Pizziconi (2007). According to Hill et al. (1986: 348), '[w]*akimae* refers to the almost automatic observation of socially agreed-upon rules applied to both verbal and non-verbal behavior', and '[a] capsule definition would be "conforming to the expected norms"'. According to Ide (2012: 136), *wakimae* literally means 'social norms according to which people are expected to behave in order to be appropriate in the society in which they live'. Matsumoto (1988, 1989) and Ide (1989) claim that Japanese politeness is different from Western politeness, challenging Brown and Levinson's (1978, 1987) theory of universal politeness. Matsumoto (1989) claims that Japanese politeness is centred on discernment (*wakimae*). Ide (1989) categorises politeness into the discernment type and the volitional type, Japanese politeness being categorised as the former (see also Hill et al. 1986).

Some scholars, especially those from non-Western countries (e.g., de Kadt 1998; Mao 1994; Nwoye 1992), agreed with the claims of Ide (1989) and Matsumoto (1988, 1989). However, such a notion of discernment was challenged by other researchers. According to Kádár and Mills (2013: 143), discernment should be seen as 'the theoretical translation of a folk-theoretical concept, which describes *the socially dominant norms of relationally constructive conventional and ritualistic behaviour*' (emphasis in original). According to Kádár (2013: 179), Ide (1989) places the interface between social ritual and politeness under the umbrella of discernment and contrasts this interface with non-ritualistic politeness, but she fails to define the relationship between politeness and ritual.[10] Indeed, some other researchers (see, e.g., Fukada and Asato 2004; Fukushima 2000: 58–59; Pizziconi 2003: 1473; 2011: 65; Watts 2003: 83) also question the validity of the notion of discernment as espoused by Ide (1989). Kádár and Mills (2013) argue that the polarisation of discernment and volition developed by Ide (1989) is problematic, as it does not capture politeness behaviour beyond certain stereotypes, and as such it fails to address the complexities with which a cross-cultural examination of politeness needs to cope (see also Section 3.2). According to Kádár and Mills (2013: 137), Ide (1989) arguably makes a cross-cultural overgeneralisation when she contrasts '*wakimae* dominant society' and 'volition dominant society'. Kádár (2013: 179) further states that 'the relational differences that the notion of discernment and volition imply are not so much related to politeness per se but rather to rituality'.

Honorifics[11] play an important role in politeness in Japanese, according to some previous studies. For example, Suzuki (2007: 71) states that politeness in Japanese almost equates to the proper use of honorifics. *Keigo* ('honorifics') was included in the conceptualisation of politeness in Japanese (Obana and Tomoda 1994). According to Haugh and Obana (2011: 147), much of the work on politeness in Japanese to date has inherited a predisposition to explicating politeness primarily in relation to honorifics. Pizziconi (2011) also demonstrates the importance of honorifics in Japanese, although her stance towards honorifics is slightly different from that of some other researchers.[12]

Indexicality of honorifics may vary, for example, showing respect for the social status of others (thereby giving rise to politeness), showing empathy, indexing the speaker's self-presentational stance among other things (Haugh and Obana 2011: 150; see also Cook 2006; Okamoto 1997, 1999; Pizziconi 2003; Yoshida and Sakurai 2005). Indexing the speaker's self-presentation through honorifics is somewhat similar to a demonstration of a polished self-presentation, which was found in politeness in English (Haugh 2004: 97). Furthermore, the data by Pizziconi (2007: 229) show that a polished self-presentation is a by-product of being polite in both English and Japanese. Indexing self-presentation through the proper use of honorifics may also show good education (see, e.g., Coulmas 2005 [1992]).

Dunn (2013) attempted to clarify the conceptualisation of politeness in Japanese through the business etiquette training provided for new employees in Japanese companies. In those training courses, three broad themes that comprise the concept of politeness are found. They are (1) displaying deference, which is closely related to the use of honorifics, (2) speaking in ways which are kind or showing consideration towards the addressee and (3) speaking in ways which are beautiful, which also includes the display of an appropriate demeanour. The second theme includes not only the use of so-called cushion words (e.g., *mooshi-wake gozaimasen* 'There is no excuse' or *osore irimasu* 'I'm sorry' before asking someone for their name or informing them that the person to whom they wished to speak was currently unavailable), but also includes speaking in ways that are easy to understand.

In relation to the second theme, Dunn (2013: 237) states that '[s]tudents in the manners classes were instructed to consider things from the other person's perspective (*aite no tachiba ni tatte, kangae*), which is similar to Lebra's (1993: 72) understandings of empathy, namely, *aite no mi ni naru* ("to stand in someone else's shoes"), and to put the other person's feelings first (*aite no kimochi wo saki ni suru*)'. Here we can see that empathy is closely involved. Dunn (2013: 237) further states that '[s]peaking kindly was not only a matter of memorizing appropriate "cushion phrases", but of actively *anticipating* customers' wants' (emphasis added). Although the term 'attentiveness' was not used, 'anticipating customers' wants' corresponds to the second stage[13] of demonstrating attentiveness, namely, inferring the other party's needs, wants and feelings (see Section 2.2.3), and is related to business-oriented attentiveness (see Example [2.17]), as noted in Section 2.2.1. We can see a close connection between attentiveness and the conceptualisation of politeness in Japanese.

4.3.2 Data and methodology

Any data elicitation methodology – for example, authentic discourse, elicited conversation, role play, discourse completion tasks, multiple choice questionnaires, rating scale questionnaires, interviews, diaries, verbal report – has advantages and disadvantages (see, e.g., Kasper 2008). We need to select a methodology which suits our research purpose. As the aim of this section is to collect data as widely as possible, open-ended questionnaires, in which the participants could write anything, were chosen. Furthermore, questionnaires were used because they offer further insights into the metalinguistic awareness of cultural insiders or members (Kádár and Haugh 2013: 193), and it would be possible to gather more general patterns through questionnaires than through situation-specific interactions (Fukushima and Sifianou 2017).

Participants

The participants were 200 Japanese people of two different age groups, who had no prior engagement with theoretical issues of politeness: 100 Japanese university students[14] (age range: 18–24; mean age: 20.51) and 100 Japanese adults (age range: 40–59; mean age: 49.92). As the age of the latter group was approximately that of the university students' parents, they are called 'Japanese parents' (JP) hereafter in order to distinguish them from 'Japanese students' (JS). In this section, the variable of generation is focused on in the investigation of politeness conceptualisation. There are many subgroups or dimensions within a culture other than generation (see Section 3.2). In order to focus on the generation, other factors (e.g., gender and social class), which may influence the conceptualisation of politeness, were controlled as much as possible. Thus, the participants were all females and they were either university students (JS) or staff working at the university (JP). The participants were considered to belong to the middle class in a broad sense.

Procedure

Open-ended questionnaires were distributed to the participants. Questionnaires were anonymous, and what the participants were asked to fill in concerning their personal background was only their age. Participants were asked how they would conceptualise politeness (*teineisa*) in Japanese.

The data obtained were categorised into the following, which was devised in Fukushima and Sifianou (2017): (1) consideration to others and (2) appropriate behaviour. The first broad category, consideration to others, includes attentiveness, empathy, respect and attitude.[15] The second major category, appropriate behaviour, includes honorifics, general use of language[16] (e.g., wording, beautiful way of speaking and greetings), good manners (including bows), demeanour/deportment (e.g., posture, good/clean appearance) and smiling/pleasant disposition. While honorifics and general use of language are considered as linguistically manifested appropriate behaviour,[17] good manners, demeanour/deportment and smiling/pleasant disposition are considered as non-linguistically manifested appropriate behaviour.

4.3.3 Results and discussion

The results (see Table 4.1) show that there were no major differences between the conceptualisation of politeness by Japanese students and that by Japanese parents overall. The conceptualisation of politeness by the participants (both Japanese students and Japanese parents) in this section did not include what has often been noted in previous research findings (e.g., vertical relations, discretion, modesty, restraint, being humble, reserve and *wakimae* ['discernment']), as noted in Section 4.3.1. Not only the Japanese students, but also the Japanese parents, who were almost 30 years older than the Japanese students, conceptualised politeness differently from a traditional view which includes vertical relations. This indicates that a shift in the conceptualisation of politeness is under way, and different views are not solely the result of young age (see Fukushima and Sifianou 2017).

Another significant similarity between the results of the Japanese students and those of the Japanese parents was that the non-linguistic aspect predominated over the linguistic one, although this should not be taken to mean that linguistically manifested aspects of politeness are not important. These results may, in part at least, confirm that 'politeness is a social practice rather than a simple manifestation of language' (Kádár and Haugh 2013: 4). It should be noted that, despite the importance of non-linguistic aspects, they have been rather neglected in previous politeness research in Japanese (but see Fukushima and Sifianou 2017).

Table 4.1: Conceptualisation of politeness by Japanese students and Japanese parents

Categories	Sub-categories		Japanese students	Japanese parents
Consideration to others		Attentiveness	29	25
		Empathy	25	33
		Respect	11	10
		Attitude	9	8
Appropriate behaviour	Linguistically appropriate behaviour	Honorifics	19	7
		General use of language	39	25
	Non-linguistically appropriate behaviour	Good manners	20	14
		Demeanour/ deportment	23	10
		Smiling/pleasant disposition	9	7

This may be partly because politeness in Japanese has been sometimes conflated with honorifics (namely, the linguistic aspect). In what follows, the results are presented according to the broad categories consideration to others and appropriate behaviour.

As mentioned above, consideration to others includes attentiveness, empathy, respect and attitude. Both Japanese students (29) and Japanese parents (25) in this section seem to consider attentiveness as an important constituent of politeness. Some responses did not include the term 'attentiveness' and some other responses included more than just 'attentiveness'. However, what all of these responses meant was attentiveness. For example, *nanigoto ni mo chuui bukaku kokoro ga iki todoite iru* ('doing anything carefully and being attentive') and *aite no ito wo kumitoru* ('inferring the other party's intention') were noted by the Japanese students. The first response is similar to the definition of *teinei* ('politeness') by Shinmura (2018: 1986), that is, *chuui bukaku kokoro ga iki todoku koto* ('attentive'). This shows a close connection between attentiveness and politeness. The second response above is inference, which is required in order to demonstrate attentiveness (see Section 2.2.2). Similar responses were noted by the Japanese parents, too; for example, *aite no ito wo kumitoru* ('inferring the other party's intention') and *kokoro wo komete saibu made shinkei ga iki todoite iru koto* ('doing something with all one's heart, sensitivity and attentiveness, even to the details'). These responses show the importance of attentiveness in the conceptualisation of politeness. Moreover, the last response also indicates the importance of the heart perspective as well in the conceptualisation of politeness.

As noted in Section 1, attentiveness has gained increasing importance in recent im/politeness research. Ogiermann (2015: 35) illustrates this, arguing that 'politeness is not so much about how we express our needs and involve others in satisfying them, but how we attend to others' needs'. Although Ogiermann does not use the term 'attentiveness', her understanding is closely related to attentiveness, as she argues that '[a]ccommodating somebody's wishes by "reading their mind" and providing them with what they need without being explicitly asked for it is certainly cooperative and considerate' (2015: 35). This is, in principle, along the same lines as the definition of attentiveness in Section 1.2, although the evaluation of attentiveness is not always positive (cooperative or considerate). The results of this section, at least in part, show that attentiveness is closely related to politeness. In other words, attentiveness is one of the major constituents of politeness in Japanese, which has not been paid much attention in previous research.

Empathy as a constituent of politeness was also frequently noted by both Japanese students (25) and Japanese parents (33). Many of them wrote just *omoiyari* ('empathy') and some others wrote *omoiyari no kokoro* ('the heart of empathy'). Since empathy is to think of others, the following responses were also included under the category of empathy: *hito wo omou kimochi* ('the feelings to think of others') and *aite no koto wo kangaete iru* ('thinking of the other party') by the Japanese students, and *hito wo daiji ni suru kokoro* ('the heart to cherish people'), *aite wo omou kimochi* ('the feelings to think of the other party') and *aite no tachiba ni natte kangaeru* ('to stand in someone else's shoes') by the Japanese parents. The last response is almost identical to Lebra's (1993: 72) definition of empathy, namely, *aite no mi ni naru* ('to stand in someone else's shoes') (see Section 4.2).

As both attentiveness and empathy are interpersonal notions, these results suggest that interpersonal aspects are important in the conceptualisation of politeness in Japanese. Empathy was noted in the conceptualisation of politeness in Japanese not only in this section, but also in some previous studies (e.g., Dunn 2013; Ide et al. 2005 [1992]; Kádár and Haugh 2013; Pizziconi 2007). This may be because empathy is cherished in Japanese culture (see, e.g., Clancy 1986, 1990; Section 4.2).

Consideration to others also includes respect and attitude. Although both Japanese students (11) and Japanese parents (10) wrote 'respect', the results of this section do not coincide with those of previous studies. For example, Haugh's (2004) results on politeness in Japanese encompass showing respect with a strong nuance of vertical respect involved. However, responses by both the Japanese students and the Japanese parents in this section did not clearly show the hierarchical emphasis. Responses by the Japanese students included *aite e no sonkei* ('respect for the other party'), *sonkei no nen* ('a sense of respect'), *aite no kokoro wo uyamau* ('respect the other party's heart') and *tanin wo omoiyari sonkei suru* ('respect the other party with empathy'). Responses by the Japanese parents included *tasha e no keii* ('respect for the other party'), *hito wo uyamau* ('respect people'), *sonkei no nen* ('a sense of respect') and *aite wo soncho suru kokoro* ('the heart to respect the other party'). These responses indicate that the traditional view of politeness, which associates respect with vertical relations, did not surface in this section.

The responses by the Japanese students (9) which could be categorised under attitude include *komakai taiou* ('a sensitive response') and *komayakasa* ('sensitivity'). The Japanese parents (8) also noted similar responses, such as *sensaisa* ('sensitivity') and *tekikaku de komayaka na taiou* ('an appropriate and sensitive response'). These responses may be related to attentiveness in a broad sense, as sensitivity towards others is required in order to demonstrate attentiveness. Furthermore, the Japanese students noted *shinshi na taido* ('sincere attitude') and *byoudou na taido* ('equal attitude'), and the Japanese parents *seijitsu na taido* ('sincere attitude') and *hito ni shinshi ni mukiau shisei* ('attitude to face people sincerely'). These responses indicate how one behaves towards others, for example, behaving sincerely towards others. Thus, they seem to be related to interpersonal relationships.

A broad category of appropriate behaviour was subcategorised into linguistically appropriate behaviour and non-linguistically appropriate behaviour. Linguistically appropriate behaviour includes honorifics and general use of language, and non-linguistically appropriate behaviour includes good manners, demeanour/deportment and smiling/pleasant disposition.

Under the sub-category of honorifics, the Japanese students (19) and the Japanese parents (7) just wrote *keigo* ('honorifics'). Thus, it cannot be verified which of the indices of honorifics (e.g., showing respect, formality, or a speaker's self-presentation) the specific participants had in mind (see n. 12).[18] The number of participants who noted honorifics as a constituent of politeness was smaller than expected. These results suggest that politeness in Japanese is expressed not only through honorifics, and that the results do not accord with some previous research. Previous research includes, for example, Ogawa and Gudykunst (1999–2000), who argue that the use of *keigo* (honorific forms) is a major strategy in demonstrating politeness in Japan, Suzuki (2007), who claims that politeness in Japanese is sometimes equated with honorifics, and Tao, Yoon and Nishijima (2016: 147), who show that '[m]any students mentioned honorific forms as their image of politeness, or *teinei*.'[19]

Under the sub-category of general use of language (JS: 39; JP: 25), both the Japanese students and the Japanese parents wrote *kotoba zukai* ('wording') most frequently. As the appropriate use of language in interacting with others has been a subject of study in Japan for hundreds of years (Haugh and Obana 2011: 49), Japanese participants may have been careful about the wording. Some Japanese students wrote *sono ba no jyookyoo ni oojita kotoba zukai* ('wording according to the situation') and *kirei na kotoba zukai* ('beautiful wording'). Those who can use words properly and beautifully are probably seen as polite in the eyes of Japanese students. Some Japanese parents assumed that one shows concern for the other party by selecting appropriate words such as *aite no kimochi wo kangaeta kotoba erabi* ('selecting words, thinking about the feelings of the other party'). This shows that the manifestation is linguistic, but the idea behind it is thinking about the feelings of the other party, which encompasses the non-linguistic aspect, namely, consideration towards others.

Non-linguistically appropriate behaviour includes good manners, demeanour/deportment and smiling/pleasant disposition. The most frequent response by both the Japanese students (20) and the Japanese parents (14) which was categorised under good manners was *reigi tadashisa* ('good manners'). The next most frequent response by them was *ojigi* ('bow'). The Japanese students noted bows with some variations, such as *teinei ni ojigi wo suru* ('to bow politely') or *fukabuka to rei wo suru* ('to bow deeply'). As for demeanour/deportment (JS: 23; JP: 10), the Japanese students often mentioned *shisei* ('posture'), *ochitsuita tachii furumai* ('calm demeanour'), and *kirei na shigusa* ('refined behaviour'). The Japanese parents noted *tachii furumai* ('demeanour'), *monogoshi* ('demeanour') and *shigusa* ('gesture/behaviour'). In Japanese society, good manners (*reigi*) are considered to be important as shown in previous research (see, e.g., Coulmas 2003: 68–69; Haugh 2004; Kádár and Haugh 2013; Obana and Tomoda 1994; Pizziconi 2007). The results of this section have confirmed the importance of good manners in Japanese society as well as the importance of demeanour/deportment. These perspectives are also related to a polished self-presentation, which was discussed earlier in relation to honorifics. Responses which were categorised under smiling/pleasant disposition (JS: 9; JP: 7) include *egao* ('smiles') by both the Japanese students and the Japanese parents. Although there were not many participants who wrote responses which can be categorised under smiling/pleasant disposition, to my knowledge, previous studies have not included such elements at all in the conceptualisation of politeness in Japanese.[20]

Although there were no major differences between the conceptualisation of politeness by the Japanese students and by the Japanese parents, some subtle differences were found in appropriate behaviour. That is, more Japanese students noted all of the sub-categories of appropriate behaviour than did Japanese parents. For example, 19 Japanese students noted honorifics, whereas only 7 Japanese parents did so, as noted above. This may be because the Japanese students had been taught (and they themselves acknowledged) the importance of the proper use of honorifics. They are expected to use honorifics properly, especially when they go to job interviews or when they talk to their superiors. According to one of the Japanese students who filled in the questionnaire, Japanese students sometimes make mistakes in the use of honorifics, and they need to be careful when they use honorifics. It is said that young Japanese people these days cannot use honorifics properly (cf. Hudson 2011). The students themselves seem to acknowledge this tendency and are concerned about it. It seems that those who can use honorifics properly are seen as polite in the eyes of Japanese students. However, it should be noted, as mentioned above, that the number of the participants who noted honorifics as a constituent of politeness in this section was smaller than expected and smaller than in previous research.

Moreover, these results may be partly due to the educational system, especially up to high school (some of the students who filled in the questionnaire reported that they were repeatedly told to bow, especially in their high school days), or to their expected behaviour at school (keeping good posture in classrooms or on ceremonial occasions is expected).[21] Or, some Japanese students may view that they could give a good impression through good posture. Actually, some Japanese students who had succeeded in job interviews reported that they were commended because of their good posture. In fact, there is an open seminar for students at our university called *manaa kouza* ('manner course') outside the curriculum. This is meant for students who want to get a good job or who are not confident about their manners. Some students think that it is important to acquire good manners for job hunting.

As mentioned earlier, the results of this section showed some differences in the conceptualisation of politeness in Japanese: a movement from the earlier emphasis on vertical distinctions (see, e.g., Haugh 2004; Obana and Tomoda 1994; Pizziconi 2007) (we can term such a view as the traditional conceptualisation of politeness in Japanese) to a less hierarchical or a more egalitarian one, which includes orientation to others. This reflects the emerging importance attached to the interpersonal aspect in the conceptualisation of politeness, which may resonate with the recent direction of politeness research (see, e.g., Haugh et al. 2013).

Some changes in the conceptualisation of politeness in Japanese were reported in some previous studies, too. For example, Haugh (2007a: 661) points out the shift from a concern for social position (*mibun*) or status (*chi'i*) to potentially less hierarchical dimensions, such as the dignity/character of others (*jinkaku*) and the place one stands (*tachiba*).[22] Marui et al. (1996: 389) argue that 'the personal and interpersonal elements in the old meaning of *teinei* have been substituted by normative ones in the newer meaning'.[23] However, some changes or the shift in the conceptualisation of politeness in Japanese found in this section did not include any of the above. Instead, the emphasis is on the orientation towards others, being manifested mainly through attentiveness and empathy. This may be similar to consideration to others, which was found to be an aspect of politeness in English in Haugh (2004). This suggests, on the one hand, that what is conceptualised as politeness varies across cultures, but, on the other, some constituents of politeness may be common across cultures, although further scrutiny on this assumption is needed.

Some of the shifts observed in the conceptualisation of politeness in Japanese in this section are somewhat similar to the results in Dunn (2013), in which a traditional conceptualisation of politeness in Japanese was not found. The traditional conceptualisation of politeness in Japanese includes, for example, vertical relations, a strong emphasis on modesty or reserve, and so on, as mentioned earlier. Instead, the results of Dunn (2013) show wider understandings of politeness in Japanese (e.g., kindness, consideration, speaking beautifully and the demeanour aspect). Moreover, some elements of attentiveness were included in Dunn (2013: 237). In relation to the above, Dunn (2013: 237) notes that empathy is an important concept for being *yasashii* ('kind' and 'considerate'). This is in tune with the contention in Section 2.2.2, that is, one of the conditions for attentiveness to arise is empathy.

4.4 Conclusion

This chapter has investigated attentiveness in Japanese relational networks. In Section 4.2, a cross-generational comparison of emic understandings of attentiveness, empathy and anticipatory inference was undertaken with the aid of metapragmatic interviews. The results tell us that the three concepts above are important for most Japanese participants. Some subtle cross-generational differences were also found. The older Japanese (JP) appear to value the three notions more highly than the younger Japanese (JS). Although the differences between these two groups were subtle,[24] this shows that generation is one of the constituents of a culture and that heterogeneity or intra-cultural variability (see Section 3.2) exists in Japanese culture.

Empathy was highly valued by most of the Japanese participants in Section 4.2, which coincides with the earlier research (see, e.g., Clancy 1986, 1990). However, there were some subtle cross-generational differences. That is, the older Japanese value empathy more highly than the younger Japanese, although this does not mean that the younger Japanese do not value empathy. The younger Japanese pointed out the possibility that showing empathy can sometimes become meddling. This is why the younger Japanese do not value empathy as highly as the older Japanese.

Both empathy and attentiveness are considered to be important in interpersonal relations by the participants in Section 4.2. These findings suggest the importance of these notions in im/politeness research, especially in interpersonal pragmatics. Furthermore, it was found that these concepts are related to morality to a certain extent, although further investigation is needed.

The findings show that the three notions investigated in Section 4.2 are related to each other to a certain extent. In particular, a close connection between empathy and attentiveness was detected. In other words, most of the participants did not clearly distinguish empathy from attentiveness. This may resonate, at least in part, with the results in Section 2.3, which would be helpful to see how or to what extent they are related.

Although there were some subtle cross-generational differences, most of the participants evaluated the three notions positively, which was treated as politeness concerns. These results suggest that the moral order on which the participants in Section 4.2 evaluate im/politeness may not differ very much in some instances. Further investigation is needed before these suggestions are confirmed, given that the number of participants was relatively small.

As noted above, there were no major cross-generational differences on the conceptualisation of the three notions, but some cross-generational differences were observed in the way the participants presented their ideas. There was a tendency for the Japanese parents to take more turns and consequently more time in answering questions than the Japanese students. For example, when JP1 in Example (4.3) was asked to cite some examples of inference, she could not give examples immediately and stated '(2.0) *A* (3.4) *uun rei wo ageru* (1.0) *sassuru hou da* (.) *uun* (2.8) *hito no jyoutai kana.*' (line 4), which can be considered as a think-aloud protocol (Kasper 2000: 336–339) or verbal report (Kasper 2008: 298–300). That is, she verbalised some thoughts before she answered the question. JP10 in Example (4.7) and JP9 in Example (4.8) repeated the questions ('*E* (1.0) *omoiyari ga naze hitsuyou ka.* (4.0)' [line 4] and '*Eeto* (.) *dono teido tte iuno wa* (.) *eeto*' [line 5]) before they answered. On the other hand, the Japanese students gave answers straight away in most examples. It cannot be clearly deduced only from the data here why this occurred. It may be interesting to investigate this issue in future research.

Section 4.3 attempted to investigate attentiveness through the conceptualisation of politeness in Japanese cross-generationally. The results show that there were not many differences in the responses given by the participants of the different age groups. The major similarity between the two groups of participants was that attentiveness and empathy, which were categorised under consideration to others, were frequently noted. Whereas empathy was noted in some previous studies (e.g., Dunn 2013; Ide et al. 2005 [1992]; Kádár and Haugh 2013; Pizziconi 2007), attentiveness was not found in the conceptualisation of politeness in previous research except for Kádár and Haugh (2013) and Fukushima and Sifianou (2017). Moreover, the traditional view (e.g., being humble, reserved, restrained, modest) entailing vertical relations did not surface in the results of Section 4.3 (in the data from both the Japanese students and the Japanese parents) in contrast to previous research (e.g., Ide et al. 2005 [1992]; Haugh 2004; Obana and Tomoda 1994; Pizziconi 2007). Although the results of Section 4.3 include honorifics, which have often been noted in previous studies and sometimes index vertical relations, they were not part of the main constituents of the conceptualisation of politeness in Section 4.3. Furthermore, both groups of participants noted some constituents which could be manifested non-linguistically, such as attentiveness,[25] empathy, good manners, demeanour and smiles. This shows the importance of the non-linguistic aspect of politeness, although many previous studies on the conceptualisation of politeness in Japanese focused on the linguistic aspect (e.g., Ide et al. 2005 [1992]). Indeed, the results in Section 4.3 included the demeanour aspect, which is also non-linguistically manifested, but such an aspect was not noted in other previous studies on politeness in Japanese except for Dunn (2013). Moreover, other constituents, such as smiles, which, to my knowledge, have not been noted in previous research on the conceptualisation of politeness in Japanese, were also included in the data in Section 4.3.

Thus, the results of Section 4.3, at least in part, suggest a shift in the conceptualisation of politeness. However, this shift is somewhat different from previous studies which noted some changes in the conceptualisation of politeness in Japanese (e.g., Haugh 2007a; Marui et al. 1996; Nishijima 1995). The shift in the conceptualisation of politeness in Japanese in Section 4.3 is from a traditional or vertical view into a more egalitarian view, which includes interpersonal perspectives such as attentiveness.

A similar tendency, a shift in the conceptualisation of politeness, was observed in Fukushima and Sifianou (2017). It was conjectured that this shift towards a less hierarchical understanding of politeness was due to the young age of the participants (Fukushima and Sifanou 2017). However, this shift in the conceptualisation of politeness is also found among the Japanese parents in Section 4.3. This indicates that this shift has been ongoing for years, and it is thus not solely noted in the data from the younger age group. These results may probably be due to some social changes as well as some incidents.[26] People's values and ideologies change over time (see, e.g., Spencer-Oatey 2005a) (see Section 3.2). However, what it is that influenced the observed shift in the conceptualisation of politeness cannot be clearly detected only from the results of Section 4.3. Further studies are needed to investigate this issue.

The data from both the Japanese students and the Japanese parents did not include negative views on politeness, such as 'feigned politeness, which is worse than impoliteness' and 'the most tolerated form of hypocrisy', which were found in the conceptualisation of politeness in Greek drawn from a corpus consisting of short messages posted to Twitter (Sifianou 2015: 27). This can also be considered as a similarity between the two groups of participants in Section 4.3.

Since, to the best of my knowledge, a cross-generational comparison on the conceptualisation of politeness in Japanese has not previously been conducted, Section 4.3 may contribute to expanding politeness research in Japanese. The results of Section 4.3 show that attentiveness is closely related to politeness. Actually, attentiveness is one of the major constituents of politeness, according to both groups of Japanese from two different generations, which resonates with the results in Fukushima and Sifianou (2017). It is hoped that attentiveness will be further investigated in relation to im/politeness.

CHAPTER 5

Conclusion

5.1 Overview and implications

This book has shed light on the importance of an interpersonal notion, namely, attentiveness, in interpersonal and cross-cultural pragmatics, and attempted to elucidate attentiveness both from theoretical and empirical points of view, the latter including data elicited through focus groups, metapragmatic interviews and questionnaires. This book has dealt with some of the important issues in pragmatics, such as im/politeness, interpersonal relationships and culture in relation to attentiveness.

This book has tried to fill some of the gaps in the field. Firstly, attention was drawn to non-linguistically manifested im/politeness, which has been rather neglected in im/politeness research. It has been shown that attentiveness entails both linguistic and non-linguistic aspects. That is, the cues for attentiveness can be linguistic and/or non-linguistic, and attentiveness can be demonstrated linguistically and/or non-linguistically. Secondly, we focused on the variable of generation or age, which has not been as popular as other variables in previous im/politeness research, and cross-generational comparisons of demonstration and evaluation of attentiveness were conducted. Thirdly, an interdisciplinary perspective was incorporated in examining attentiveness. Although the recent trend in im/politeness research goes in this direction, research in this fashion may still be wanting. It has been shown that attentiveness and some other similar concepts are sometimes located beyond the boundary of pragmatics or linguistics and are found in multiple disciplines. For this reason, an interdisciplinary perspective is definitely needed in the investigation of attentiveness.

Attentiveness has been considered in various ways in this volume, and some important issues have been raised. Among those issues were the intentionality of a potential recipient of attentiveness, the discrepancy between some different kinds of attentiveness, and the outcomes (or influences) of attentiveness. With respect to the intentionality of a potential recipient of attentiveness, it has been shown that it is not always clear whether a potential recipient of attentiveness solicits attentiveness or not. As for different kinds of attentiveness, genuine attentiveness, reflexive attentiveness and business-oriented attentiveness have been explained. It is sometimes difficult to observe the difference between genuine attentiveness and reflexive attentiveness. In other words, it is difficult to discern whether the demonstrator of attentiveness would demonstrate attentiveness merely for the well-being of the other party or for the sake of the demonstrator. Attentiveness contributes not only to establishing or maintaining interpersonal relationships, but it also plays a significant role in making profits in the business context. The data on business-oriented attentiveness, which has been taken up in this volume, revealed that profits included financial gain as well as the efficiency of work and so on.

Culture, which is elusive as well as heterogeneous, is important in considering and understanding attentiveness. Culture is composed of a number of variables, such as nation, generation and so on. Cross-cultural comparisons (among the participants of different national backgrounds, namely, Japanese, British and Americans) of attentiveness showed some differences and similarities. Likewise, cross-generational comparisons (between the Japanese participants of two different generations) of the demonstration and evaluation of attentiveness revealed some differences and similarities in the same culture (Japanese). It is worth noting that similarities outweighed differences in both cross-cultural and cross-generational comparisons. This may partly be due to the following reasons: (1) the participants (for cross-cultural comparisons) shared similar generational and educational backgrounds, namely, young university students; and (2) the Japanese participants of the two different generations were born after World War II; they received democratic education and may have been more or less influenced by American culture. This indicates that the Japanese people of two different generations shared the same sub-culture to a certain degree, although they differed in age. Cross-cultural similarities suggest that attentiveness, which was thought to be a virtue in Japanese culture, is not unique to Japanese culture, and that attentiveness is an important interpersonal notion elsewhere, too. The fact that the concept of attentiveness was not clear in other cultures may be because there are no single terms for attentiveness in some other cultures, although the concept exists, and people sometimes behave accordingly. In some other disciplines (e.g., social psychology), a similar concept to attentiveness is sometimes referred to as 'helping behaviour' or 'prosocial behaviour', which can be found also in other cultures, although they are not exactly the same as attentiveness, as the data in this volume has shown.

5.2 Prospects for future research

There are several issues which can be incorporated into future research on attentiveness. According to Haugh (2011: 253), the key features of the discursive approach are (1) the use of discourse data (i.e. longer fragments of authentic interaction) as opposed to single utterances that are often made up; (2) a greater focus on the hearer's evaluation of behaviour, not simply the speaker's production of utterances; (3) an increasing amount of research on impoliteness; and, perhaps most importantly, (4) greater emphasis on the need to analyse lay or first-order interpretations of politeness in theorising (second-order) conclusions (see also Kádár and Mills 2011; Mills 2011a; van der Bom and Mills 2015, among others). In this volume, the focus has been on the hearer's (or a recipient's) evaluation. Moreover, lay interpretations of politeness were addressed through the lens of attentiveness. Although some interview data was used in the analysis, naturally occurring data on attentiveness may be needed to draw a more definite conclusion on attentiveness in relation to theorising politeness. As attentiveness is sometimes demonstrated subtly and evaluation of attentiveness is not always explicitly articulated in our daily life, it may not be easy to obtain such kind of data, though. I am not suggesting that a certain type of data is better than another type of data. Every type of data has advantages and disadvantages (see, e.g., Jucker et al. 2018 for an overview of methods). Indeed, '[t]he strengths and weaknesses of a particular research methodology always have to be considered in relation to the types of research questions one wants to answer' (Golato and Golato 2018: 379). Focus groups, metapragmatic interviews and questionnaire data in this volume are significant in the sense that such kinds of data can offer more general patterns than situation-specific interactions and are the outcomes of what the participants think, whereas naturally occurring data is spontaneous. In other words, participants in the above-mentioned data types are conscious about what they say or write, whereas those in naturally occurring data may not always be conscious about what they say. By the use of different types of data in research it would be possible to add more depth and credibility to the data, compensating for the respective disadvantages. In this way, attentiveness could be further clarified.

In the present volume, the intentionality of the potential recipient of attentiveness has been discussed. The difference between two types of attentiveness, namely, one in which the potential recipient solicits attentiveness and another in which s/he does not solicit attentiveness, is difficult to observe. As the difference between the two does not appear ostensibly, future studies, which might incorporate follow-up interviews investigating the intentionality of the potential recipient of attentiveness, would be helpful in understanding these two types of attentiveness further.

It has been shown in this volume that attentiveness and im/politeness are related. For instance, a positive evaluation of attentiveness by the recipient occasions politeness, whereas a negative evaluation occasions impoliteness. The results set out in this book show that a positive evaluation of attentiveness is made when the attentiveness was what the recipient needed or expected. A negative evaluation is made when the attentiveness did not match the recipient's expectations, or when attentiveness was meddlesome, intrusive and so on. Future studies might investigate how a recipient of attentiveness would act or respond to the attentiveness demonstrated or to the demonstrator of attentiveness, after attentiveness is demonstrated. It is likely that the recipient may thank the demonstrator should the recipient evaluate the attentiveness positively. When the recipient makes a negative evaluation of the attentiveness demonstrated, would s/he say something to the demonstrator? If so, in what way? Or, would s/he show a negative evaluation only non-linguistically, or would s/he hold back from saying/doing anything? Some interactional data on this issue may be helpful in understanding the further processes of attentiveness.

The results in this book have shown the importance of attentiveness in Japanese relational networks. However, investigation of attentiveness in other cultures seems to be still wanting (but see, e.g., Fukushima and Haugh 2014; Chang and Fukushima 2017). The following issues can be further investigated in other cultures: whether or when attentiveness is demonstrated, how frequently it is demonstrated, whether it is expected, how attentiveness is evaluated, and how attentiveness is related to im/politeness.

As some of the data on business-oriented attentiveness have shown, attentiveness is an important issue also in the business world in Japan. New employees (mostly young people) at some companies in Japan may not be aware of the importance of attentiveness in the business setting or may not be accustomed to demonstrating attentiveness. Two directions of research can be pursued from this. One of them would be concerned with the issue of cross-culture and another that of cross-generation in the business context. Demonstration of attentiveness may give a good impression to customers in Japan, and that might lead to financial gain. However, customers' expectations may differ cross-culturally. Whether attentiveness is valued in the business world in other cultures needs to be further investigated. It may be interesting to investigate attentiveness from the perspectives of cross-cultural as well as intercultural business communication. Moreover, an exploration into whether there is any difference in the demonstration and the evaluation of attentiveness between new and experienced employees could be carried out.

We have investigated attentiveness with regards to culture. The variables of nation and generation were incorporated into the examination of attentiveness.

As this volume has shown, there are many other constituents of culture, for example, gender and social class. Although the variable of gender was incorporated in the questionnaire data in Sections 2.3 and 3.3, the participants in other sections were all females in order to focus on the central issues investigated in each section, attempting to reduce possible gender-based influences. As the participants in this volume were university students, librarians and staff in most cases, the social class investigated was considered to be roughly middle class.[1]

In future research, there may be a need to investigate attentiveness from the perspectives of gender and social class further. With respect to gender, Peterson and Seligman (2004: 384) state that females are more likely than males to feel guilty for failure to attend to the needs of others, drawing on Beutel and Marini (1995). Would that influence the gender difference in the demonstration or the evaluation of attentiveness? Although the issue of gender is not as straightforward as in the past, it may be included in a future investigation of attentiveness. Social class can also be incorporated into future research. As culture is sometimes about good upbringing (see, e.g., Eelen 2001: 168) and politeness1 norms typically emanate from the upper classes (Terkourafi 2011a: 176), is attentiveness related to any social class? Or, are there any differences in the frequency of the demonstration of attentiveness or in the evaluation of attentiveness according to social class? We must admit, however, the difficulty of assigning someone to a certain class (see Mills 2017: 81).

Moreover, we also need to take into account the factors of globalisation, easy mobility and the advanced technology of communication, which make it easier for us to share many things than before. We may need to consider culture from more diverse perspectives, as culture is getting more complicated than in the past. For example, people of different national backgrounds may share some sub-culture via the Internet. Here there may be the necessity to investigate attentiveness also from the perspective of Internet pragmatics. So, attentiveness may be further investigated having all of the above in mind.

The investigation of interpersonal pragmatics as well as cross-cultural pragmatics through the lens of attentiveness may help us make complicated and sometimes difficult interpersonal relationships in different cultures[2] a little easier. This is because attentiveness plays a significant role in establishing and maintaining interpersonal relationships, as this volume has shown. Through attentiveness, we can show our concern to other people, and that will be returned to us (even if it is not reflexive attentiveness) as *ki* ('spirit'), which is needed in demonstrating attentiveness, surrounds us. In the era of technological developments, artificial intelligence (AI)[3] replaces some of the work which human beings used to do. This sometimes makes our life easier and may compensate for the labour shortage. However, at the same time, some people may lose their jobs. I wonder whether AI can demonstrate attentiveness, thinking of the other party. It seems that AI can learn some behavioural patterns and can pre-empt some acts. AI can accumulate the data from behaviours of individuals. Here is an example. After someone has printed out something, s/he staples the papers together. After AI has learned this pattern of behaviour, AI would be able to pre-empt the act of handing a stapler to that person when s/he has finished printing. This is a pre-emptive response, but this is only the result of an accumulation of data. Although a pre-emptive response is a major feature of attentiveness, a pre-emptive response here is different from that in attentiveness. Even if AI has human intelligence, can AI demonstrate attentiveness as humans do, considering the other party? If attentiveness, which is demonstrated from the heart, is the privilege of human beings, why do we not use it and restore our human relationships in a real sense? As I wrote at the very beginning, we cannot live alone. It would be great if we could pursue a better life by helping each other through attentiveness. I hope people will be interested in attentiveness and that further research on attentiveness will be conducted. As has been shown in this volume, attentiveness is related not only to pragmatics, but also to some other disciplines such as social psychology, anthropology, communication and so on. Although an interdisciplinary aspect has been incorporated in this volume, more research on attentiveness taking an interdisciplinary perspective will be needed to further the understanding of attentiveness and im/politeness.

Attentiveness is a fascinating interpersonal notion and has lots to offer.

Appendices

Appendix 1: Transcription conventions

[ ]	overlapping speech
(0.5)	numbers in brackets indicate pause length
(.)	micropause
?	rising intonation
↑	sharp rising intonation
underlining	contrastive stress or emphasis
:	stretching of sound
> <	rushed or compressed talk
°	markedly soft speech
h	laughter

Appendix 2: Transcription conventions used in Cook and Burdelski (2017), which appear in Section 2.2.1

[Wo]rd	Brackets indicate overlapping talk.
Wo::rd	Colon marks phonological lengthening (each colon is approx. 0.1sec.).
Wo-	Hyphen indicates sound cutoff.
((bows))	Nonverbal actions and comments are shown in double parentheses.
h	Indicates laughter.
(1.2)	Number in parentheses indicates silence in seconds/tenths of a second.
(.)	Full stop inside parentheses indicates a micro-pause (less than 0.2 second).
>word<	Greater-than/less-than signs mark fast-paced speech.
=	An equals sign indicates latching between turns.
.	Full stop marks falling intonation.
,	Comma marks a continuing intonation.

?	Question mark indicates a rising intonation.
(Word)	Word in parentheses indicates transcriber uncertainty of hearing and a tentative reconstruction.
( )	Empty parentheses indicate an inaudible word or words.
°Word°	Circles around an utterance mark reduced volume.

(Cook and Burdelski 2017: 482)

Notes

Chapter 1

1. Culpeper, Marti, Mei, Nevala and Schauer (2010: 599) point out that what recent studies (Locher and Watts 2005; Holmes and Schnurr 2005; Spencer-Oatey 2000) have in common is a central focus on interpersonal relations, although the terms they use differ ('relational work' in Locher and Watts 2005; 'relational practice' in Holmes and Schnurr 2005; or 'rapport management' in Spencer-Oatey 2000). Locher and Graham (2010) termed these lines of research 'interpersonal pragmatics', which is used to designate examinations of the relational aspect of interactions between people that both affect and are affected by their understandings of culture, society, and their own and others' interpretations (Locher and Graham 2010: 2). Interpersonal pragmatics is a perspective on language in use which particularly highlights the interpersonal aspect of communication (Locher 2012: 38).

2. According to Watts (2003: 1), there is a surprising amount of disagreement in what people imagine polite behaviour to be. There are both positive and negative views of politeness. For instance, the positive view includes 'an inherent virtue coming from the heart' (Sifianou 2015: 27), and the negative view 'non-altruistic and clearly egocentric' (Watts 2005 [1992]: 69). Along the same lines, attentiveness can be evaluated either positively or negatively (see Sections 3 and 4). Attentiveness is, for instance, evaluated negatively when it is perceived as meddling, although Ogiermann (2015: 35) has focused only on its positive view, saying that it is cooperative and considerate.

3. According to Brown and Levinson (1987: 211), '[a] communicative act is done off record if it is done in such a way that it is not possible to attribute only one clear communicative intention to the act. In other words, the actor leaves himself an "out" by providing himself with a number of defensible interpretations … if a speaker wants to do an FTA [face-threatening act], but wants to avoid the responsibility for doing it, he can do it off record and leave it up to the addressee to decide how to interpret it'. Weizman (1989) uses the term 'requestive hints' in a similar sense. The attention to responses to

off-record requests indicates the importance of the hearer, which is in accord with a discursive approach.

4. The term 'solicitousness' was employed in the same sense as attentiveness in Fukushima (2000).

5. As off-record requests force heavy inferential demands on the addressee (see Blum-Kulka 1987: 133; Pinker 2007: 442), they are considered to be the most indirect among request strategies.

6. In previous research, it was shown that off-record indirectness is not universally or uncontroversially perceived as polite (see, e.g., Blum-Kulka 1987: 136; Holtgraves and Yang 1990: 724; Weizman 1993: 125; Turner 1996: 5–6; Márquez-Reiter 2000). Lee and Pinker (2010: 787) also argue that politeness and indirectness do not reside on the same scale but are rather distinct mechanisms elicited by different kinds of social encounters (see also Terkourafi 2011b).

Chapter 2

1. It was translated as 'I missed the class recently' in Haugh (2015: 258); however, *konoaida* here means 'the last class' or 'last time'. Thus, it can be translated as 'I missed the last class'.

2. The example was originally from Xie (2000).

3. The pre-emptive offer here means 'attentiveness' in my terms.

4. Haugh (2016b: 182) makes further comments on this conversation: '[w]hether the mother was talking to herself, thereby positioning her daughter as an overhearer, or alternatively, was directing the noticing at her daughter remained ambivalent. Nevertheless, the daughter offered the desired object to her mother, and in that sense, the reporting here prompted an offer of immediate assistance, namely, procuring a handkerchief.'

5. See also Vauclair, Wilson and Fischer (2014), who found cultural differences and similarities on the conception of morality between individualistic- (New Zealand and Germany) and collectivistic-oriented cultures (the Philippines and Brazil), which are also related to Chapter 3.

6. According to Hara (pers. com.), *kokoro* is closer to 'mind' rather than 'heart'. In this volume, *kokoro* is translated as 'heart', which is in line with other studies referred to here. Further support for this interpretation is offered in the following definitions: Whereas heart is 'the place where emotions are felt', mind is 'used to describe the ways a person thinks or the intelligence of a person' (www.merriam webster com). *Kokoro* here is used in the sense of emotions and feelings, rather than intelligence, although *kokoro* sometimes entails intelligence. Haugh (2015: 252) translates *kokoro* as 'heart-mind'

and argues that in some cases an orientation to their respective heart-mind (*kokoro*) underpins evaluations of politeness in Japanese.

7. This may be related to the different ways of making requests, i.e., making direct and indirect requests (including off-record requests in Brown and Levinson's [1987] terms, or hinting). Sifianou (1993) also mentions an understanding similar to attentiveness in response to off-record requests, although the term 'attentiveness' is not used.

8. When a potential recipient of attentiveness solicits attentiveness (see the discussion on the intentionality of a potential recipient of attentiveness), the following types of linguistic cues are considered to be possible: 'my side telling', 'reportings', 'topicalising troubles' and 'noticing a deficiency' (see Haugh 2015: 262–266). Lines 1–2 in Example (2.2) show a case of noticing a deficiency.

9. JP stands for Japanese parent, but JP does not have to be a parent of one of the students. It indicates someone, who is about the same age as a parent of a Japanese university student (JS).

10. Although pre-emptive features are not necessarily required in social support, as mentioned earlier, social support and attentiveness are similar in that both are, in principle, for the well-being of the other party.

11. Horike (1991: 151–152) defines social skill as 'knowledge', 'ability' or 'communication skills' which help interpersonal relationships move smoothly.

12. *Mitaina* is one of the hedges and is translated as 'like' in Shigeko Okamoto (2016: 19). When *mitaina* appears in the utterance final position, as shown here, it is translated as 'something like that' in this volume. This is because *mitaina* here 'dangles' by not being followed by a normatively expected head noun, which Matsumoto (2018) advocates.

13. Prior to Example (2.14), an older Japanese (in her fifties) stated that she would demonstrate attentiveness naturally (data is not included here). However, a young Japanese (a university student) stated that she would not demonstrate attentiveness naturally, but she would demonstrate attentiveness in order not to be excluded from the group. Here we can see a cross-generational difference in demonstrating attentiveness.

14. Transcription conventions have been preserved from the original text (see Appendix 2).

15. Transcription conventions have been preserved from the original text (see Appendix 2).

16. According to Iwamoto and Takahashi (2015), hospitality and *omotenashi* are often used as similar concepts, but they differ from each other in the following sense: whereas *omotenashi* tends to imply more selfless service, hospitality refers to fee-paying services in today's tourism industry. How-

ever, there may be also some similarities between *omotenashi* and hospitality. Morikoshi (2014: 24) argues that, in general, the concepts of *omotenashi* and hospitality are associated with the appropriate manners of hosts. Hotels and service-related companies in Japan provide so-called 'hospitality' training which focuses on employees learning the appropriate manners, polite greetings and anticipation of the guest's needs (Morikoshi 2014: 24). Anticipation of the guest's needs is related to anticipatory inference, which is one of the conditions for attentiveness to arise (see Section 2.2.2).

17. The meaning of *motenashi* includes demeanour developed by one's cultural appreciation and character (Yamajo 2008: 3). Yamajo (2008: 4–6) argues that demeanour consists of greeting, bowing and smiling. These are needed for people who engage in the hospitality industry, according to Yamajo (2008: 4). Demeanour and good manners are closely related to the conceptualisation of politeness in Japanese relational networks (see Section 4.3).

18. According to Terasaka and Inaba (2014: 96), *sarigenasa* ('unpretentiousness' or 'subtleness'), which is based on Japanese culture and does not necessarily apply to hospitality, is one of the features of *omotenashi*. The service in *Kagaya* (a Japanese-style inn) is given subtly. This is because there is the possibility of making the other party feel unpleasant by imposing (Terasaka and Inaba 2014: 106). Subtleness prevents the unpleasant imposition of *omotenashi*. Here another similarity between *omotenashi* and attentiveness can be found. Both attentiveness and *omotenashi* can be imposing or meddling, which leads to a negative evaluation. When attentiveness is demonstrated subtly, it may be less likely to be negatively evaluated than attentiveness demonstrated without subtleness.

19. Customer orientation represents a server's level of commitment to customers. That is, servers who routinely modify their service to anticipate and meet the needs of their customers are described as customer oriented (Lee 2015: 135).

20. Customer satisfaction is defined as an overall emotional reaction to a service that results from customers' evaluative comparisons of actual outcomes with expected ones (Lee 2015: 136).

21. An unobtrusive check-back style means that a server watches his or her tables carefully after serving the food to check, for example, whether beverages are running low or whether guests need new plates, instead of directly asking the guests (Lee 2015: 135).

22. In the case of business-oriented attentiveness, there may be instances in which a demonstrator does not have willingness. S/he may demonstrate business-oriented attentiveness merely to fulfil their duties at work.

23. According to Batson's (2010) empathy-altruism hypothesis, the decision of

helping or not depends primarily on whether you feel empathy for the person and secondarily on the costs and rewards (social exchange concerns).

24. 'Empathy' is widely used as a translation of *omoiyari* (e.g. Burdelski 2013; Lebra 1976; Takada 2013; Travis 1998); see Section 2.3.

25. It can be considered that attentiveness is in the realm of prosocial behaviour. In the classification of prosocial behaviour, Harada (1991: 50) lists attentiveness as one of the behavioural types. It includes behaviours such as attending to the state of the other party, worrying about the physical state (of the other party), and visiting someone when s/he is ill.

26. 'Consideration' is sometimes used as a translation of *hairyo* (see Section 2.3). Dunn (2013: 237) uses both 'consideration' and 'empathy' as a gloss for *omoiyari*.

27. These reasons are found among the negative evaluations of attentiveness in Sections 3.3 and 3.5.

28. Although the original version was in Chinese, only an English translation is presented here.

29. For example, the following studies investigated attentiveness and its similar concepts in different languages: Fukushima (2004) in Japanese, British English and Swiss German; Haugh (2016a) in Japanese; Fukushima and Haugh (2014) in Japanese and Chinese; Chang and Fukushima (2017) in Chinese; Sifianou (1993, 1995, 1997a) and Sifianou and Tzanne (2010) in Greek; Ogiermann (2015) in Polish; and Işik-Güler (2008) in Turkish. The terminologies used in these studies varied: 'attentiveness' was used in Fukushima (2004), Chang and Fukushima (2017), Fukushima and Haugh (2014), Haugh (2016a) and Işik-Güler (2008); 'solicitude' was used in Sifianou (1993, 1997a); and no single term to mean attentiveness was used in the other studies.

30. Miyake (2011: 6–7) also includes negative linguistic behaviour of consideration, such as fooling the other party and hurting the other party. However, in this section, such an aspect is not included.

31. Batson (2011: 11) uses 'empathic concern' and, as a shorthand, 'empathy' to refer to 'other-oriented emotion elicited by and congruent with the perceived welfare of someone in need'.

32. By this, Leech means genuine altruism. Leech (2014: 4) argues that politeness is communicative altruism, which is conveyed via communication and should not be equated with genuine altruism. However, Leech admits that communicative altruism and genuine altruism often coincide.

33. I would like to tell a personal anecdote as an example of helping behaviour. When I was walking back home one day, I suddenly felt ill. I fell unconscious and suffered a subarachnoid haemorrhage. I was lying on a busy street near a railway station. Obviously, I was in need of help. Someone unknown to me

called an ambulance. A nurse, who was on his way home, happened to pass by and gave me emergency treatment with an AED (Automated External Defibrillator), which was installed at the station. Of course, I found out about all of this only after I returned home from hospital. These strangers demonstrated helping behaviour, without which I would not have been able to write this book. I thank them all.

34. These participants are the same as those in Fukushima (2019).

Chapter 3

1. The terms 'cross-cultural' and 'intercultural' are sometimes used without any clear definition or interchangeably in the literature (see, e.g., Kecskes 2004: 1; Wolf 2015: 445). In this chapter, 'cross-cultural' is used, as British, Japanese and American data were obtained independently. This is in line with Spencer-Oatey (2008: 6), who argues that the term 'cross-cultural' is used to refer to comparative data, in other words, to data obtained independently from two different cultural groups; the term 'intercultural' is used to refer to interactional data, in other words, data obtained when members of two different cultural groups interact with each other. See Kádár and Bargiela-Chiappini (2011) who addressed the problematic nature of culture as well as the challenges posed by cross-cultural and intercultural research. See also Chen (2010) and Leech (2007).

2. According to Kádár and Mills (2011: 7), the 'discursive' turn in politeness research was initiated by three influential monographs by Eelen (2001), Mills (2003) and Watts (2003), which were followed by others such as Locher (2004), Locher and Watts (2005), Terkourafi (2005), Bousfield (2008) and collections such as Bousfield and Locher (2008). See also Culpeper (2011a) for an overview of politeness and impoliteness, including a shift to a discursive approach, Garcés-Conejos Blitvich (2010) for the status quo of im/ politeness research, Watts (2010) for recent research trails of politeness theory, and Grainger (2013) for an explanation of the discursive approach, especially in relation to interpersonal pragmatics.

3. A key claim in theorising im/politeness as social practice is that the moral order is what grounds our evaluations of social actions and meanings as 'good' or 'bad', 'normal' or 'exceptional', 'appropriate' or 'inappropriate' and so on, and, of course, as 'polite', 'impolite', 'over-polite' and so on (Haugh 2015: 173).

4. According to Žegarac (2008: 51), the term 'a culture' is more often used to describe an ethnic group or a nation.

5. When we use the term 'cross-cultural comparison', we may mean a compar-

ison between people of different national, ethnic, regional or generational backgrounds. In many previous 'cross-cultural' studies, however, the term 'cross-cultural comparison' has been used to mean a comparison among people of different nations (see, e.g., Blum-Kulka, House and Kasper 1989; Hickey and Stewart 2005a). Thus, in this chapter, the term 'cross-cultural comparison' is used to mean a comparison among people of different national backgrounds which differentiates from a cross-generational comparison, although cross-cultural comparisons may encompass cross-generational comparisons. Indeed, Tannen (2015) argues that cross-generations are also cross-cultures.

6. The contention by Thomas (1983) is worth noting. For Thomas, 'cross-cultural' is not just native–non–native interactions, but 'any communication between two people who, in any particular domain, do not share a common linguistic or cultural background' (Thomas 1983: 91).

7. Behaviours of people may also constitute a culture.

8. According to Mills (2017: 47), politeness, because of this association with the moral order, is linked to notions of appropriate behaviour. See also Schneider (2012), who shows that appropriateness and inappropriateness are more salient notions than politeness and impoliteness or rudeness.

9. Small culture is a dynamic, ongoing group process which operates in changing circumstances to enable group members to make sense of and operate meaningfully within those circumstances. It can be said to have a small culture when there is a discernible set of behaviours and understandings connected with group cohesion (Holliday 1999: 248).

10. Social-class level is associated with educational opportunities and with a person's occupation or profession (Hofstede 1991: 10).

11. This view of culture as an elite group may relate to Eelen's (2001: 168) statement on culture: culture is about good upbringing, good breeding and good human beings in general. Culture is not only a quantitative, but also an ethically correct entity.

12. This may be related to Terkourafi's (2011a: 176) following argument: 'Politeness1 norms typically emanate from the upper classes and are a reflection of their power. This allows them to play a gate-keeping role which is central to the smooth operation of society …'

13. Mills (pers. com.) suggests that it is really the ideologies associated with middle-class behaviours and working-class behaviours which are different rather than the behaviours themselves. She suggests that it is not possible to distinguish between working-class and middle-class linguistic behaviour at any simple level, but they are discussed differently.

14. See also Mills (2011b) and Wenger (1998). According to Wenger (1998),

there are three criteria for defining a community of practice: mutual engagement of members, members' jointly negotiated enterprise, and members' shared repertoire.

15. This means that Eelen's (2001) view on culture acknowledges the heterogeneity of a culture.

16. See Spencer-Oatey and Franklin (2009: 36–37) for further discussion on regularity and variability.

17. The dimension to be identified with individualism versus collectivism was most strongly associated with the relative importance attached to the following work goal items. For the individualist pole: (1) Personal time: Have a job which leaves you sufficient time for your personal or family life. (2) Freedom: Have considerable freedom to adopt your own approach to the job. (3) Challenge: Have challenging work to do – work from which you can achieve a personal sense of accomplishment. For the collectivist pole: (4) Training: Have training opportunities (to improve your skills or learn new skills). (5) Physical conditions: Have good physical working conditions. (6) Use of skills: Fully use your skills and abilities on the job (Hofstede 1991: 51–52).

18. Referring to cultures, some scholars use 'collectivist' and 'individualist', and some other 'collectivistic' and 'individualistic'. They are used as each researcher chooses in this section.

19. See also Marra (2015: 33), who contends that '[c]ulture influences interaction via distinctive values and norms for communicating'.

20. *Kuuki* is a very rich concept which includes both the prevailing movement of minds from moment to moment and the external atmosphere in both a physical and a social sense (Tsujimura 1987: 126).

21. The United States is classified into a low-context and Japan into a high-context communication framework (Ting-Toomey 1999: 100–111; see also Okabe 1983: 35).

22. Here is another example to show that inference is more valued in Japanese culture than in American culture. Azuma (2009: 176–178) states that Japanese society belongs to a high-context culture, whereas American culture belongs to a low-context culture and that *kigakiku* (i.e., being attentive) belongs to a high-context culture. He cites as examples the situation where one invites someone to his/her home in Japan and in the United States. In Japan, a host/hostess serves cold barley tea or juice in summer and hot tea or coffee in winter, without asking the guest. A host/hostess, who infers what a guest wants and serves a drink, is *kigakiku* ('attentive'), getting a positive evaluation for his/her attentiveness. In the United States, on the other hand, the host asks the guest what s/he would like to drink, saying, for example, 'I have Coke, Seven-Up, orange juice, apple juice, milk, ice tea. What would

you like?' (Azuma 2009: 178). If the host serves an American guest a drink without asking her/him what s/he would like to drink, the guest may not evaluate that positively.

23. Features of collectivist and individualist cultures should be viewed as differing in emphasis rather than as strictly dichotomous in substance (see Okabe 1983: 22).

24. Social and political changes include war, as shown here, but they also include other phenomena, such as industrialisation, which can bring about individualism (see, e.g., Culpeper and Kádár 2010).

25. See Stewart (2005), for example.

26. Brown and Levinson (1987: 230–231) acknowledge the possibility of a mixture of positive and negative politeness strategies, namely, 'a kind of hybrid strategy somewhere in between the two'.

27. Access to education is considered to be one of the factors which may constitute a culture (see, e.g., Hofstede 1991: 10). People with higher education and those without it may belong to different subgroups in a culture.

28. Japanese participants were recruited from a university located in Yamanashi, Japan, and British participants were recruited from two universities, one being located in the south of England and the other in the north of England. (My sincere thanks are due to Rosina Márquez-Reiter and Derek Bousfield.)

29. Sifianou (1997b: 68) referred to 'doing things for others without being requested to', but what she meant was attentiveness in my terms.

30. According to Hatch and Lazaraton (1991: 57), most researchers who use scales prefer to use a 5-point, 7-point or 9-point scale, as the wider range encourages respondents to show greater discrimination in their judgments. I have decided to use a 5-point scale, as the participants would be confused if they were given too many options and it would be easy for the participants to interpret the following: 3 on a 5-point scale is neutral, 1 is very positive evaluation of attentiveness and 5 is very negative evaluation on the scale.

31. For the situations, post hoc tests (Scheffe tests for the comparison of situations) were conducted. The results showed the following significant differences in the degree of imposition required to demonstrate attentiveness. The mean score of Situation 1 was significantly higher than the scores in Situations 2, 3, 4 and 5; the mean score of Situation 2 was significantly lower than those in Situations 4, 5 and 6; the mean score of Situation 3 was significantly lower than those in Situations 4, 5 and 6; the mean score of Situation 4 was significantly higher than that in Situation 5; and the mean score of Situation 5 was significantly lower than that in Situation 6.

32. The degree of imposition required to demonstrate attentiveness in Situations 1, 4, 5 and 6 was evaluated as follows. Situation 1: British 3.8; Japanese 4.0;

Situation 4: British 3.4; Japanese 3.6; Situation 5: British 2.4; Japanese 2.5; Situation 6: British 3.6; Japanese 3.8. Situation 5 had a lower degree of imposition than Situations 1, 4 and 6, but Situation 5 was evaluated as having a higher degree of imposition than Situations 2 (British 1.8; Japanese 2.1) and 3 (British 1.6; Japanese 1.8) (see also n. 31).

33. Whereas multiple choices were given in the questionnaire, the participants talked freely in the interviews. If the results of the interviews coincide with (or are similar to) those of the questionnaire, it can be said that the results of multiple-choice questionnaires, which were ordered to match the options in Questions 1 and 2, have high levels of reliability.

34. They are undergraduates of Tsuru University in Yamanashi, Japan.

35. It was intended to collect data from those who were older than the students. The participants of this group did not have to be related to the students, but they had to be from an older generation than the students. They included parents, relatives and acquaintances, the parents being the majority of this group (68.5%). For this reason, this group was called Japanese parents.

36. They are undergraduates of University of California and are all native speakers of English. It was hoped to obtain data from American parents, too, but their marital situations were more complex than those of Japanese parents. For example, some were divorced or remarried. There were students who did not have close contact with their parents, or some of them said that they did not know which father or mother (their biological one or their new one) they should contact. Thus, the idea of obtaining American parents' data was abandoned.

37. As mentioned in n. 30, the participants would be confused if they were given too many options. Moreover, the same choice (e.g., 7 on a 9-point scale) can mean different judgments according to different participants. A five-point scale may be able to avoid this kind of obscurity, 1 being the lowest imposition and 5 being the highest.

38. For example, in Situation 2 in the students' questionnaire they have lunch at a canteen, and in the parents' questionnaire they have lunch at a restaurant near their company. In Situation 3 in the students' questionnaire the book was for a thesis, and in the parents' questionnaire it was for a project. Situation 4 in the students' questionnaire relates to a part-time job, and in the parents' questionnaire it involves working for a company. In Situation 5 in the students' questionnaire papers were submitted to a professor, and in the parents' questionnaire papers were submitted to a section chief at a project meeting.

39. Priority seats are for the elderly and the handicapped, therefore, those who are carrying a lot of baggage are not candidates for priority seats.

40. They are (1) pre-empting a request from the other party and demonstrating attentiveness, (2) suggesting an alternative means other than doing something (e.g., giving advice or making suggestions), and (3) refusing a request from the other party.

41. Although it could be assumed that those who selected Choice 1 (demonstration of attentiveness) in Question 1 would select the first reason in Question 2, it was necessary to confirm this. And more detailed reasons can be obtained by giving Choice 4 (other) in Question 2.

42. In Situations 1, 3, 4 and 5, two factors (participants and participants' choices) were used for the analysis. In Situations 2 and 6, however, participants' choices could not be used as a factor for the analysis, because most participants selected the same choice for Question 1 in these situations. This is why a one-way ANOVA was conducted in Situations 2 and 6.

43. Choice 4 (other) in each situation included the following. Situation 1 (seat): 'It would depend on how old A was and how much s/he appeared to be struggling with her/his baggage' (JP and AS); 'It depends on how I feel' (JP). Situation 2 (lunch): 'I would ask B, "Shall I treat you to lunch?"' (JS); 'Pay for B's lunch but expect them to pay back or return the favor in the future' (AS). Situation 3 (book): 'Call C to see if C needs the book' (JS, JP and AS); 'Suggest using Amazon' (JS). Situation 4 (work schedule): 'I would work if they asked' (JS, JP and AS); 'I would work if I did not have any particular schedule' (JS and JP); 'We would consult among colleagues and adjust the schedule' (JS and JP); 'Suggest that we switch work shifts for the week' (AS). Situation 5 (papers): 'If the professor asks for some assistance, then I would help' (JS and AS); 'It depends on the relationship between the professor and me' (JS); 'It is natural to help the boss' (JP); 'It would be a problem if some important papers went missing when I helped' (JP). Situation 6 (rail pass): 'I would let the station staff know about that' (JS).

44. Choice 4 (other) in each situation included the following. Situation 1 (seat): 'Because A is an acquaintance of mine' (JS, JP and AS); 'I feel bad, if only I remain seated' (JS); 'It depends on whether A is older or younger than me' (JP); 'That is what I want to be offered' (JP). Situation 2 (lunch): 'It is natural' (JS, JP and AS); 'It is mutual' (*otagai sama*) (JS and JP); 'It is all right if B pays me back' (JS, JP and AS); 'B is a friend/colleague' (JS, JP and AS); 'It would be troublesome to wait for B' (JS and JP). Situation 3 (book): 'S/he may no longer need it or s/he may have it already' (JS, JP and AS); 'It would be imposing' (JS and JP); 'It would be a burden on the recipient' (*ki wo tsukawa seru*) (JS). Situation 4 (work schedule): 'It is mutual' (*otagai sama*) (JS and JP); 'It is for the company and for everybody' (JS and JP); 'It is natural' (JS and JP); 'I would be in trouble if I were D' (JP); 'It is up to the company to

assign people to cover D's job' (JS, JP and AS); 'I want to work, because I can get extra pay' (JS, JP and AS). Situation 5 (papers): 'It is natural to help her/ him' (JP); 'I probably wouldn't think about it unless they asked' (JS and AS); 'If the professor needed help, he would ask' (AS); 'I will assume that the professor already has TA's helping him/her' (AS); 'The professor should be aware that a lot of papers would be turned in, so he should have brought something to carry them with' (AS). Situation 6 (rail pass): 'It's the right thing to do' (JS, JP and AS).

45. The results of ANOVA showed that the main effect of the participants was significant in Situations 1 (df = 2/277, F = 6.666. p < 0.01), 3 (df = 2/277, F = 5.339, p < 0.01) and 5 (df = 2/278, F = 3.329, p < 0.05). A post hoc test (Bonferroni test) was conducted, and the results showed that there were significant differences between the Japanese students and the Japanese parents and between the Japanese students and the American students in Situation 1 (p < 0.05), between the Japanese students and the Japanese parents in Situation 3 (p < 0.05) and between the Japanese students and the Japanese parents in Situation 5 (p < 0.05).

46. The results of ANOVA in Situation 1 showed that the main effect of the participants' factor was significant (df = 2/263, F = 6.637, p < 0.01). The main effect of Question 1 was significant (df = 2/263, F = 4.904, p < 0.01). The interaction was also significant (df = 4/263, F = 4.216, p < 0.01). Since the interaction was significant, a one-way ANOVA (participants' choice in Question 1) and a post hoc test (Scheffe test) were conducted. The results showed that the Japanese parents who selected Choice 3 ('keep reading a book') achieved a high score (4.50) (p < 0.05). There were no significant differences between the demonstration of attentiveness and the degree of imposition required to demonstrate attentiveness among Japanese students and American students. The results in Situations 2 and 6 showed that there were no significant differences among the participants. The results in Situations 3, 4 and 5 showed that only the main effect of Question 1 was significant: Situation 3 (df = 1/189, F = 11.759, p < 0.001); Situation 4 (df = 2/216, F = 23.295, p < 0.0001); Situation 5 (df = 1/262, F = 42.601, p < 0.0001).

47. Kyono (2017: 40) states that *ki wo tsukau* literally means 'to use mind/heart/ attention' and functions to convey 'be careful about, worry about, and be solicitous for somebody's welfare'. *Ki wo tsukawa seru* here means that the demonstrator makes the recipient use mind/heart/attention and, in consequence, the recipient may have to do something for the demonstrator in return, or give the demonstrator a gift in return, in other words, reimbursement, as noted in Section 3.3.

48. The following is an email I received from a staff member at university con-

cerning a class which was cancelled because of a heavy snowfall: *Itsumo <u>o</u> <u>sewa ni natte ori masu</u>. 1 gatsu 22 nichi no kousetsu ni yori kyuukou ni natta jyugyou ni taishite hokou/repooto taiou ga hitsuyou na baai wa gakusei ni shuuchi suru hitsuyou ga arimasu node 1 gatsu 26 nichi made ni kyoumu tan-tou made go renraku kudasai*. ('Thank you for your constant cooperation. If you need to make up a class or assign students a paper to replace a class which was cancelled on 22 January because of the snowfall, could you let us {academic affairs section} know about that by 26 January, as we need to inform students?) In this email, *o se wa ni natte ori masu* does not have any specific meaning, but it is rather an idiomatic expression or an introductory remark. The idea of *o sewa ni naru* may be related to collectivist features as noted in Section 3.2, as *o sewa ni naru* can mean that I am taken care of by you or somebody, which indicates that one depends on the other party or the group. This needs further scrutiny, though.

49. According to Himeno (2003), a recipient of attentiveness sometimes feels guilty when attentiveness is demonstrated by somebody who is not close.

50. Although it could be assumed that those who evaluated attentiveness posi-tively would select the first choice ('I needed that' or 'that was helpful') and those who evaluated attentiveness negatively would select the second choice ('I felt it as a burden' or 'it was imposing'), multiple choices were used. This was partly because the participants in Section 3.3, who could write any rea-son, wrote too many reasons, some of which could not be classified into either positive or negative reasons. The participants could also write some other reasons in Choice 3, if they thought their reason would not match either Choice 1 or Choice 2.

51. In Locher and Watts' (2005: 11) view, relational work 'comprises the entire continuum of verbal behavior from direct, impolite, rude or aggressive inter-action through to polite interaction' (Darics 2010: 132). Relational work is a term that covers the entire spectrum of behaviour and cannot be simply reduced to a dichotomy of impolite and polite behaviour (Locher 2006: 255). Following this idea of a continuum, this section does not ask the participants to evaluate whether attentiveness is positive or negative (which may lead to politeness or impoliteness) as a binary choice, but on a scale ranging from 'very appreciative' to 'not at all appreciative'.

52. The results of ANOVA showed that the main effect of the participants was significant in Situations 5 ($df = 2/279$, $F = 8.047$, $p < 0.01$) and 6 ($df = 2/280$, $F = 4.942$, $p < 0.01$). A post hoc test (Bonferroni test) was conducted, and the results showed that there were significant differences among the Japanese students, Japanese parents and American students ($p < 0.05$) both in Situa-tions 5 and 6.

53. These results may be due to the fact that the American students attended University of California, where many people use their cars (i.e., they may not use a rail pass very much).

54. Choice 3 ('other') in each situation included the following. Situation 1 (seat): 'Giving the seat is the right thing to do and not giving up the seat would be rude' (JS: 0%; JP: 2.2%; AS: 3.1%); 'It was helpful, but also sort of expected' (only by AS: 3.1%). Situation 2 (lunch): 'It is mutual' (*otagaisama*) (JS: 0.6%; JP: 2.2%; AS: 0%); 'If we are friends, it should be expected' (JS: 0%; JP: 1.1%; AS: 3.1%). Situation 3 (book): 'I want to decide myself whether the book is necessary or not' (JS: 0.6%; JP: 2.2%; AS: 0%); 'If someone bought that book for me, it would be a favour above and beyond the norm for such good acts; I would be so appreciative and do something extra in return' (only by AS: 3.1%). Situation 4 (work schedule): 'Employer should have enough staff to cover incidents like this' (only by AS: 3.1%); 'It is natural' (only by JP: 2.2%); 'It is mutual' (*otagaisama*) (JS: 0.6%; JP: 1.1%; AS: 0%). Situation 5 (papers): 'It is natural to do so' (only by JP: 4.3%); 'I do not want to be brown-nosing' (only by AS: 6.3%); 'The professor should be aware that a lot of papers would be turned in, so he should have brought something to carry them with' (only by AS: 3.1%); 'I would feel awkward with my Prof' (only by AS: 3.1%); 'I feel considerate' (only by JS: 0.6%). Situation 6 (rail pass): 'It is the right thing to do' (JS: 5.1%; JP: 7.6%; AS: 3.1%); 'If I were the one who lost a rail pass, I would like someone to hand it in' (JS: 1.3%; JP: 1.1%; AS: 0%); 'As a rail pass costs a lot, it would be a problem if we lost that' (only JS: 0.6%); 'We can solve the problem on the spot, by handing in the rail pass' (JS: 0.6%; JP: 1.1%; AS: 0%).

55. As the situations were the same as in Section 3.4, the degree of imposition required to demonstrate attentiveness was also the same as in Section 3.4 (see Table 3.5).

56. Holliday (1999) maintains the importance of a small culture paradigm, which attaches culture to small social groupings or activities wherever there is cohesive behaviour, and thus avoids culturist ethnic, national or international stereotyping (see the discussion in Section 3.2).

Chapter 4

1. Kádár and Haugh (2013) argue that both first-order and second-order understandings potentially correspond to analysts as well as lay interlocutors, and that they are needed to better theorise im/politeness. In relation to politeness, Kádár and Haugh (2013: 84) consider the understandings of metaparticipants: 'people whose evaluations of politeness arise through

vicariously taking part in the interaction by viewing it on television or on the internet, for instance. Both participant and metaparticipant understandings are first-order in the sense that they involve some kind of *participation* in the evaluative moment. On the other hand, there is the view of those who *observe* evaluative moments through which politeness arises. The *lay observer* can observe such moments spontaneously in an ad hoc manner' (emphasis in the original). 'However, there is another more formalized way of observing that involves more systematic and evidenced interpretations of evaluative moments. An understanding that arises through systematic and evidenced observation is that of an *analyst*. Both lay observer and analyst understandings are second-order in that they involve *observation* rather than participation in the social world' (Kádár and Haugh 2013: 85) (emphasis in the original). In relation to the argument above, Davies (2018: 127) raises the question of what particular behaviours count as involvement in the evaluative moment (first-order) as compared to observationally based theorising about folklinguistic systems (second-order).

2. Attentiveness and empathy are discussed in relation to the metapragmatics of politeness in Japanese in Haugh (2016a).

3. 'Metapragmatics can be broadly defined as the study of *awareness* on the part of ordinary or *lay observers* about the ways in which they use language to interact and communicate with others' (Kádár and Haugh 2013: 181, original emphasis). '[M]etapragmatic interviews and questionnaires have also been utilised to offer further insights into the metalinguistic awareness of cultural insiders or members' (Kádár and Haugh 2013: 193).

4. Moral order refers to what members of a sociocultural group or relational network 'take for granted' (Kádár and Haugh 2013: 67) or 'seen but unnoticed' expected background features of everyday scenes in Garfinkel's terms (1967: 36; see also Haugh 2013; Wuthnow 1987). A key claim in theorising im/politeness as social practice is that the moral order is what grounds our evaluations of social actions and meanings as 'good' or 'bad', 'normal' or 'exceptional', 'appropriate' or 'inappropriate' and so on, and of course, as 'polite', 'impolite', 'over-polite' and so on (Haugh 2015: 173). Moral order lies at the heart of politeness as social practice (Kádár and Haugh 2013: 204) (see also Section 2.2.1).

5. *Teineisa* is used as a translation of 'politeness' in this chapter, as *teineisa* ('politeness') or *teinei* ('polite') was widely used in previous research (see, e.g., Haugh 2004, 2005, 2007a; Haugh and Obana 2011; Ide et al. 2005 [1992]; Kádár and Haugh 2013; Pizziconi 2007).

6. I take the standpoint that empathy itself does not include a demonstration of attentiveness.

7. The importance of emotions in im/politeness research, especially in interpersonal pragmatics, is pointed out by Locher and Langoltz (2008) and Langlotz and Locher (2013). However, research into how emotions would influence the evaluation of im/politeness may be still wanting.

8. This interview took place in October 2011. As shown in n. 26, the earthquake in March 2011 caused heavy damage and many casualties.

9. *Omoiyari no aru* is an adjective which stems from the noun *omoiyari*. *Omoiyari no aru* is translated as 'considerate' in Ide et al. (2005 [1992]) and Pizziconi (2007), but *omoiyari* is often glossed as 'empathy' (see, e.g., Lebra 1976, 1993). Haugh (2016a: 51) argues that *omoiyari no aru* lies within its own semantic field that overlaps with, yet is nevertheless distinct from, that of *teineina*. According to Haugh (2016a: 51), the 'willingness to respond to other people's unspoken feelings, wants, and needs' that is said to underpin *omoiyari* (Lebra 1976: 39; Wierzbicka 1997: 275) intersects with the notion of *kikubari/kizukai* ('attentiveness') (Fukushima and Haugh 2014). In reaching an understanding of the term *omoiyari* and its relationship with *teineina*, we must therefore make recourse to a range of other terms such as *ki wo kubaru* ('be attentive'), *hairyo ga aru* ('have consideration'), *kigakiku* ('attentive'), *shinsetsuna* ('kind'), *yasashii* ('gentle') and so on (Haugh 2016a: 51). There is a difference in meaning between *omoiyari* and *hairyo* ('consideration') (see Section 2.3).

10. The reason why Ide's framework intermixes social ritual and politeness is likely to be that social conventions/rituals (which trigger the use of honorifics in Japanese dominant ideologies) are often represented as normative 'etiquette' (and as culture-specific equivalents of etiquette such as *reigi* in Japanese), which triggers their association with politeness (Kádár and Mills 2013: 150).

11. The origin of Japanese honorifics is derived from ritual prayers used in the act of praising and worshipping gods and goddesses in animism, which later developed as Shintoism (see Obana 2017). The distance indexed by honorifics may derive from this origin.

12. For example, Ide (2005: 61) argues that the use of honorifics indexes the appropriate relationship between the speaker and the hearer, the formality of the situation and the speaker's attributes and the speaker's identity. This is related to Ide's (1989) claim, namely, *wakimae* ('discernment'). However, Pizziconi (2011: 70) argues that '*wakimae*, or a principle of discernment of social relations said to govern the appropriate use of Japanese honorifics, is not a sufficient principle for defining any specific feature of Japanese politeness'. According to Pizziconi (2011: 69), '[t]ypically, honorifics are understood to be indices of deferential, humble or polite stance; typically they are

said to mark vertical distance, but other typical reports involve horizontal distance; however, we have examined one case of honorifics used to convey the affective stance of anger, and by the same mechanisms they can be used to index irony, flattery, annoyance, formality (concern for the situation) and "hypocritical politeness" (*inginburei*) etc.'

13. There are several stages leading up to the demonstration of attentiveness: (1) observation of a situation by a potential demonstrator (considering verbal and non-verbal cues and reading the atmosphere of the situation), (2) anticipatory inference by the potential demonstrator (reading the other party's needs, wants and feelings), (3) evaluation of attentiveness by the potential demonstrator (checking the attentiveness against the moral order and evaluating the possible outcomes) and (4) demonstration of attentiveness.

14. These participants (JS) are the same as those in Fukushima and Sifianou (2017), as Section 4.3 is part of an extended project by Fukushima and Sifianou (2017).

15. Although helping behaviour was found in the Greek data in Fukushima and Sifianou (2017), it was not found in the Japanese data. Thus, helping behaviour, which was grouped together with attentiveness in Fukushima and Sifianou (2017), is omitted in Section 4.3. Respect was included in the broad category of consideration to others, as 'respect for someone always involves the willingness to show some kind of consideration for that person' (Simon 2007: 310).

16. General use of language includes linguistic features other than honorifics. This sub-category was labelled as miscellaneous in Fukushima and Sifianou (2017).

17. According to Haugh and Obana (2011: 149), '[m]ost of the "proto-scientific" work on appropriate behaviour in Japan was focused on honorifics, which are termed *keigo* (lit. "respect language") in both popular and academic discourse, or less commonly *taigu hyogen* (lit. "treatment expressions"), the latter term being largely restricted to academic circles'. However, in Section 4.3, appropriate behaviour is used in a broader sense. That is, it includes both linguistically (not only honorifics but also other aspects of linguistic features which are categorised as general use of language) and non-linguistically manifested appropriate behaviour.

18. Further investigation is needed on the indices of honorifics in Japanese in relation to the conceptualisation of politeness.

19. By 'many students' Tao et al. (2016) mean that 21 male Japanese participants out of 55 participants (25.0%) (Tao et al. 2016: 140) and 67 female Japanese participants out of 105 participants (39.8%) (Tao et al. 2016: 141) mentioned honorifics and polite expressions. However, in the categorisation (what they

call 'type') Tao et al. (2016) included expressions, which were not categorised under honorifics in Section 4.3. For example, they included 'respect', which was found in the responses by male Japanese students, and 'Good morning', which was found in the responses by female Japanese students. These two were categorised under the sub-categories of respect and general use of language respectively in Section 4.3. In the categorisation of honorifics and polite expressions in Tao et al. (2016), only 1 male Japanese student mentioned 'honorifics' and 17 female Japanese students mentioned 'honorifics and honorific language'. If only these responses are counted as honorifics, it could be said that the number of Japanese students who stated honorifics as the conceptualisation of politeness in Japanese would not be high. Thus, it depends very much on how the responses are categorised.

20. Smiles were viewed as acts of politeness by Israelis (Blum-Kulka 2005 [1992]: 261) and Greeks (Sifianou 1992: 91).

21. This may be related to Kádár and Mills' (2013: 151) statement, that, in Japan, many social conventional/ritual practices form part of general education.

22. Haugh (2005) advocates the importance of place, which is composed of (1) the place where one belongs (inclusion or being part of a group) and (2) the place where one stands (distinction or being different from others) in Japanese politeness. Similarly, Haugh and Obana (2011) have shown that the notion of *tachiba* ('the place where one stands') can account for a broad range of normative politeness behaviours, not only in more formal situations where it is expected that honorifics will be used, but also in instances where the use of honorifics is not generally expected, such as in interactions between family or close friends of a similar age (2011: 148).

23. Thus, it is necessary to take historicity (see, e.g., Kádár and Paternoster 2015) of such terms into consideration. See also Nishijima (1995), who advocates a shift in the conceptualisation of politeness in Japanese.

24. The mean ages of the Japanese participants of the two generations were 21.4 years and 52.6 years old respectively. If the age difference between them had been greater, the difference on the three concepts might have been greater. People in a certain culture may have different values over the course of time. How long values take to change may vary. Not only elapsing time, but economic states or historical events may also influence the changes of people's values and ideologies (see also n. 26). For example, Yamaguchi (1994: 184) pointed out that Japanese culture has become more individualistic than before due to economic growth, which Japan has achieved since World War II, a significant historical event (see Section 3.2). This is related to the moral order, which changes over time (see, e.g., Kádár and Haugh 2013: 67). Further investigation is still needed.

25. Attentiveness entails both linguistic and non-linguistic politeness. Attentiveness can be demonstrated linguistically (e.g., offering help linguistically, giving advice), non-linguistically (e.g., doing something for the other party) or both linguistically and non-linguistically (see Section 2.2.1).

26. For instance, the great East Japan earthquake hit Japan in March 2011. The casualties were 15,894, and 2,562 people were still unaccounted for as of 8 December 2017 (https://hinansyameibo.katata.info/article/after-311-japan-earthquake-20180110.html) (last accessed on 16 January 2019). *Kizuna*, which can be translated as 'bond', 'human ties' or 'solidarity', was a keyword when we tried to help and cheer each other up. Stickers, saying 'Hang in there, Japan! Bond' were sold to help the sufferers. People who placed an importance on material aspects may have realised the importance of the bond among people. This kind of change of people's ideologies may have led to the concern for other people, which is related to moral order (see, e.g., Spencer-Oatey and Kádár 2016: 92), although this assumption needs further scrutiny.

Chapter 5

1. Mills (2017: 61) also focused on middle-class respondents. However, it should be noted that middle-class respondents are not representative of the whole of society or culture, as Mills (2017: 85) rightly argues that '[m]iddle-class politeness does not constitute all of the relational work within English politeness'.

2. As it may be clear from the discussion in this volume, different cultures can exist even among people of the same national background.

3. According to Cummings (2005: 213), pragmatics is in a position to influence the development of AI models of language processing. However, attentiveness is not an issue of language processing.

References

Akasu, K., & Asano, K. (1993). Sociolinguistic factors influencing communication in Japan and the United States. In W. B. Gudykunst (Ed.), *Communication in Japan and the United States* (pp. 88–121). Albany, NY: State University of New York Press.

Aronson, E., Wilson, T. D., & Akert, R. A. (2013). *Social Psychology* (8th ed.). Boston: Pearson Education, Inc.

Azuma, S. (2009). *Shakai gengogaku nyuumon* [Introduction to sociolinguistics]. Tokyo: Kenkyusha.

Babbie, E. (1998). *The practice of social research* (8th ed.). Belmont, CA: Wadsworth.

Bargiela-Chiappini, F. (2010). Facing the future: some reflections. In F. Bargiela-Chiappini & M. Haugh (Eds.), *Face, communication and social interaction* (pp. 307–326). London: Equinox.

Bargiela-Chiappini, F., & Harris, S. (2006). Politeness at work: Issues and challenges. *Journal of Politeness Research, 2*(1), 7–33. https://doi.org/10.1515/pr.2006.002

Barros García, M. J., & Terkourafi, M. (2014). First-order politeness in rapprochement and distancing cultures: Understandings and uses of politeness by Spanish native speakers from Spain and Spanish nonnative speakers from the U.S. *Pragmatics, 24*(1), 1–34. https://doi.org/10.1075/prag.24.1.01bar

Batson, C. D. (2010). Empathy-induced altruistic motivation. In M. Mikulincer & P. R. Shaver (Eds.), *Prosocial motives, emotions, and behavior: The better angels of our nature* (pp. 15-34). Washington, DC: American Psychological Association. https://doi.org/10.1037/12061-001

Batson, C. D. (2011). *Altruism in humans.* Oxford: Oxford University Press.

Batson, C. D., Chang, J., Orr, R., & Rowland J. (2002). Empathy, attitudes, and action: Can feeling for a member of a stigmatized group motivate one to help the group? *Personality and Social Psychology Bulletin, 28*(12), 1656–1666. https://doi.org/10.1177/014616702237647

Bella, S. (2009). Invitations and politeness in Greek: The age variable. *Journal of Politeness Research, 5*(2), 243–271. https://doi.org/10.1515/jplr.2009.013

Bergmann, J. R. (1998). Introduction: Morality in discourse. *Research on Language and Social Interaction, 31*(3-4), 279–294. https://doi.org/10.1080/08351813.1998.9683594

Beutel, A. M., & Marini, M. M. (1995). Gender and values. *American Sociological Review, 60*, 436–448.

Blum-Kulka, S. (1987). Indirectness and politeness in requests: Same or different? *Journal of Pragmatics, 11*(2), 131–146. https://doi.org/10.1016/0378-2166(87)90192-5

Blum-Kulka, S. (2005 [1992]). The metapragmatics of politeness in Israeli society. In R. J. Watts, S. Ide, & K. Ehlich (Eds.), *Politeness in language: Studies in its history, theory and practice* (pp. 255–280). Berlin: Mouton de Gruyter. https://doi.org/10.1515/9783110886542-013

Blum-Kulka, S., House, J., & Kasper, G. (1989). *Cross-cultural pragmatics: Requests and apologies*. Norwood, NJ: Ablex Publishing Corporation.

Bolger, N., Zuckerman, A., & Kessler, R. C. (2000). Invisible support and adjustment to stress. *Journal of Personality and Social Psychology, 79*(6), 953–961. https://doi.org/10.1037//0022-3514.79.6.953

Bond, M. H., Žegarac, V., & Spencer-Oatey, H. (2000). Culture as an explanatory variable: Problems and possibilities. In H. Spencer-Oatey (Ed.), *Culturally speaking: Managing rapport through talk across cultures* (pp. 47–71). London: Continuum.

Bousfield, D. (2007a). Impoliteness, preference organization and conductivity. *Multilingua, 26*(1), 1–33.

Bousfield, D. (2007b). Beginnings, middles and ends: A biopsy of the dynamics of impolite exchanges. *Journal of Pragmatics, 39*(12), 2185–2216. https://doi.org/10.1016/j.pragma.2006.11.005

Bousfield, D. (2008). *Impoliteness in interaction*. Amsterdam: John Benjamins.

Bousfield, D. (2016). Welcome introduction to the 4th Linguistic Impoliteness, Aggression and Rudeness (LIAR IV). Manchester Metropolitan University, Manchester, UK, 12–14 July 2016.

Bousfield, D., & Locher, M. (Eds.) (2008). *Impoliteness in language*. Berlin: Mouton de Gruyter.

Brown, P., & Levinson. S. C. (1978). Universals in language usage: Politeness phenomena. In E. N. Goody (Eds.), *Questions and politeness: Strategies in social interaction* (pp. 56–310). Cambridge: Cambridge University Press.

Brown, P., & Levinson, S. C. (1987). *Politeness: Some universals in language usage*. Cambridge: Cambridge University Press.

Brown, S., Hayashi, B., & Yamamoto, K. (2012). Japan/Anglo-American cross-cultural communication. In C. B. Paulston, S. F. Kiesling, & E. S. Rangel (Eds.), *The handbook of intercultural discourse and communication* (pp. 252–271). Oxford: Wiley-Blackwell. https://doi.org/10.1002/9781118247273.ch13

Burdelski, M. (2010). Socializing politeness routines: Action, other-orientation, and embodiment in a Japanese preschool. *Journal of Pragmatics, 42*(6), 1606–1621. https://doi.org/10.1016/j.pragma.2009.11.007

Burdelski, M. (2013). 'I'm sorry, flower': Socializing apology, relationships, and empathy in Japan. *Pragmatics and Society, 4*(1), 54–81. https://doi.org/10.1075/ps.4.1.03bur

Burdelski, M., & Mitsuhashi, K. (2010). 'She thinks you're *kawaii*': Socializing affect, gender, and relationships in a Japanese preschool. *Language in Society, 39*(1), 65–93. https://doi.org/10.1017/s0047404509990650

Burger, J. M., Sanchez, J., Imberi, J. E., & Grande, L. R. (2009). The norm of reciprocity as an internalized social norm: Returning favors even when no one finds out. *Social Influence, 4*(1), 11–17. https://doi.org/10.1080/15534510802131004

Caffi, C. (2009). Metapragmatics. In J. L. Mey (Eds.), *Concise encyclopedia of pragmatics* (pp. 625–630). Amsterdam: Elsevier.

Caffi, C. (2015). (Un)expected behavior: Some general issues and a papal example. *Journal of Pragmatics, 86*, 19–24. https://doi.org/10.1016/j.pragma.2015.06.008

Chang, W.-L. M., & Fukushima, S. (2017). 'Your care and concern are my burden!': Accounting for the emic concepts of 'attentiveness' and 'empathy' in interpersonal relationships among Taiwanese females. *East Asian Pragmatics, 2*(1), 1–23. https://doi.org/10.1558/eap.33081

Chen, R. (2010). Pragmatics East and West: Similar or different? In A. Trosborg (Ed.), *Pragmatics across languages and cultures* (pp. 167–188). Berlin: De Gruyter Mouton. https://doi.org/10.1515/9783110214444.1.167

Clancy, P. (1986). The acquisition of communicative style in Japanese. In B. Schieffelin & E. Ochs (Eds.), *Language socialization across cultures* (pp. 213–250). Cambridge: Cambridge University Press. https://doi.org/10.1017/cbo9780511620898.011

Clancy, P. (1990). Acquiring communicative style in Japanese. In R. C. Scarcella, E. S. Andersen, & S. D. Krashen (Eds.), *Developing communicative competence in a second language* (pp. 27–35). New York: Newbury House Publishers.

Cohen, R. (1978). Altruism: Human, cultural, or what? In L. Wispé (Ed.), *Altruism, sympathy, and helping: Psychological and sociological principles* (pp. 79–98). New York: Academic Press.

Cook, H. M. (2006). Japanese politeness as an interactional achievement: Academic consultation sessions in Japanese universities. *Multilingua, 25*(3), 269–292. https://doi.org/10.1515/multi.2006.016

Cook, H. M., & Burdelski, M. (2017). (Im)politeness: Language socialization. In J. Culpeper, M. Haugh & D. Z. Kádár (Eds.), *The Palgrave handbook of linguistic (im)politeness* (pp. 461–488). Basingstoke: Palgrave Macmillan. https://doi.org/10.1057/978-1-137-37508-7_18

Coulmas, F. (2005 [1992]). Linguistic etiquette in Japanese society. In R. J. Watts, S. Ide, & R. Ehlich (Eds.), *Politeness in language: Studies in its history, theory and practice* (pp. 299–323). Berlin: Mouton de Gruyter. https://doi.org/10.1515/9783110886542-015

Coulmas, F. (2003). *Die Kultur Japans: Tradition und Moderne*. Munich: Verlag C. H. Beck.

Coupland, N. (2010). Introduction: Sociolinguistics in the global era. In N. Coupland (Ed.), *The handbook of language and globalization* (pp. 1–27). Chichester: Wiley-Blackwell. https://doi.org/10.1002/9781444324068.ch

Culpeper, J. (1996). Towards an anatomy of impoliteness. *Journal of Pragmatics, 25*(3), 349–367. https://doi.org/10.1016/0378-2166(95)00014-3

Culpeper, J. (2003). Impoliteness revisited: With special reference to dynamic and prosodic aspects. *Journal of Pragmatics, 35*(10–11), 1545–1579. https://doi.org/10.1016/s0378-2166(02)00118-2

Culpeper, J. (2005). Impoliteness and entertainment in the television quiz show: *The Weakest Link. Journal of Politeness Research, 1*(1), 35–72. https://doi.org/10.1515/jplr.2005.1.1.35

Culpeper, J. (2011a). Politeness and impoliteness. In G. Andersen & K. Aijmer (Eds.), *Pragmatics of Society* (pp. 393–438). Berlin: Mouton de Gruyter. https://doi.org/10.1515/9783110214420.393

Culpeper, J. (2011b). *Impoliteness: Using language to cause offence.* Cambridge: Cambridge University Press.

Culpeper, J., & Haugh, M. (2014). *Pragmatics and the English language.* Basingstoke: Palgrave Macmillan.

Culpeper, J., & Kádár, D. Z. (2010). *Historical (im)politeness.* Bern: Peter Lang.

Culpeper, J., Marti, L., Mei, M., Nevala, M., & Schauer, G. (2010). Cross-cultural variation in the perception of impoliteness: A study of impoliteness events reported by students in England, China, Finland, Germany and Turkey. *Intercultural Pragmatics, 7*(4), 597–624. https://doi.org/10.1515/iprg.2010.027

Culpeper, J., & Tantucci, V. (2018). On reciprocity and (im)politeness. A paper presented at the 11th International Conference on Im/politeness, University of Valencia, 4–6 July 2018.

Cummings, L. (2005). *Pragmatics: A multidisciplinary perspective.* Edinburgh: Edinburgh University Press.

Cutrona, C. E., & Suhr, J. A. (1992). Controllability of stressful events and satisfaction with spouse support behaviors. *Communication Research, 19*(2), 154–174. https://doi.org/10.1177/009365092019002002

Daibou, I. (2012). Taijin kankei ni okeru hairyo koudou no shinrigaku: Taijin komyunikeeshon no shiten. [Psychology of considerate behaviour in interpersonal relationships: A perspective of interpersonal communication]. In K. Miyake, H. Noda, & N. Ogoshi (Eds.), *Hairyo wa donoyou ni shime sareru ka* [How is consideration expressed?] (pp. 51–67). Tokyo: Hituzi Syobo.

Darics, E. (2010). Politeness in computer-mediated discourse of a virtual team. *Journal of Politeness Research, 6*(1), 129–150. https://doi.org/10.1515/jplr.2010.007

Davies, B. L. (2018). Evaluating evaluations: What different types of metapragmatic behaviour can tell us about participants' understandings of the moral order. *Journal of Politeness Research, 14*(1), 121–151. https://doi.org/10.1515/pr-2017-0037

de Kadt, E. (1998). The concept of face and its applicability to the Zulu language. *Journal of Pragmatics, 29*(2), 173–191. https://doi.org/10.1016/s0378-2166(97)00021-0

Duan, C., & Hill, C. E. (1996). The current state of empathy research. *Journal of Counselling Psychology, 43*, 261–274.

Dunn, C. D. (2013). Speaking politely, kindly, and beautifully: Ideologies of politeness in Japanese business etiquette training. *Multilingua, 32*(2), 225–245. https://doi.org/10.1515/multi-2013-0011

Eelen, G. (2001). *A critique of politeness theories.* Manchester: St. Jerome Publishing.

Floyd, K., & Ray, C. D. (2017). Thanks, but no thanks: Negotiating face threats when rejecting offers of unwanted social support. *Journal of Social and Personal Relationships, 34*(8), 1260–1276. https://doi.org/10.1177/0265407516673161

Fukada, A., & Asato, N. (2004). Universal politeness theory: Application to the use of Japanese honorifics. *Journal of Pragmatics, 36*(11), 1991–2002. https://doi.org/10.1016/j.pragma.2003.11.006

Fukushima, S. (2000). *Requests and culture: Politeness in British English and Japanese.* Bern: Peter Lang.

Fukushima, S. (2004). Evaluation of politeness: The case of attentiveness. *Multilingua, 23*(4), 365–387. https://doi.org/10.1515/mult.2004.23.4.365

Fukushima, S. (2009). Evaluation of politeness: Do the Japanese evaluate attentiveness more positively than the British? *Pragmatics, 19*(4), 501–518. https://doi.org/10.1075/prag.19.4.01fuk

Fukushima, S. (2011). A cross-generational and cross-cultural study on demonstration of attentiveness. *Pragmatics, 21*(4), 549–571. https://doi.org/10.1075/prag.21.4.03fuk

Fukushima, S. (2013). Evaluation of (im)politeness: A comparative study among Japanese students, Japanese parents and American students on evaluation of attentiveness. *Pragmatics, 23*(2), 275–299. https://doi.org/10.1075/prag.23.2.04fuk

Fukushima, S. (2014). An investigation of attentiveness. Paper presented at the 8th International Symposium on Politeness, University of Huddersfield, 9–11 July 2014.

Fukushima, S. (2015). In search of another understanding of politeness: From the perspective of attentiveness. *Journal of Politeness Research, 11*(2), 261–287. https://doi.org/10.1515/pr-2015-0011

Fukushima, S. (2016). Emic understandings of attentiveness and its related concepts among Japanese. *East Asian Pragmatics, 1*(2), 181–208. https://doi.org/10.1558/eap.v1i2.31762

Fukushima, S. (2019). A metapragmatic aspect of politeness: With a special emphasis on attentiveness in Japanese. In E. Ogiermann & P. Garcés-Conejos Blitvich (Eds.), *From speech acts to lay understandings of politeness: Multilingual and multicultural perspectives* (pp. 226–247). Cambridge: Cambridge University Press. https://doi.org/10.1017/9781108182119.010

Fukushima, S., & Haugh, M. (2014). The role of emic understandings in theorizing im/politeness: The metapragmatics of attentiveness, empathy and anticipatory inference in Japanese and Chinese. *Journal of Pragmatics, 74,* 165–179. https://doi.org/10.1016/j.pragma.2014.08.004

Fukushima, S., & Sifianou, M. (2017). Conceptualizing politeness in Japanese and Greek. *Intercultural Pragmatics, 14*(4), 525–555. https://doi.org/10.1515/ip-2017-0024

Furuhata, K. (Ed.). (1994). *Shakai shinrigaku shoojiten* [A small dictionary of social psychology]. Tokyo: Yuhikaku.

Gao, G. (1996). Self and OTHER: A Chinese perspective on interpersonal relationships. In W. B. Gudykunst, S. Ting-Toomey, & T. Nishida (Eds.), *Communication in personal relationships across cultures* (pp. 81–101). Thousand Oaks, CA: Sage.

Garcés-Conejos Blitvich, P. (2010). Introduction: The *status-quo* and *quo vadis* of impoliteness research. *Intercultural Pragmatics, 7*(4), 535–559. https://doi.org/10.1515/iprg.2010.025

Garcés-Conejos Blitvich, P., Lorenzo-Dus, N., & Bou-Franch, P. (2010). A genre approach to impoliteness in a Spanish television talk show: Evidence from corpus-based analysis, questionnaires and focus groups. *Intercultural Pragmatics, 7*(4), 689–723. https://doi.org/10.1515/iprg.2010.030

Garfinkel, H. (1967). *Studies in ethnomethodology.* Englewood Cliffs, NJ: Prentice-Hall.

Garrett, P. (2010). Meanings of 'globalization': East and West. In N. Coupland (Ed.), *The handbook of language and globalization* (pp. 447–474). Chichester: Wiley-Blackwell. https://doi.org/10.1002/9781444324068.ch20

Gladkova, A. (2010). Sympathy, compassion, and empathy in English and Russian: A linguistic and cultural analysis. *Culture & Psychology, 16*(2), 267–285. https://doi.org/10.1177/1354067x10361396

Golato, A., & Golato, P. (2018). Ethnomethodology and conversation analysis. In A. H. Jucker, K. P. Schneider, & W. Bublitz (Eds.), *Methods in pragmatics* (pp. 367–394). Berlin: De Gruyter Mouton. https://doi.org/10.1515/9783110424928-015

Goldsmith, D. J. (1992). Managing conflicting goals in supportive interaction: An integrative theoretical framework. *Communication Research, 19*(2), 246–286. https://doi.org/10.1177/009365092019002007

Gouldner, A. W. (1960). The norm of reciprocity: A preliminary statement. *American Sociological Review, 25*(2), 161–178. https://doi.org/10.2307/2092623

Grainger, K. (2013). Of babies and bath water: Is there any place for Austin and Grice in interpersonal pragmatics? *Journal of Pragmatics, 58,* 27–38. https://doi.org/10.1016/j.pragma.2013.08.008

Grainger, K. (2014). Rethinking conventional indirectness: The view from interactional sociolinguistics. Paper presented at the 8th International Symposium on Politeness, University of Huddersfield, 9–11 July 2014.

Grainger, K., & Mills, S. (2016). *Directness and indirectness across cultures.* Basingstoke: Palgrave Macmillan.

Grainger, K., Mills, S., & Sibanda, M. (2010). 'Just tell us what to do': Southern African face and its relevance to intercultural communication. *Journal of Pragmatics, 42*(8), 2158–2171. https://doi.org/10.1016/j.pragma.2009.12.017

Gu, Y. (1990). Politeness phenomena in modern Chinese. *Journal of Pragmatics, 14*(2), 237–257.

Gudykunst, W. B. (1993). *Communication in Japan and the United States.* Albany, NY: State University of New York Press.

Gudykunst, W. B., Matsumoto, Y., Ting-Toomey, S., Nishida, T., Kim, K., & Heyman, S. (1996). The influence of cultural individualism–collectivism, self construals, and individual values on communication styles across cultures. *Human Communication Research, 22*(4), 510–543. https://doi.org/10.1111/j.1468-2958.1996.tb00377.x

Gudykunst, W. B., & Nishida, T. (1993). Interpersonal and intergroup communication in Japan and the United States. In W. B. Gudykunst (Ed.), *Communication in Japan and the United States* (pp. 149–214). Albany, NY: State University of New York Press.

Gudykunst, W. B., & San Antonio, P. (1993). Approaches to the study of communication in Japan and the United States. In W. B. Gudykunst (Ed.), *Communication in Japan and the United States* (pp. 18–48). Albany, NY: State University of New York Press.

Gudykunst, W. B., Yoon, Y.-C., & Nishida, T. (1987). The influence of individualism-collectivism on perceptions of communication in ingroup and outgroup relationships. *Communication Monographs, 54*(3), 295–306. https://doi.org/10.1080/03637758709390234

Haidt, J., & Graham, J. (2007). When morality opposes justice: Conservatives have moral intuitions that liberals may not recognize. *Social Justice Research, 20*(1), 98–116. https://doi.org/10.1007/s11211-007-0034-z

Haidt, J., & Kesebir, S. (2010). Morality. In S. Fiske, D. Gilbert, & G. Lindzey (Eds.), *Handbook of social psychology* (5th ed., pp. 797–832). Hoboken, NJ: Wiley. https://doi.org/10.1002/9780470561119.socpsy002022

Hall, E. T. (1976). *Beyond culture.* Garden City, NY: Doubleday.

Hamano, K. (1987). *Ki*: A key concept for Japanese interpersonal relationships. *Psychologia, 30*(2), 101–112.

Hara, K. (2006). The concept of *omoiyari* (altruistic sensitivity) in Japanese relational communication. *Intercultural Communication Studies, 15*(1), 24–32.

Hara, K., & Kim, M. (2004). The effect of self-construals on conversational indirectness. *International Journal of Intercultural Relations, 28*(1), 1–18. https://doi.org/10.1016/j.ijintrel.2003.12.005

Harada, J. (1991). Omoiyari no jikken de wakaru koto [What we learn from the experiments of empathy]. *Gendai no esupuri, 291*, 48–56.

Hatch, E., & Lazaraton, A. (1991). *The research manual: Design and statistics for applied linguistics.* Boston: Heinle and Heinle Publishers.

Haugh, M. (2003). Anticipated versus inferred politeness. *Multilingua, 22*(4), 399–413. https://doi.org/10.1515/mult.2003.020

Haugh, M. (2004). Revisiting the conceptualization of politeness in English and Japanese. *Multilingua, 23*(2), 85–109.

Haugh, M. (2005). The importance of 'place' in Japanese politeness: Implications for cross-cultural and intercultural analyses. *Intercultural Pragmatics, 2*(1), 41–68. https://doi.org/10.1515/iprg.2005.2.1.41

Haugh, M. (2007a). Emic conceptualisations of (im)politeness and face in Japanese: Implications for the discursive negotiation of second language learner identities. *Journal of Pragmatics, 39*(4), 657–680. https://doi.org/10.1016/j.pragma.2006.12.005

Haugh, M. (2007b). The co-constitution of politeness implicature in conversation. *Journal of Pragmatics, 39*(1), 84–110. https://doi.org/10.1016/j.pragma.2006.07.004

Haugh, M. (2007c). The discursive challenge to politeness research: An interactional alternative. *Journal of Politeness Research, 3*(2), 295–317. https://doi.org/10.1515/pr.2007.013

Haugh, M. (2010). Intercultural (im)politeness and the micro-macro issue. In A. Trosborg (Ed.), *Pragmatics across languages and cultures* (pp. 139–166). Berlin: De Gruyter Mouton. https://doi.org/10.1515/9783110214444.1.139

Haugh, M. (2011). Epilogue: Culture and norms in politeness research. In D. Z. Kádár & S. Mills (Eds.), *Politeness in East Asia* (pp. 252–264) Cambridge: Cambridge University Press. https://doi.org/10.1017/cbo9780511977886.013

Haugh, M. (2012). Epilogue: The first–second order distinction in face and politeness research. *Journal of Politeness Research, 8*(1), 111–134. https://doi.org/10.1515/pr-2012-0007

Haugh, M. (2013). Im/politeness, social practice and the participation order. *Journal of Pragmatics, 58*, 52–72. https://doi.org/10.1016/j.pragma.2013.07.003

Haugh, M. (2015). *Im/politeness implicatures*. Berlin: Mouton de Gruyter.

Haugh, M. (2016a). The role of English as a scientific metalanguage for research in pragmatics: Reflections on the metapragmatics of 'politeness' in Japanese. *East Asian Pragmatics, 1*(1), 39–71. https://doi.org/10.1558/eap.v1i1.27610

Haugh, M. (2016b). Prompting social action as a higher-order pragmatic act. In K. Allan, A. Capone, & I. Kecskes (Eds.), *Pragmemes and theories of language use* (pp. 167–190). Switzerland: Springer International Publishing. https://doi.org/10.1007/978-3-319-43491-9_10

Haugh, M. (2017). Prompting offers of assistance in interaction. *Pragmatics and Society, 8*(2), 183–207. https://doi.org/10.1075/ps.8.2.02hau

Haugh, M. (2018). Afterword: Theorizing (im)politeness. *Journal of Politeness Research, 14*(1), 153–165. https://doi.org/10.1515/pr-2017-0058

Haugh, M. (2019). The metapragmatics of *consideration* in (Australian and New Zealand) English. In E. Ogiermann & P. Garcés-Conejos Blitvich (Eds.), *From speech acts to lay concepts of politeness: Multilingual and multicultural perspectives* (pp. 201–225). Cambridge: Cambridge University Press. https://doi.org/10.1017/9781108182119.009

Haugh, M., & Culpeper, J. (2018). Integrative pragmatics and (im)politeness theory. In C. Ilie & N. R. Norrick (Eds.), *Pragmatics and its interfaces* (pp. 213–239). Amsterdam: John Benjamins. https://doi.org/10.1075/pbns.294.10hau

Haugh, M., & Hinze, C. (2003). A metalinguistic approach to deconstructing the concepts of 'face' and 'politeness' in Chinese, English and Japanese. *Journal of Pragmatics, 35*(10–11), 1581–1611. https://doi.org/10.1016/s0378-2166(03)00049-3

Haugh, M., & Kádár, D. Z. (2017). Intercultural (im)politeness. In J. Culpeper, M. Haugh, & D. Z. Kádár (Eds.), *The Palgrave handbook of linguistic (im)politeness* (pp. 601–632). Basingstoke: Palgrave Macmillan. https://doi.org/10.1057/978-1-137-37508-7_23

Haugh, M., Kádár, D. Z., & Mills, S. (2013). Interpersonal pragmatics: Issues and debates. *Journal of Pragmatics, 58*, 1–11. https://doi.org/10.1016/j.pragma.2013.09.009

Haugh, M., & Obana, Y. (2011). Politeness in Japan. In D. Z. Kádár & S. Mills (Eds.), *Politeness in East Asia* (pp. 147–175). Cambridge: Cambridge University Press. https://doi.org/10.1017/cbo9780511977886.009

He, Y. (2012). Different generations, different face? A discursive approach to naturally occurring compliment responses in Chinese. *Journal of Politeness Research, 8*(1): 29–51. https://doi.org/10.1515/pr-2012-0003

He, Z., & Ren, W. (2016). Current address behaviour in China. *East Asian Pragmatics, 1*(2), 163–180. https://doi.org/10.1558/eap.v1i2.29537

Held, G. (2005 [1992]). Politeness in linguistic research. In R. J. Watts, S. Ide, & K. Ehlich (Eds.), *Politeness in language: Studies in its history, theory and practice* (pp. 131–153). Berlin: Mouton de Gruyter. https://doi.org/10.1515/9783110886542-008

Hermanns, F. (1993). Mit freundlichen Grüßen: Bemerkungen zum Geltungswandel einer kommunikativen Tugend. In W. P. Klein & I. Paul (Eds.), *Sprachliche Aufmerksamkeit: Glossen und Marginalien zur Sprache der Gegenwart* (pp. 81–85). Heidelberg: Universitätsverlag C. Winter.

Hickey, L., & Stewart, M. (2005a). *Politeness in Europe*. Clevedon: Multilingual Matters.

Hickey, L., & Stewart, M. (2005b). Introduction. In L. Hickey & M. Stewart (Eds.), *Politeness in Europe* (pp.1–12). Clevedon: Multilingual Matters. https://doi. org/10.21832/9781853597398-002

Hill, B., Ide, S., Ikuta, S., Kawasaki, A., & Ogino, T. (1986). Universals of linguistic politeness: Quantitative evidence from Japanese and American English. *Journal of Pragmatics, 10*(3), 347–371. https://doi.org/10.1016/0378-2166(86)90006-8

Himeno, T. (2003). Hairyo hyoogen kara mita nihongo [The Japanese language from the perspective of expressions of consideration]. *Gekkan Nihongo, 16*(4), 66–69.

Hirschon, R. (2001). Freedom, solidarity and obligation: The socio-cultural context of Greek politeness. In A. Bayraktaroglu & M. Sifianou (Eds.), *Linguistic politeness across boundaries: The case of Greek and Turkish.* (pp. 17–42). Amsterdam: John Benjamins. https://doi.org/10.1075/pbns.88.03hir

Hofstede, G. (1980). *Culture's consequences: International differences in work-related values.* Newbury Park: Sage.

Hofstede, G. (1991). *Cultures and organizations: Software of the mind.* London: McGraw-Hill Book Company.

Hofstede, G. (2001). *Culture's consequences: Comparing values, behaviors, institutions, and organizations across nations* (2nd ed.). Thousand Oaks, CA: Sage.

Holliday, A. (1999). Small cultures. *Applied Linguistics, 20*(2), 237–264. https://doi. org/10.1093/applin/20.2.237

Holmes, J., & Schnurr, S. (2005). Politeness, humor and gender in the workplace: Negotiating norms and identifying contestation. *Journal of Politeness Research, 1*(1), 121–149. https://doi.org/10.1515/jplr.2005.1.1.121

Holtgraves, T., & Yang, J.-N. (1990). Politeness as universal: Cross-cultural perceptions of request strategies and inferences based on their use. *Journal of Personality and Social Psychology, 59*(4), 719–729. https://doi.org/10.1037/0022-3514.59.4.719

Horike, K. (1991). Shakaiteki sukiru to shite no omoiyari [Omoiyari as a social skill]. *Gendai no esupuri, 291*, 150–160.

Huang, Y. (2012). *The Oxford dictionary of pragmatics.* Oxford: Oxford University Press.

Hübler, A. (2011). Metapragmatics. In W. Bublitz, A. H. Jucker, & K. P. Schneider (Eds.), *Foundation of pragmatics* (pp. 107–136). Berlin: De Gruyter Mouton.

Hübler, A., & Bublitz, W. (2007). Introducing metapragmatics in use. In W. Bublitz & A. Hübler (Eds.), *Metapragmatics in use* (pp. 1–26). Amsterdam: John Benjamins. https://doi.org/10.1075/pbns.165.02hub

Hudson, M. E. (2011). Student honorifics usage in conversations with professors. *Journal of Pragmatics, 43*(15), 3689–3706. https://doi.org/10.1016/j.pragma.2011.09.004

Ide, S. (1989). Formal forms and discernment: Two neglected aspects of universals of linguistic politeness. *Multilingua, 8*(2–3), 223–248. https://doi.org/10.1515/mult.1989.8.2-3.223

Ide, S. (2005). How and why honorifics can signify dignity and elegance: The indexicality and reflexivity of linguistic rituals. In R. T. Lakoff & S. Ide (Eds.), *Broadening the horizon of linguistic politeness* (pp. 45–64). Amsterdam: John Benjamins. https://doi. org/10.1075/pbns.139.06ide

Ide, S. (2012). Roots of the *wakimae* aspect of linguistic politeness: Modal expressions and Japanese sense of self. In M. Meeuwis & J.-O. Östman (Eds.), *Pragmaticizing understanding: Studies for Jef Verschueren* (pp. 121–138). Amsterdam: John Benjamins. https://doi.org/10.1075/z.170.08ide

Ide, S., Hills, B., Carnes, Y. M., Ogino, T., & Kawasaki, A. (2005 [1992]). The concept of politeness: An empirical study of American English and Japanese. In R. J. Watts, S. Ide, & K. Ehlich (Eds.), *Politeness in language: Studies in its history, theory and practice* (pp. 281–297). Berlin: Mouton de Gruyter. https://doi.org/10.1515/9783110886542-014

Ide, S., & Ueno, K. (2012). Ba no riron de kangaeru hairyo gengo koudou [Linguistic behaviour of consideration thinking from the theory of ba]. In K. Miyake, H. Noda, & N. Ogoshi (Eds.), *Hairyo wa donoyouni shime sareru ka* [How is consideration expressed?] (pp. 29–50). Tokyo: Hituzi shobo.

Intachakra, S. (2012). Politeness motivated by the 'heart' and 'binary rationality' in Thai culture. *Journal of Pragmatics, 44*(5), 619–635. https://doi.org/10.1016/j.pragma.2011.07.016

Ishii, S. (1984). Enryo-sasshi communication: A key to understanding Japanese interpersonal relations. *Cross Currents, 11*, 49–58.

Ishii, S. (1987). Taijin kankei to ibunka komyunikeeshion [Interpersonal relationships and intercultural communication]. In G. Furuta (Ed.), *Ibunka komyunikeeshion* [Intercultural communication] (2nd ed., pp. 121–140). Tokyo: Yuhikaku.

Işik-Güler, H. (2008). *Metapragmatics of (im)politeness in Turkish: An exploratory emic investigation* (PhD dissertation). Middle East Technical University, Ankara.

Işik-Güler, H., & Ruhi, Ş. (2010). Face and impoliteness at the intersection with emotions: A corpus-based study in Turkish. *Intercultural Pragmatics, 7*(4), 625–660. https://doi.org/10.1515/iprg.2010.028

Iwamoto, H., & Takahashi, K. (2015). Nihon no omotenashi to seiyou no hosupitaritii no kenkai ni kansuru ichi kousatsu [A study on omotenashi in Japan and hospitality in the West]. *Jyousai Kokusai Daigaku Kiyou, 23*(6), 17–26.

Jinnai, M. (2006). Bokashi hyougen no nimensei: Chikazukanai hairyo to chikazuku hairyo [Two aspects of blurry expressions: Consideration of distancing and consideration of approaching]. In Kokuritsu kokugo kenkyuujyo [National Institute for Japanese Language and Linguistics] (Ed.), *Gengo koudou ni okeru hairyo no shosou* [Consideration in linguistic behaviours] (pp. 115–131). Tokyo: Kuroshio.

Jucker, A. H., Schneider, K. P., & Bublitz, W. (Eds.). (2018). *Methods in pragmatics.* Berlin: De Gruyter Mouton. https://doi.org/10.1007/s41701-019-00054-z

Kádár, D. Z. (2013). *Relational rituals and communication: Ritual interaction in groups.* Basingstoke: Palgrave Macmillan.

Kádár, D. Z. (2017). *Politeness, impoliteness and ritual: Maintaining the moral order in interpersonal interaction.* Cambridge: Cambridge University Press. https://doi.org/10.1017/9781107280465

Kádár, D. Z., & Bargiela-Chiappini, F. (2011). Introduction: Politeness research in and across cultures. In F. Bargiela-Chiappini & D. Z. Kádár (Eds.), *Politeness across cultures* (pp. 1–14). Basingstoke: Palgrave Macmillan. https://doi.org/10.1057/9780230305939_1

Kádár, D. Z., & Fukushima, S. (2018). The meta-conventionalisation and moral order of e-practices: A Japanese case study. *Internet Pragmatics, 1*(2), 352–378. https://doi.org/10.1075/ip.00016.kad

Kádár, D. Z., & Haugh, M. (2013). *Understanding politeness.* Cambridge: Cambridge University Press. http://dx.doi.org/10.1017/CBO9781139382717

Kádár, D. Z., & Márquez-Reiter, R. (2015). (Im)politeness and (im)morality: Insights from intervention. *Journal of Politeness Research, 11*(2), 239–260. http://dx.doi.org/10.1515/pr-2015-0010

Kádár, D. Z., & Mills, S. (2011). Introduction. In D. Z. Kádár & S. Mills (Eds.), *Politeness in East Asia* (pp. 1–17). Cambridge: Cambridge University Press.

Kádár, D. Z., & Mills, S. (2013). Rethinking discernment. *Journal of Politeness Research, 9*(2), 133–158. http://dx.doi.org/10.1515/pr-2013-0007.

Kádár, D. Z., Parvaresh, V., & Ning, P. (2019). Morality, moral order, and language conflict and aggression: A position paper. *Journal of Language Aggression and Conflict, 7*(1), 6–30. https://doi.org/10.1075/jlac.00017.kad

Kádár, D. Z., & Paternoster, A. (2015). Historicity in metapragmatics – A study on 'discernment' in Italian metadiscourse. *Pragmatics, 25*(3), 369–391. https://doi.org/10.1075/prag.25.3.03kad

Kasper, G. (2000). Data collection in pragmatics research. In H. Spencer-Oatey (Ed.), *Culturally speaking: Managing rapport through talk across cultures* (pp. 316–341). London: Continuum.

Kasper, G. (2008). Data collection in pragmatics research. In H. Spencer-Oatey (Ed.), *Culturally speaking: Culture, communication and politeness theory* (2nd ed., pp. 279–303). London: Continuum.

Kecskes, I. (2004). Editorial: Lexical merging, conceptual blending, and cultural crossing. *Intercultural Pragmatics, 1*(1), 1–26. https://doi.org/10.1515/iprg.2004.005

Kerkam, Z. (2007). *Indirectness and directness in English and Arabic* (PhD thesis). Sheffield Hallam University, Sheffield.

Kinjyo, N. (2014). Omotenashi no nihon: Garapagosuka kara no dakkyaku ni mukete [Japan of *omotenashi*: Towards a way out from becoming Galapagos] https://eyi.eyjapan.jp/knowledge/omotenashi/column/pdf/2014-06-23.pdf

Krippendorff, K. (2013). *Content analysis: An introduction to its methodology* (3rd ed.). Thousand Oaks, CA: Sage Publications.

Krueger, R. A., & Casey, M. A. (2009). *Focus groups: A practical guide for applied research* (4th ed.). Thousand Oaks, CA: Sage Publications.

Kupetz, M. (2014). Empathy displays as interactional achievements – Multimodal and sequential aspects. *Journal of Pragmatics, 61*, 4–34. https://doi.org/10.1016/j.pragma.2013.11.006

Kyono, C. (2017). Japanese politeness situated in thanking a benefactor: Examining the use of four types of Japanese benefactive auxiliary verbs. *East Asian Pragmatics, 2*(1), 25–57. https://doi.org/10.1558/eap.30468

Lakoff, R. T. (2005). Civility and its discontents: Or, getting in your face. In R. T. Lakoff & S. Ide (Eds.), *Broadening the horizon of linguistic politeness* (pp. 23–43). Amsterdam: John Benjamins. https://doi.org/10.1075/pbns.139.05lak

Langer, E. J. (1989). *Mindfulness*. Cambridge, MA: Perseus Books.

Langlotz, A., & Locher, M. A. (2013). The role of emotions in relational work. *Journal of Pragmatics, 58*, 87–107. https://doi.org/10.1016/j.pragma.2013.05.014

Lebra, T. S. (1976). *Japanese patterns of behavior*. Honolulu: University of Hawai'i Press.

Lebra, T. S. (1993). Culture, self, and communication in Japan and the United States. In W. B. Gudykunst (Ed.), *Communication in Japan and the United States* (pp. 51–87). Albany, NY: State University of New York Press.

Lebra, T. S. (2004). *The Japanese self in cultural logic*. Honolulu: University of Hawai'i Press.

Lee, H. E. (2015). Does a server's attentiveness matter? Understanding intercultural service encounters in restaurants. *International Journal of Hospitality Management, 50*, 134–144. https://doi.org/10.1016/j.ijhm.2015.08.003

Lee, J., & Pinker, S. (2010). Rationales for indirect speech: The theory of the strategic speaker. *Psychological Review, 117*(3), 785–807. https://doi.org/10.1037/a0019688

Leech, G. (2007). Politeness: Is there an East–West divide? *Journal of Politeness Research, 3*(2), 167–206. https://doi.org/10.1515/PR.2007.009

Leech, G. (2014). *The pragmatics of politeness*. Oxford: Oxford University Press.

Lempert, M. (2012). Indirectness. In C. B. Paulston, S. F. Kiesling, & E. S. Rangel (Eds.), *The handbook of intercultural discourse and communication* (pp. 108–204). Oxford: Wiley-Blackwell. https://doi.org/10.1002/9781118247273.ch10

Lempert, M. (2013). No ordinary ethics. *Anthropological Theory, 13*(4), 370–393.

Lim, T., & Ahn, S. (2015). Dialectics of culture and dynamic balancing between individuality and collectivity. *Journal of Asian Pacific Communication, 25*(1), 63–77. https://doi.org/10.1075/japc.25.1.04lim

Linguistic Politeness Research Group (Eds.). (2011). *Discursive approaches to politeness*. Berlin: Mouton de Gruyter. https://doi.org/10.1515/9783110238679.1

Locher, M. A. (2004). *Power and politeness in action: Disagreements in oral communication*. Berlin: Mouton de Gruyter.

Locher, M. A. (2006). Polite behavior within relational work: The discursive approach to politeness. *Multilingua, 25*(3), 249–267. https://doi.org/10.1515/multi.2006.015

Locher, M. A. (2012). Politeness research from past to future, with a special focus on the discursive approach. In L. F. Amaya, M. de la O. H. López, R. G. Morón, M. P. Cruz, M. M. Borrero, & M. R. Barranca (Eds.), *New perspectives on (im)politeness and interpersonal communication* (pp. 36–60). Cambridge: Cambridge Scholars Publishing.

Locher, M. A. (2015). Interpersonal pragmatics and its link to (im)politeness research. *Journal of Pragmatics, 86*, 5–10. https://doi.org/10.1016/j.pragma.2015.05.010

Locher, M. A., & Bousfield, D. (2008). Impoliteness in power in language. In D. Bousfield & M. A. Locher (Eds.), *Impoliteness in language: Studies on its interplay with power in theory and practice* (pp. 1–13). Berlin: Mouton de Gruyter.

Locher, M. A., & Graham, S. L. (2010). Introduction to interpersonal pragmatics. In M. A. Locher & S. L. Graham (Eds.), *Interpersonal pragmatics* (pp. 1–13). Berlin: Mouton de Gruyter. https://doi.org/10.1515/9783110214338.0.1

Locher, M. A., & Langlotz, A. (2008). Relational work: At the intersection of cognition, interaction and emotion. *Bulletin Suisse de linguistique appliqué, 88*, 165–191.

Locher, M. A., & Watts, R. J. (2005). Politeness theory and relational work. *Journal of Politeness Research, 1*(1), 9–33. https://doi.org/10.1515/jplr.2005.1.1.9

Long, C., Fukushima, S., Kádár, D. Z., & Márquez-Reiter, R. (in preparation). Japanese and non-Japanese understandings of service in Japan.

MacGeorge, E. L., Feng, B., & Burleson, B. R. (2011). Supportive communication. In M. L. Knapp & J. A. Daly (Eds.), *The Sage handbook of interpersonal communication* (4th ed., pp. 317–354). Thousand Oaks, CA: Sage.

Mao, L. R. (1994). Beyond politeness theory: 'Face' revisited and renewed. *Journal of Pragmatics, 21*(5), 451–486. https://doi.org/10.1016/0378-2166(94)90025-6

Markus, H. R., & Kitayama, S. (1991). Culture and the self: Implications for cognition, emotion, and motivation. *Psychological Review, 98*(2), 224–253. https://doi. org/10.1037//0033-295x.98.2.224

Márquez-Reiter, R. (2000). *Linguistic politeness in Britain and Uruguay: A contrastive study of requests and apologies.* Amsterdam: John Benjamins. https://doi.org/10.1075/ pbns.83

Marra, M. (2015). Language and culture in sociolinguistics. In F. Sharifian (Ed.), *The Routledge handbook of language and culture* (pp. 373–385). London: Routledge.

Marsella, A. J. (1993). Counseling and psychotherapy with Japanese Americans: Cross-cultural considerations. *American Journal of Orthopsychiatry, 63*(2), 200–208. https:// doi.org/10.1037/h0079431

Marui, I., Nishijima, Y., Noro, K., Reinelt, R., & Yamashita, H. (1996). Concepts of communicative virtues (CCV) in Japanese and German. In M. Hellinger & U. Ammon (Eds.), *Contrastive sociolinguistics* (pp. 385–409). Berlin: Mouton de Gruyter. https:// doi.org/10.1515/9783110811551.385.

Matsui, Y. (1991). Omoiyari no kouzou [The anatomy of empathy]. *Gendai no esupuri, 291*, 27–37.

Matsumoto, D. (2002). *The new Japan: Debunking seven cultural stereotypes.* Boston, MA: Intercultural Press.

Matsumoto, Y. (1988). Reexamination of the universality of face: Politeness phenomena in Japanese. *Journal of Pragmatics, 12*(4), 403–426. https://doi.org/10.1016/0378-2166(88)90003-3

Matsumoto, Y. (1989). Politeness and conversational universals: Observations from Japanese. *Multilingua, 8*(2–3), 207–221. https://doi.org/10.1515/mult.1989.8.2-3.207

Matsumoto, Y. (2018). The form and meaning of the dangling *mitaina* construction in a network of constructions. In M. E. Hudson, Y. Matsumoto, & J. Mori (Eds.), *Pragmatics of Japanese: Perspectives on grammar, interaction and culture* (pp. 75–98). Amsterdam: John Benjamins. https://doi.org/10.1075/pbns.285.03mat

Mills, S. (2003). *Gender and politeness.* Cambridge: Cambridge University Press. http:// dx.doi.org/10.1017/CBO9780511615238

Mills, S. (2004). Class, gender and politeness. *Multilingua, 23*(1–2), 171–191. http:// dx.doi.org/10.1515/mult.2004.004

Mills, S. (2009). Impoliteness in a cultural context. *Journal of Pragmatics, 41*, 1047–1060.

Mills, S. (2011a). Discursive approaches to politeness and impoliteness. In Linguistic Politeness Research Group (Eds.), *Discursive approaches to politeness* (pp. 19–56). Berlin: Mouton de Gruyter. https://doi.org/10.1515/9783110238679.19

Mills, S. (2011b). Communities of practice and politeness. In B. Davies, M. Haugh, & A. J. Merrison (Eds.), *Situated politeness* (pp. 73–87). London: Continuum.

Mills, S. (2015). Language, culture, and politeness. In F. Sharifian (Ed.), *The Routledge handbook of language and culture* (pp. 129–140). London: Routledge.

Mills, S. (2017). *English politeness and class.* Cambridge: Cambridge University Press.

Mills, S., & Kádár, D. Z. (2011). Politeness and culture. In D. Z. Kádár & S. Mills (Eds.), *Politeness in East Asia* (pp. 21–44). Cambridge: Cambridge University Press. https://doi.org/10.1017/cbo9780511977886.004

Miyahara, A. (2004). Toward theorizing Japanese interpersonal communication competence from a non-Western perspective. In F. E. Jandt (Ed.), *Intercultural communication: A global reader* (pp. 279–292). Thousand Oaks, CA: Sage Publications.

Miyake, K. (2011). *Nihongo no taijin kankei haaku to hairyo gengo koudou* [A proper understanding of interpersonal relationships in Japanese and linguistic behaviour of consideration]. Tokyo: Hituzi shobo.

Miyashita, K. (2011). Ryokan 'Kagaya' no bijinesu moderu: 'Omotenashi' wa sekai no moderu ni narieru ka [The business model of the Japanese style inn 'Kagaya': Can *omotenashi* serve as a world model?]. *Obirin Keiei Kenkyuu, 2*, 33–50.

Mizutani, N. (1993). 'Kyowa' kara 'taiwa' e. [From mutual utterance to dialogue]. *Nihongogaku, 12*(4), 4–10.

Mizutani, O., & Mizutani, N. (1987). *How to be polite in Japanese.* Tokyo: Japan Times.

Morgan, D. L. (1997). *Focus groups as qualitative research.* Thousand Oaks, CA: Sage Publications.

Morikoshi, K. (2014). A review of the concepts and definitions regarding hospitality and tourism in Japan. *Hokusei Gakuen Daigaku Tanki Daigakubu Hokusei Ronshuu, 12*, 17–28.

Muneuchi, A. (2017). *Essei de yomi toku kyouiku/shidou no essensu* [The essence of education and guidance: Through the understanding of essays]. Tokyo: Shoshisaikou.

Murphy, B. (2010). *Corpus and sociolinguistics: Investigating age and gender in female talk.* Amsterdam: John Benjamins.

Nagao, Y., & Umemuro, H. (2012). Elements constructing omotenashi and development of omotenashi evaluation tool. *Journal of Japan Industrial Management Association, 63*, 126–137.

Nakamura, H., & Takagi, O. (Eds.). (1987). *Hito wo tasukeru koudou no shinrigaku* [Psychology of behaviour of helping others]. Tokyo: Kouseikan.

Naotsuka, R., Sakamoto, N., Hirose, T., Hagihara, H., Ohta, J., Maeda, S., Hara, T., & Iwasaki, K. (1981). *Mutual understanding of different cultures.* Tokyo: Taishukan.

Nishida, T. (1977). An analysis of a cultural concept affecting Japanese interpersonal communication. *Communication, 6*, 69–80.

Nishijima, Y. (1995). Über den Bedeutungswandel von 'teinei' – Zum internationalen Vergleich der Konzepte von kommunikativen Tugenden. In Ronbunshū Kanko Iinkai [Committee for Festschrift Publication] (Ed.), *Koumura Fujihiko Kyōju Taikan Kinen Ronbunshū* [Festschrift for Emeritus Professor Fujihiko Koumura] (pp. 207–220). Matsuyama: Committee for Festschrift Publication.

Norrick, N., & Haugh, M. (2015). Interdisciplinary perspectives on pragmatics: A festschrift for Jonathan Culpeper (Editorial). *Journal of Pragmatics, 86*, 1–4. https://doi.org/10.1016/j.pragma.2015.07.007

Nwoye, O. G. (1992). Linguistic politeness and socio-cultural variations of the notion of face. *Journal of Pragmatics, 18*(4), 309–328. https://doi.org/10.1016/0378-2166(92)90092-p

Obana, Y. (2017). Japanese honorifics re-re-visited. *Journal of Politeness Research, 13*(2), 281–311. https://doi.org/10.1515/pr-2016-0022

Obana, Y., & Tomoda, T. (1994). The sociological significance of 'politeness' in English and Japanese languages – Report from a pilot study. *Japanese Studies Bulletin, 14*(2), 37–49. https://doi.org/10.1080/10371399408727576

O'Driscoll, J. (2013). The role of language in interpersonal pragmatics. *Journal of Pragmatics, 58*, 170–181. https://doi.org/10.1016/j.pragma.2013.09.008

Ogawa, N., & Gudykunst, W. B. (1999–2000). Politeness rules in Japan and the United States. *Intercultural Communication Studies, 9*, 47–69.

Ogiermann, E. (2009). *On apologizing in negative and positive politeness cultures.* Amsterdam: John Benjamins.

Ogiermann, E. (2012). About Polish politeness. In L. Ruiz de Zarobe & Y. Ruiz de Zarobe (Eds.), *Speech acts and politeness across languages and cultures* (pp. 27–52). Bern: Peter Lang. https://doi.org/10.3726/978-3-0351-0438-7

Ogiermann, E. (2015). Direct off-record requests? – 'Hinting' in family interactions. *Journal of Pragmatics, 86*, 31–35. https://doi.org/10.1016/j.pragma.2015.06.006

Ogiermann, E., & Suszczyńska, M. (2011). On im/politeness behind the iron curtain. In F. Bargiela-Chiappini & D. Z. Kádár (Eds.), *Politeness across cultures* (pp. 194–215). Basingstoke: Palgrave Macmillan. https://doi.org/10.1057/9780230305939_10

Ohashi, J. (2008). Linguistic rituals for thanking in Japanese: Balancing obligations. *Journal of Pragmatics, 40*(12), 2150–2174. https://doi.org/10.1016/j.pragma.2008.04.001

Ohashi, J. (2010). Balancing obligations: Bowing and linguistic features in thanking in Japanese. *Journal of Politeness Research, 6*(2), 183–214. https://doi.org/10.1515/jplr.2010.010

Ohashi, J. (2013). *Thanking and politeness in Japanese: Balancing acts in interaction.* Basingstoke: Palgrave Macmillan.

Okabe, R. (1983). Cultural assumptions of East and West: Japan and the United States. In W. B. Gudykunst (Ed.), *Intercultural communication theory: Current perspectives* (pp. 21–44). Beverly Hills, CA: Sage.

Okamoto, S. (1997). Social context, linguistic ideology, and indexical expressions in Japanese. *Journal of Pragmatics, 28*(6), 795–817. https://doi.org/10.1016/s0378-2166(97)81491-9

Okamoto, S. (1999). Situated politeness: Manipulating honorific and non-honorific expressions in Japanese conversations. *Pragmatics, 9*(1), 51–74. https://doi.org/10.1075/prag.9.1.05oka

Okamoto, S. [Shigeko]. (2016). Variability and multiplicity in the meanings of stereotypical gendered speech in Japanese. *East Asian Pragmatics, 1*(1), 5–37. https://doi.org/10.1558/eap.v1i1.28747

Okamoto, S. [Shinichiro]. (2016). *Akui no shinrigaku* [Psychology of malice]. Tokyo: Chuokoron Shinsha.

Okano, E., & Brown, L. (2018). Did Becky really need to apologise? Intercultural evaluations of politeness. *East Asian Pragmatics, 3*(2), 151–178. https://doi.org/10.1558/eap.35178

Overstreet, M. (2010). Metapragmatics. In L. Cummings (Ed.), *Pragmatics encyclopedia* (pp. 266–268). London: Routledge.

Pan, Y., & Kádár, D. Z. (2011). *Politeness in historical and contemporary Chinese*. London: Continuum.

Peterson, C., & Seligman, M. E. P. (2004). *Character strengths and virtues: A handbook and classification*. Oxford: Oxford University Press.

Pinker, S. (2007). The evolutionary social psychology of off-record indirect speech acts. *Intercultural Pragmatics, 4*(4), 437–461. https://doi.org/10.1515/ip.2007.023

Pizziconi, B. (2003). Re-examining politeness, face and the Japanese language. *Journal of Pragmatics, 35*(10–11), 1471–1506. https://doi.org/10.1016/s0378-2166(02)00200-x

Pizziconi, B. (2007). The lexical mapping of politeness in British English and Japanese. *Journal of Politeness Research, 3*(2), 207–241. https://doi.org/10.1515/pr.2007.010

Pizziconi, B. (2011). Honorifics: The cultural specificity of a universal mechanism in Japanese. In D. Z. Kádár & S. Mills (Eds.), *Politeness in East Asia* (pp. 45–71). Cambridge: Cambridge University Press. https://doi.org/10.1017/cbo9780511977886.005

Pizziconi, B. (2012). The regulation of normative interpersonal behaviour and public morality in Japanese public service encounters. http://www.liar3.illinois.edu/revabs/LIAR3Pizziconi.pdf (accessed on 28 February 2016).

Pon, F. (1996). 'Ki' 'kikubari hyougen' wo megutte [On *ki* and expressions of *kikubari*]. *Nihongogaku, 15*, 76–83.

Pon, F. (2005). *Nihongo no 'hairyo hyougen' ni kansuru kenkyuu: Chuugokugo to no hikaku kenkyuu ni okeru shomondai* [A study on 'expressions of consideration' in Japanese: Some problems concerning a comparison with Chinese]. Osaka: Izumi Shoin.

Pudlinski, C. (2005). Doing empathy and sympathy: Caring responses to troubles tellings on a peer support line. *Discourse Studies, 7*(3), 267–288. https://doi.org/10.1177/1461445605052177

Ran, Y. (2016). 'Equity rights im/politeness' revisited: Evidence from rapport management in Chinese folk mediation. Plenary lecture at the 4th Linguistic Impoliteness, Aggression and Rudeness conference (LIAR IV), Manchester Metropolitan University, 12–14 July 2016.

Riley, P. (2007). *Language, culture and identity*. London: Continuum.

Ruhi, Ş., & Işik-Güler, H. (2007). Conceptualizing face and relational work in (im) politeness: Revelations from politeness lexemes and idioms in Turkish. *Journal of Pragmatics, 39*(4), 681–711. https://doi.org/10.1016/j.pragma.2006.11.013

Sarkhosh, M., & Alizadeh, A. (2017). Compliment response patterns between younger and older generations of Persian speakers. *Pragmatics and Society, 8*(3): 421–446. https://doi.org/10.1075/ps.8.3.05sar

Schneider, K. P. (2012). Appropriate behaviour across varieties of English. *Journal of Pragmatics, 44*(9), 1022–1037. https://doi.org/10.1016/j.pragma.2011.09.015

Schwartz, S. H. (1977). Normative influences on altruism. In L. Berkowitz (Ed.), *Advances in experimental social psychology* (pp. 221–279). New York: Academic Press. https://doi.org/10.1016/s0065-2601(08)60358-5

Schwartz, S. H. (1990). Individualism-collectivism: Critique and proposed refinements. *Journal of Cross-Cultural Psychology, 21*(2), 139–157. https://doi.org/10.1177/0022022190212001

Schwartz, S. H. (1994). Beyond individualism/collectivism: New cultural dimensions of values. In U. Kim, H. C. Triandis, Ç. Kağitçibaşi, S.-C. Choi, & G. Yoon (Eds.), *Individualism and collectivism: Theory, method, and applications* (pp. 85–119). Thousand Oaks, CA: Sage.

Schwartz, S. H. (2007). Universalism values and the inclusiveness of our moral universe. *Journal of Cross-Cultural Psychology, 38*(6), 711–728. https://doi.org/10.1177/0022022107308992

Scollon, R., & Scollon, S. W. (1995). *Intercultural communication: A discourse approach.* Malden: Blackwell.

Scollon, R., Scollon, S. W., & Jones, R. H. (2012). *Intercultural communication: A discourse approach* (3rd ed.). Oxford: Wiley-Blackwell.

Shimizu, H. (1993). *Adolescents in Japanese school: An ethnographic approach to achievement, morality, and behavioral inhibition* (Unpublished doctoral dissertation). Harvard University, Cambridge, MA.

Shimizu, H. (2000). Japanese cultural psychology and empathic understanding: Implications for academic and cultural psychology. *Ethos, 28*(2), 224–247. https://doi.org/10.1525/eth.2000.28.2.224

Shinmura, I. (Ed.). (2018). *Kojien* (7th ed.). Tokyo: Iwanami shoten.

Sifianou, M. (1992). *Politeness phenomena in England and Greece: A cross-cultural perspective.* Oxford: Clarendon Press.

Sifianou, M. (1993). Off-record indirectness and the notion of imposition. *Multilingua, 12*(1), 69–79. https://doi.org/10.1515/mult.1993.12.1.69

Sifianou, M. (1995). Indirectness and politeness: The case of English and Greek. *Reading Working Papers in Linguistics, 2*, 241–253.

Sifianou, M. (1997a). Politeness and off-record indirectness. *International Journal of the Sociology of Language, 126*(1), 163–179. https://doi.org/10.1515/ijsl.1997.126.163

Sifianou, M. (1997b). Silence and politeness. In A. Jaworski (Ed.), *Silence: Interdisciplinary perspectives* (pp. 63–84). Berlin: Mouton de Gruyter.

Sifianou, M. (2011). On the concept of face and politeness. In F. Bargiela-Chiappini & D. Z. Kádár (Eds.), *Politeness across cultures* (pp. 42–58). Basingstoke: Palgrave Macmillan. https://doi.org/10.1057/9780230305939_3

Sifianou, M. (2013). The impact of globalisation on politeness and impoliteness. *Journal of Pragmatics, 55*, 86–102. https://doi.org/10.1016/j.pragma.2013.05.016

Sifianou, M. (2015). Conceptualizing politeness in Greek: Evidence from Twitter corpora. *Journal of Pragmatics, 86*, 25–30. https://doi.org/10.1016/j.pragma.2015.05.019

Sifianou, M., & Garcés-Conejos Blitvich, P. (2017). (Im)politeness and cultural variation. In J. Culpeper, M. Haugh, & D. Z. Kádár (Eds.), *The Palgrave handbook of linguistic (im)politeness* (pp. 571–597). Basingstoke: Palgrave Macmillan. https://doi.org/10.1057/978-1-137-37508-7_22

Sifianou, M., & Garcés-Conejos Blitvich, P. (2018). Introduction: Im/politeness and globalisation. *Journal of Pragmatics, 134*, 113–119. https://doi.org/10.1016/j.pragma.2018.06.014

Sifianou, M., & Tzanne, A. (2010). Conceptualizations of politeness and impoliteness in Greek. *Intercultural Pragmatics, 7*(4), 661–687. https://doi.org/10.1515/iprg.2010.029

Simon, B. (2007). Respect, equality, and power: A social psychological perspective. *Gruppendynamik und Organisationsberatung, 38*(3), 309–326.

Somucho Seishonen Taisaku Honbu [Headquarters of measure for the young, Ministry of internal affairs and communication]. (1995). Kodomo to kazoku ni kansuru kokusai hikaku chousa [A survey of international comparison on children and family]. http:www8.cao.go.jp/youth/kenkyu/kodomo/kodomo.htm (accessed on 17 January 2016).

Spencer-Oatey, H. (2000). *Culturally speaking: Managing rapport through talk across cultures*. London: Continuum.

Spencer-Oatey, H. (2005a). Rapport management theory and culture. *Intercultural Pragmatics, 2*(3), 335–346. https://doi.org/10.1515/iprg.2005.2.3.335

Spencer-Oatey, H. (2005b). (Im)politeness, face and perceptions of rapport: Unpackaging their bases and interrelationships. *Journal of Politeness Research, 1*(1), 95–119. https://doi.org/10.1515/jplr.2005.1.1.95

Spencer-Oatey, H. (2008). Introduction. In H. Spencer-Oatey (Ed.), *Culturally speaking: Culture, communication and politeness theory* (2nd ed., pp. 1–8). London: Continuum.

Spencer-Oatey, H., & Franklin, P. (2009). *Intercultural interaction: A multidisciplinary approach to intercultural communication*. Basingstoke: Palgrave Macmillan.

Spencer-Oatey, H., & Kádár, D. Z. (2016). The bases of (im)politeness evaluations: Culture, the moral order and the East–West debate. *East Asian Pragmatics, 1*(1), 73–106. https://doi.org/10.1558/eap.v1i1.29084

Stewart, M. (2005). Politeness in Britain: 'It's only a suggestion …'. In L. Hickey & M. Stewart (Eds.), *Politeness in Europe* (pp. 116–129). Clevedon: Multilingual Matters. https://doi.org/10.21832/9781853597398-010

Stewart, D. W., Shamdasani, P. N., & Rook, D. W. (2007). *Focus groups: Theory and practice* (2nd ed.). Thousand Oaks, CA: Sage Publications.

Sugito, S., & Ozaki, Y. (2006). Keii hyougen kara gengo koudou ni okeru hairyo e [From honorifics to consideration in linguistic behaviour]. In Kokuritsu kokugo kenkyuujyo [National Institute for Japanese Language and Linguistics] (Ed.), *Gengo koudou ni okeru hairyo no shosou* [Consideration in linguistic behaviours] (pp. 1–18). Tokyo: Kuroshio.

Sun, Y. (2018). The acceptability of American politeness from a native and non-native comparative perspective. *East Asian Pragmatics, 3*(2), 263–287. https://doi.org/10.1558/eap.36664

Suzuki, T. (2007). *A pragmatic approach to the generation and gender gap in Japanese politeness strategies.* Tokyo: Hituzi shobo.

Takada, A. (2013). Generating morality in directive sequences: Distinctive strategies for developing communicative competence in Japanese caregiver–child interactions. *Language and Communication, 33*(4), 420–438. https://doi.org/10.1016/j.langcom.2013.03.012

Takagi, O. (1998). *Hito wo tasukeru kokoro: Enjyo koudou no shakai shinrigaku* [Heart to help people: Social psychology of helping behaviour]. Tokyo: Saiensusha.

Takano, Y., & Osaka, E. (1999). An unsupported common view: Comparing Japan and the U.S. on individualism/collectivism. *Asian Journal of Social Psychology, 2*(3), 311–341. https://doi.org/10.1111/1467-839x.00043

Takemura, K. (1991). Kenketsu/zouki teikyou koudou to aitashin [Blood/organ donation behaviour and altruism]. *Gendai no esupuri, 291*, 86–97.

Tannen, D. (2015). The ambiguity and polysemy of im/politeness in professor–students emails. A plenary talk at the 9th International Im/politeness Conference. National Kapodistrian University of Athens. 1–3 July 2015.

Tao, L. (2010). Komyunikeeshon koudou hyouka gainen 'omoiyari' no nicchu hikaku [Omoiyari as an evaluative concept of communicative behaviour: A contrastive analysis of Japanese and Chinese]. *Kanagawa Daigaku Gengo Kenkyuu, 32*, 93–108.

Tao, L., Yoon, S., & Nishijima, Y. (2016). *Teinei, Limao,* and *Kongson*: A comparison of Japanese, Chinese, and Korean concepts of politeness. *Intercultural Communication Studies, 25*(3): 134–155.

Terasaka, K., & Inaba, Y. (2014). Hosupitaritii to omotenashi saabisu no hikaku bunseki: Omotenashi no tokuchoo to manejimento [The comparison of hospitality and Japanese hospitality 'omotenashi': Characteristics and management of omotenashi]. *The Journal of Social Sicences, 78*, 85–120.

Terkourafi, M. (2005). Beyond the micro-level in politeness research. *Journal of Politeness Research, 1*(2), 237–262. https://doi.org/10.1515/jplr.2005.1.2.237

Terkourafi, M. (2011a). From Politeness1 to Politeness2: Tracking norms of im/politeness across time and space. *Journal of Politeness Research, 7*(2), 159–185. https://doi.org/10.1515/jplr.2011.009

Terkourafi, M. (2011b). The puzzle of indirect speech. *Journal of Pragmatics, 43*(11), 2861–2865. https://doi.org/10.1016/j.pragma.2011.05.003

Terkourafi, M. (2012). Politeness and pragmatics. In K. Allan & K. M. Jaszczolt (Eds.), *The Cambridge handbook of pragmatics* (pp. 617–637). Cambridge: Cambridge University Press. https://doi.org/10.1017/cbo9781139022453.034

Thomas, J. (1983). Cross-cultural pragmatic failure. *Applied Linguistics, 4*(2), 91–112.

Ting-Toomey, S. (1999). *Communicating across cultures.* New York: The Guilford Press.

Travis, C. (1997). Kind, considerate, thoughtful: A semantic analysis. *Lexiko, 7*, 130–152.

Travis, C. (1998). *Omoiyari* as a core Japanese value: Japanese-style empathy? In A. Athanasiadou & E. Tabakowska (Eds.), *Speaking of emotions: Conceptualisation and expression* (pp. 55–81). Berlin: Mouton de Gruyter. https://doi. org/10.1515/9783110806007.55

Triandis, H. C. (1994). Theoretical and methodological approaches to the study of collectivism and individualism. In U. Kim, H. C. Triandis, Ç. Kağitçibaşi, S.-C. Choi, & G. Yoon (Eds.), *Individualism and collectivism: Theory, method, and applications* (pp. 41–51). Thousand Oaks, CA: Sage.

Triandis, H. C., & Gelfand, M. J. (2012). A theory of individualism and collectivism. In P. A. M. Van Lange, A. W. Kruglanski, & E. T. Higgins (Eds.), *Handbook of theories of social psychology* (pp. 498–520). Los Angeles, CA: Sage. https://doi. org/10.4135/9781446249222.n51

Tsujimura, A. (1987). Some characteristics of the Japanese way of communication. In D. L. Kincaid (Ed.), *Communication theory: Eastern and western perspectives* (pp. 115–126). San Diego, CA: Academic Press. https://doi.org/10.1016/b978-0-12-407470-5.50014-1

Turner, B. S., & Holton, R. J. (2016). Theories of globalization: Issues and origins. In B. S. Turner & R. J. Holton (Eds.), *The Routledge international handbook of globalization studies* (2nd ed., pp. 3–23). London: Routledge.

Turner, K. (1996). The principal principles of pragmatic inference: Politeness. *Language Teaching, 29*(1), 1–13. https://doi.org/10.1017/s0261444800008211

Uchida, Y. (2011). Sympathy in Japanese cultural context: A cross-cultural perspective. *Kagaku, 81*(1), 51–53.

Uchida, Y., & Kitayama, S. (2001). Development and validation of a sympathy scale. *The Japanese Journal of Psychology, 72*(4), 275–282. http://dx.doi.org/10.4992/jjpsy.72.275

van der Bom, I., & Mills, S. (2015). A discursive approach to the analysis of politeness data. *Journal of Politeness Research, 11*(2), 179–206. https://doi.org/10.1515/pr-2015-0008

Vauclair, C.-M., Wilson, M., & Fischer, R. (2014). Cultural conceptions of morality: Examining lay people's associations of moral character. *Journal of Moral Education, 43*(1), 54–74. https://doi.org/10.1080/03057240.2013.873365

Verschueren, J. (2000). Notes on the role of metapragmatic awareness in language use. *Pragmatics, 10*(4), 439–456. https://doi.org/10.1075/prag.10.4.02ver

Watanabe, S. (2005). Cultural differences in framing: American and Japanese group discussions. In S. F. Kiesling & C. B. Paulston (Eds.), *Intercultural discourse and communication: The essential readings* (pp. 226–247). Oxford: Blackwell. https://doi. org/10.1002/9780470758434.ch15

Watanabe, T., Skrzypczak, E. R., & Snowden, P. (Eds.). (2003). *Kenkyusha's new Japanese–English dictionary* (5th ed.). Tokyo: Kenkyusha.

Watts, R. J. (2003). *Politeness.* Cambridge: Cambridge University Press. http://dx.doi. org/10.1017/CBO9780511615184

Watts, R. J. (2005). Linguistic politeness research: *Quo vadis?* In R. Watts, S. Ide, & K. Ehlich (Eds.), *Politeness in language: Studies in history, theory and practice* (2nd ed., pp. xi–xlvii). Berlin: Mouton de Gruyter. https://doi.org/10.1515/9783110199819.xi

Watts, R. J. (2005 [1992]). Linguistic politeness and politic verbal behavior: Reconsidering claims for universality. In R. Watts, S. Ide, & K. Ehlich (Eds.), *Politeness in language: Studies in its history, theory and practice* (pp. 43–69). Berlin: Mouton de Gruyter. https://doi.org/10.1515/9783110886542-005

Watts, R. J. (2010). Linguistic politeness theory and its aftermath: Recent research trails. In M. A. Locher & S. Graham (Eds.), *Interpersonal pragmatics* (pp. 43–70). Berlin: De Gruyter Mouton. https://doi.org/10.1515/9783110214338.1.43

Watts, R. J., Ide, S., & Ehlich, K. (2005 [1992]). Introduction. In R. J. Watts, S. Ide, & K. Ehlich (Eds.), *Politeness in language: Studies in its history, theory and practice* (pp. 1–17). Berlin: Mouton de Gruyter. https://doi.org/10.1515/9783110886542-003

Weizman, E. (1989). Requestive hints. In S. Blum-Kulka, J. House, & G. Kasper (Eds.), *Cross-cultural pragmatics: Requests and apologies* (pp. 71–95). Norwood, NJ: Ablex.

Weizman, E. (1993). Interlanguage requestive hints. In G. Kasper & S. Blum-Kulka (Eds.), *Interlanguage pragmatics* (pp. 123–137). Oxford: Oxford University Press.

Wenger, E. (1998). *Communities of practice: Learning, meaning, and identity.* Cambridge: Cambridge University Press.

Wierzbicka, A. (1997). *Understanding cultures through their key words.* Oxford: Oxford University Press.

Wierzbicka, A. (2003). *Cross-cultural pragmatics* (2nd ed.). Berlin: Mouton de Gruyter.

Wolf, H.-G. (2015). Language and culture in intercultural communication. In F. Sharifian (Ed.), *The Routledge handbook of language and culture* (pp. 445–459). London: Routledge.

Wong, P. T. P., Wong, L.C. J., & Scott, C. (2006). Beyond stress and coping: The positive psychology of transformation. In P. T. P. Wong & L. C. J. Wong (Eds.), *Handbook of multicultural perspectives on stress and coping* (pp. 1–26). New York: Springer. https://doi.org/10.1007/0-387-26238-5_1

Wuthnow, R. (1987). *Meaning and moral order: Explorations in cultural analysis.* Berkeley: University of California Press.

Wynn, R., & Wynn, M. (2006). Empathy as an interactionally achieved phenomenon in psychotherapy: Characteristics of some conversational resources. *Journal of Pragmatics, 38*(9), 1385–1397. https://doi.org/10.1016/j.pragma.2005.09.008

Xie, Y. (2000). *Irai koui: Nicchu taishou kenkyuu* [A comparative study of requests in Japanese and Mandarin Chinese] (Master's thesis). Tokyo University of Foreign Studies, Tokyo.

Yamada, H. (1997). *Different games, different rules.* Oxford: Oxford University Press.

Yamaguchi, S. (1994). Collectivism among the Japanese: A perspective from the self. In U. Kim, H. C. Triandis, Ç. Kağitçibaşi, S. Choi, & G. Yoon (Eds.), *Individualism and collectivism: Theory, method, and applications* (pp. 175–188). Thousand Oaks, CA: Sage Publications.

Yamajo, T. (2008). *Hosupitaritii seishin no shinka* [Deepening hospitality spirit]. Tokyo: Horitsu bunka sha.

Yamaoka, M., Makihara, T., & Ono, M. (2010). *Komyunikeeshon to hairyo hyougen* [Communication and expressions of consideration]. Tokyo: Meiji shoin.

Yoshida, T. (1994). Interpersonal versus non-interpersonal realities: An effective tool individualists can use to better understand collectivists. In R. W. Brislin & T. Yoshida (Eds.), *Improving intercultural interactions: Modules for cross-cultural training programs* (pp. 243–267). Thousand Oaks, CA: Sage. https://doi.org/10.4135/9781452204857.n13

Yoshida, M., & Sakurai, C. (2005). Japanese honorifics as a marker of sociocultural identity: A view from non-Western perspectives. In R. T. Lakoff & S. Ide (Eds.), *Broadening the horizon of linguistic politeness* (pp. 197–215). Amsterdam: John Benjamins. https://doi.org/10.1075/pbns.139.18yos

Yuuki, T. (1991). Omoiyari no shisoo [Thought on omoiyari]. *Gendai no esupuri, 291*, 161–170.

Žegarac, V. (2008). Culture and communication. In H. Spencer-Oatey (Ed.), *Culturally speaking: Culture, communication and politeness theory* (2nd ed., pp. 48–70). London: Continuum.

Žegarac, V., & Spencer-Oatey, H. (2013). Achieving mutual understanding in intercultural project partnerships: Cooperation, self-orientation, and fragility. *Intercultural Pragmatics, 10*(3), 433–458. https://doi.org/10.1515/ip-2013-0019

Žegarac, V., Spencer-Oatey, H., & Ushioda, E. (2014). Conceptualizing mindfulness-mindlessness in intercultural interaction. *International Journal of Language and Culture, 1*(1), 75–97. https://doi.org/10.1075/ijolc.1.1.05zeg

Zhang, M., & Wu, D. D. (2018). A cross-cultural analysis of celebrity practice in microblogging. *East Asian Pragmatics, 3*(2), 179–200. https://doi.org/10.1558/eap.33060

CPSIA information can be obtained
at www.ICGtesting.com
Printed in the USA
JSHW020812180220
4291JS00001B/2